IMAGES
of America

LONG PRAIRIE

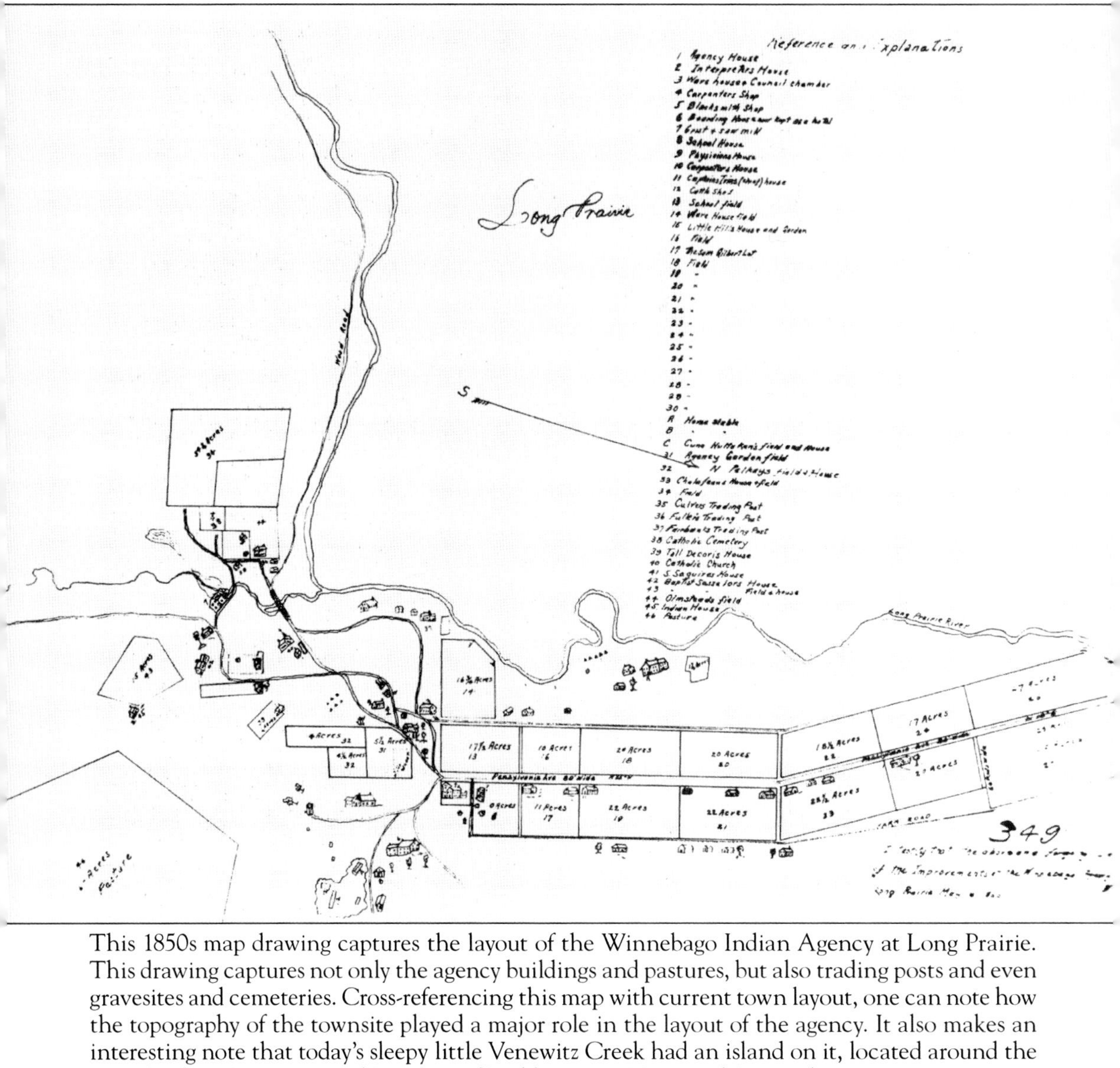

This 1850s map drawing captures the layout of the Winnebago Indian Agency at Long Prairie. This drawing captures not only the agency buildings and pastures, but also trading posts and even gravesites and cemeteries. Cross-referencing this map with current town layout, one can note how the topography of the townsite played a major role in the layout of the agency. It also makes an interesting note that today's sleepy little Venewitz Creek had an island on it, located around the site of today's Burger King. (Courtesy of Todd County Historical Society.)

ON THE COVER: The Reichert Hotel building is a focal landmark on the Main Street of Long Prairie. Not just a hotel, this building housed many other businesses—some private, some government-owned, some utility-owned. One of the early telephone companies used space in the Reichert Hotel building for its switchboard and operators. (Author's collection.)

IMAGES
of America

LONG PRAIRIE

Jeff Lucas

ARCADIA
PUBLISHING

ISBN 978-1-4671-2903-9

Published by Arcadia Publishing
Charleston, South Carolina

Printed in the United States of America

Library of Congress Control Number: 2017964140

For all general information, please contact Arcadia Publishing:
Telephone 843-853-2070
Fax 843-853-0044
E-mail sales@arcadiapublishing.com
For customer service and orders:
Toll-Free 1-888-313-2665

Visit us on the Internet at www.arcadiapublishing.com

Contents

Acknowledgments

I would like to thank all the people that have helped me in compiling the photographs, recollections, and information relating to the history of Long Prairie, Minnesota. Through the participation of the members of the Historic Long Prairie Facebook group, a treasure of first-hand accounts and sharing of stories has resulted in a collection of information that has made this book project possible. The shared photographs and stories have kept me excited about our hometown history.

I would like to thank my parents, Jerry and Glenda Lucas, for raising me and my siblings in such a warm and friendly town; and my wife, Amy Berg, for putting up with my "sickness" that is this fascination with Long Prairie history. I would like to thank Lorna Hunter, my alter-ego history fanatic in Long Prairie, for constantly feeding me photographs and information that she digs up in her searches through the annals of Long Prairie history.

A great deal of gratitude goes out to the small staff of the Todd County Historical Society, especially De Eberle, always willing to help me locate the most random bits of information and giving permission to use many of the photographs in this book.

Unless otherwise indicated, the majority of images appear courtesy of the Todd County Historical Society, noted with TCHS.

There are many others who have supplied and given me permission to use their collections of photographs and related information. They include Ron Wienhold, Brian Cowdery, Barb Hamel, Jim Notch, John Kroll, the staff at St. Benedict Monastery, Rich and Marge Wall, the Christie Home Museum, Arden Truby, Val Hoeschen, Jeremy and Sarah Weber, Sally Pesta, and Kathy Gugat Harris.

In memoriam, I would like to thank those no longer with us that contributed so much historical information for this project. These include Wally Olson; O.B. DeLaurier, who captured the history of Long Prairie and Todd County in the 1930s and 1940s; I.F. "Neats" Lano, a lifelong resident whose past writings answered so many questions; and former neighbor and family friend Bill Colby, who was a large contributor to the Facebook group. Space does not allow me to thank everyone here. So, to all others involved, please know that your help is not forgotten and is truly appreciated.

And to my title manager, Caroline Anderson of Arcadia Publishing, thank you for holding my hand in my first foray through this process.

Introduction

Long Prairie is located in central Minnesota. This area lies within the transition zone between the great fertile prairie of southern Minnesota and the rolling hardwood forest ranges to the north. Dotted with lakes and outlined by gentle rivers and streams and forest, this region has much to offer the sportsman and outdoorsman alike. Its history is rich, beautiful, and at times, tragic. The stories this area could tell would hold the attention of even the most wandering soul.

Prior to the pioneer days of the mid-1800s, the area surrounding Long Prairie had been the "warring grounds" of Sioux and Chippewa tribes. Before this time, recorded history is a bit sparse, found in bits and pieces here and there. Human occupation has been noted to exist before the last glaciers approached, covered, and retreated from the area around Long Prairie. The finding of human bones embedded in the glacial drift proves that man had wandered the area before the glaciers. It has been recorded that approximately eight miles east of Long Prairie, there may be found mounds pronounced by the Minnesota Geological Survey as belonging to the work of humans known as the Mound Builders. The exact location of these mounds has been lost, but may one day be relocated and possibly explored to help record this yet unknown era within the local history books of central Minnesota. As early as 1656, French explorers and traders were known to be in Minnesota, utilizing the rivers for transportation with the Long Prairie River more than likely being an exploited route. However, it was nearly a hundred years later that the first known trader made connections with the Native Americans in what is now Todd County. O.B. DeLaurier tells of a story, published in the *Long Prairie Leader* newspaper in 1941, of some early area history associated with the clash between the Pillager and Sioux tribes at a camp at Long Prairie around 1791. During the winter, a Sioux chief of the Wahpeton tribe gave presents to Yellow Hair (a Pillager elder) and requested to be called his brother. The presents were accepted, and the tribes discussed lasting peace between the otherwise hostile tribes. As spring approached, it was decided that peace should be preserved, and the two tribes separated. Yellow Hair decided to stay behind in the vicinity of Long Prairie with his people. His camp consisted of four lodges on the woody, east side of a small lake, believed to be present-day Lake Charlotte. Having no fear of danger due to the truce, the children of the lodges played on the snow and still frozen lake, sliding down the bluffs on the east side of the lake. One morning while Yellow Hair went hunting and the mother of his children attended to her domestic work, the children again played on the lake. Moaning was heard at the door of the lodge, and the mother rushed to see what was happening. As she opened the door, she beheld her eldest son crawling through the snow, bleeding and scalpless. The other children had been scalped and killed on the ice of the lake at the hands of the Sioux. Yellow Hair, for the rest of his days, avenged the death of his children. Sometimes, it is hard to believe that such a beautiful and peaceful place such as Long Prairie could have been such a savage place as well.

The US government decided that the warring must stop and, in 1846, removed the Winnebago Indian tribe from Fort Atkinson, Iowa, to Long Prairie, Minnesota, as the Winnebagos were known to be neutral towards the warring tribes, thus creating a buffer. An interesting story as to how the agency became located where it was in the region may be found in the writings of William E. Reed, titled *Narrative of the march of Morgan's Mounted Volunteers from Fort Atkinson, Iowa, to Long Prairie, Minnesota, guarding removal of the Winnebago Indians*. In the book, the author talks about the march reaching the east side of Osakis Lake. From there, the march turned east and came to a deep, miry spring and made camp. The next morning, Sergeant Hume took eight men and followed a trail to the northeast. Hume, with his squad, had struck out on a prairie when an elk jumped from the grass in front of him. Hume took chase, and just as he was getting ready to fire with his pistol, the elk jumped a little creek. Hume's horse did not see the creek in the tall grass and dove in. Hume went head over heels and lay there after "rolling about two rods." His men rushed to his aid and helped him into a wagon. They made camp as soon as they could find a convenient place to care for Hume, which happened to be on the big bend in the Long Prairie River (the current site of today's Long Prairie). As the scouts came into this camp, they all became in favor of establishing the mission right there. However, earlier that summer, some men were sent ahead to locate a mission place for the Winnebagos. While this camp stayed at the bend in the river, a man named Olmstead sent men downstream (north) to locate the other men, as they "certainly must have found a better place than this." They started down the river and passed over sandy barrens, where there were pine trees here and there and huckleberries by the million, and found the men cutting wood and putting up hay. These men found little fish and game, so they ate huckleberries by the handfuls. They searched the country all around, but could find no other area as agreeable as Long Prairie. They took a bath in the river, and while there, a Mr. Reed was called by Captain Morgan to come up to the hill where a meeting was taking place. When Reed made it up to the hill, there was debate going on between the leadership about where in the country they should establish the mission, and they wanted to know his opinion. Reed stated that he "considered that this was the last time the Winnebago's would be moved, at least in my day; that it was so far north; that the whites would never want this land for settlement." The next morning, they loaded up the wagons, picked huckleberries, and located the mission back where they first struck the Long Prairie River to take care of Hume. This is how the Winnebago Indian Agency was established at present-day Long Prairie. The agency was maintained until 1854, when disturbances between the Winnebagos and Chippewas became frequent. The Winnebagos were removed, and the government land was sold. The land was purchased by Anson Northrup and sold by him to the Long Prairie Land Company, headquartered in Cincinnati, Ohio.

One of the first settlers that came to Long Prairie after the Winnebagos departed was Gen. Horatio Van Cleve, along with his wife, Charlotte, and their family, arriving in 1856. The Van Cleves were prominent in the charitable and public movements in Minnesota. Charlotte Van Cleve captured her experiences of their time at Long Prairie in her book *Three Score Years and Ten*, a must-read for anyone interested in Long Prairie history. Lake Charlotte, located just south of Long Prairie, was named for Charlotte Van Cleve. Her first sighting of Long Prairie is described in her book as follows:

> The term prairie is a misnomer. We found a beautiful fruitful valley, lying between two low ranges of hills, interspersed with groves of trees and picturesque lakes and watered by a river winding gracefully through its whole length. It had been the seat of the Winnebago Indian Reservation and there were still standing in pretty good order, a large number of houses. These houses, empty though they were, gave the idea of a settlement, dispelling everything like a feeling of loneliness or isolation.

A.J. Gibson, who arrived in Long Prairie with his family at the age of five in the early winter of 1857, was another of the first to arrive back in Long Prairie after the Winnebago Agency had departed. Gibson is likely the one man who witnessed the most change in Long Prairie history throughout his over 80 years in the community. In articles for the *Leader* published between March 29 and April 26, 1934, Gibson notes his first sight and recollections of Long

Prairie, as his family came over the hill from the east. Interesting snippets from these articles include the following:

> I can recall my first site of Long Prairie. The road came out of the forest about where the Lutheran church hill is located and as we arrived at the top of the hill, there came suddenly to view the valley of the river and the long open prairie from which the village takes its name.
>
> So I say it was an impressive scene that greeted our family as we drove out over the hill and got our first glimpse of Long Prairie. There spread out before us was a little village of several hundred houses, a great number of small farms and garden tracts, all fenced neatly with white oak rails. . . . It was a deserted village.

The government had done a good and thorough job in building the town or reservation for the Indians. Everything was complete for all needs and the buildings were substantial. One of the warehouses was located about where St. Mary's Catholic School now stands. Another was situated on the site of the Reichert Hotel and the third was down near the river about where the Hansmann factory (Southside Auto) is located.

Long Prairie did not always go by the name given to it by the long prairie that extends up the river valley. In the spring of 1860, A.D. Brower came to Long Prairie with a few others to celebrate the Fourth of July. The total population of the county at the time was 27. They all gathered in Long Prairie to celebrate the nation's birthday, and on that day, they erected a pole atop the hill on the present site of the courthouse, this pole being known for many years as the "Liberty Pole." For a time after that, the village of Long Prairie was known as Liberty Pole. This first pole was damaged by fire in 1869, but with the citizens not to be deterred, a new pole was raised and stood until about the time the courthouse was built in 1883.

As time rolled forward, so did the continued development of Long Prairie. Although many alterations of the original townsite have taken place, today's Long Prairie would still be recognizable to those early settlers who painstakingly and lovingly created their new hometown. And I think they would be pleased. Today's and future generations can make these settlers proud by protecting their heritage and preserving the buildings that our ancestors built, with a sense of community pride and sense of place in Long Prairie.

On a personal note, my earliest recollections of my interest in Long Prairie history come from a time when my parents owned and operated the Snack Shack, a local teen hangout during the early 1970s. Weekday afternoons and Saturday mornings, I would go to work with my parents. While they were tending to customers, I oftentimes would wander the nooks and crannies of downtown Long Prairie. The sweet smells coming from a local bakery and the salty scents wafting out from the meat markets are forever etched in my mind from those days on bustling Main Street. To this day, when I walk into a bakery or a meat market, I am immediately taken back to those days of my youth exploring the welcoming streets of Long Prairie.

These wanderings oftentimes led me to the Todd County courthouse. A tunnel built by the Works Progress Administration in 1938 leads from street level up into the basement of the courthouse where the Todd County Historical Society museum was located. I recall it being a fairly small room dedicated to the history of the county and Long Prairie. The gentleman that oversaw and worked in the museum at that time was Morrie Olson. I remember him as kind and welcoming to this little kid who would just show up and snoop through everything. I recall flipping through the photographs on the swinging poster boards that lined the walls in the courthouse museum and looking at the objects that were sitting around on tables, rusty, with that "old smell." As the adolescence of teen years deviated my interests, and military service in the US Coast Guard took me away from Long Prairie, I never really gave the history of Long Prairie much thought.

Fast forward to a day in 2011: While sitting at home mindlessly surfing the Internet, I searched the term "Long Prairie" in eBay just to see what would pop up. I found an old black-and-white real-photo postcard of Long Prairie and, in that photograph, saw buildings that I did not recognize from the days of my youth growing up in this small midwestern town. That got me wondering what those unfamiliar buildings were, what was in them, and who owned them? As a way to try and get answers to these questions, I started a Historic Long Prairie group on this thing called Facebook that was becoming all the rage of the day. A few people joined, and then a few more. This group was a place where we could post and ask questions about all things Long Prairie that we had heard or wondered about but did not know if they were real or just urban legends. The more questions that were asked and researched, the more I found and the more questions there were to answer.

Of particular interest to me was finding old photographs of Long Prairie. When returning to visit family in Long Prairie, I would take these photographs and search for the location of the place the photograph was taken from. To stand in the spot that the photographer was standing in so many years ago, looking at the people in the image who were standing "right there" back then, made this small uninteresting town that I had grown up in "new" again. I was hooked and wanted others to be as well. As the Facebook group has grown, I have been asked if I was ever going to do something with all this information and stories collected. This book is my attempt at doing just that. I have tried to provide the best, most accurate information I could. Please excuse any inaccuracies that you may find.

Take this book with you on a walk through Long Prairie, and take a kid. Go to the locations these photographs were taken from and see and learn what has been here in the past. By learning, knowing, and understanding Long Prairie's history, it will make the most mundane and routine stroll through this "boring" Midwestern town captivating again to even those lifelong residents. The images and stories captured in this book will cause the eyes to see "ordinary Long Prairie" differently. Leave the mind to wonder and reflect on the heritage of this town. My hope is that this book will make Long Prairie "new" again to you as well and spark an interest to help honor and preserve these places that our ancestors created for us. Enjoy the journey!

One

Early Long Prairie and Its People

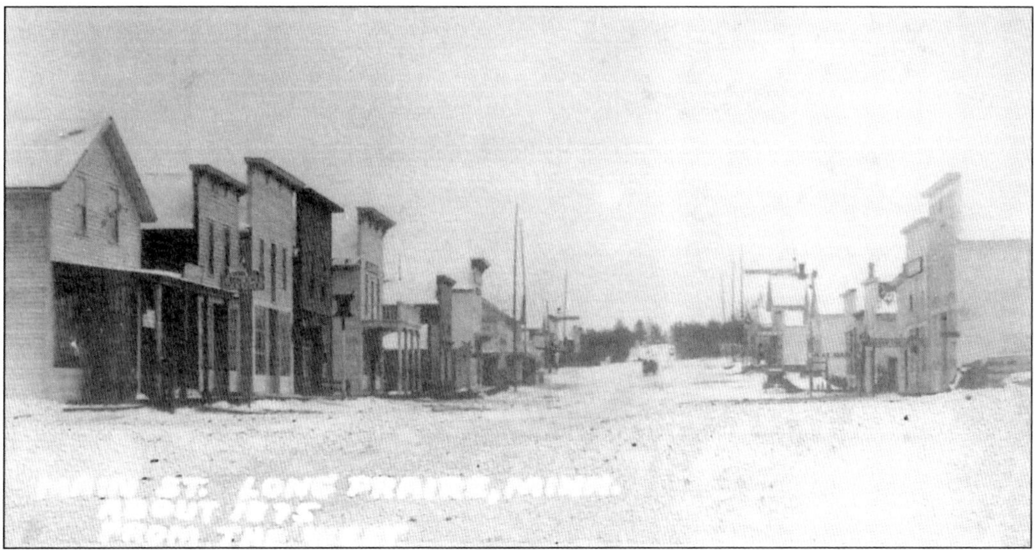

Long Prairie's Main Street in 1875 looked quite different than today. On the left side of the street, one may be able to see the letters "ouse" on the side of a building. That is the Long Prairie House, the precursor to the Reichert. The man responsible for shaving down Osakis Street (Central Avenue), leveling it to its current grade and probably making the most dramatic change in the appearance of Long Prairie, was Silas Lake. The street was shaved down in 1881. Lake died in 1900 and is buried in the Clotho cemetery. (Courtesy of TCHS.)

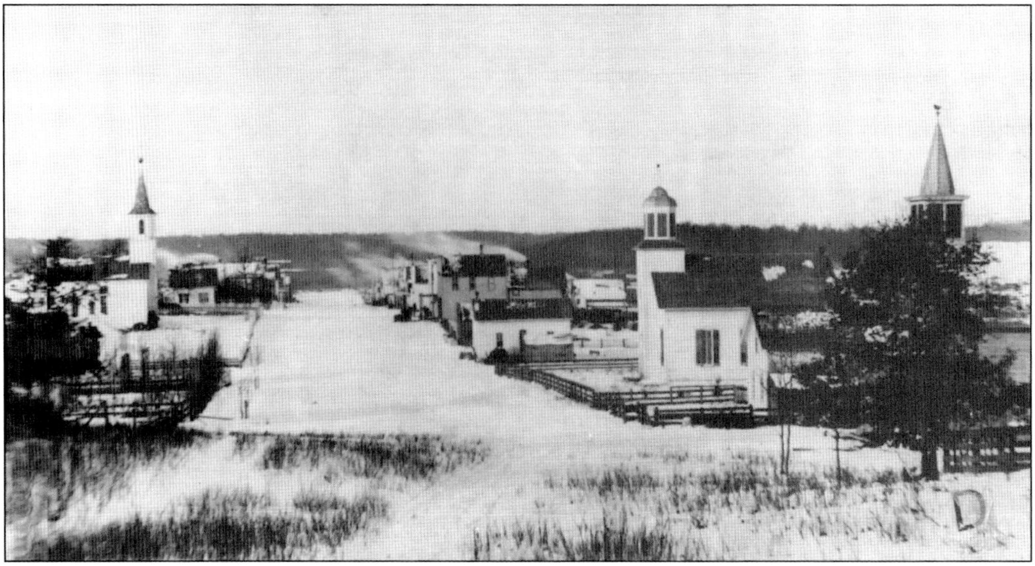

This is one of the earliest known photographs of Long Prairie, taken about 1875. The view looks west down Osakis Street (Central Avenue) prior to the street being shaved down and leveled. The second church on the right with the rounded steeple is the Baptist church, which sat at today's 510 Central Avenue address. The small church at the left is St. Mary's Church, which sat at the current location of St. Mary's Parochial School. (Courtesy of TCHS.)

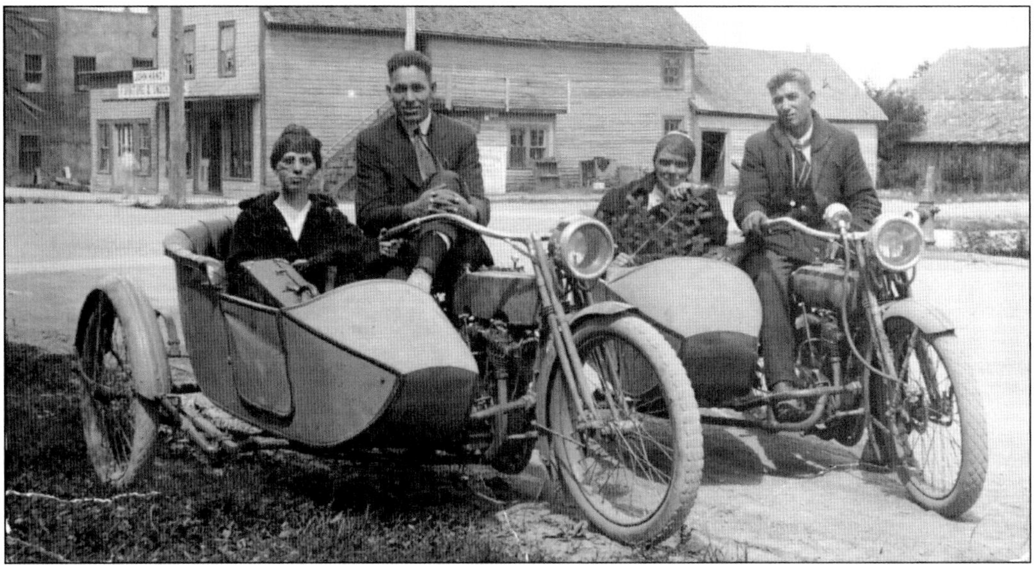

In the 1800s, the site of the current post office was home to Handy Brothers Hardware and Furniture, captured here in the background of this undated photograph. For perspective, this photograph was taken from out front of the St. Mary's rectory, with a view looking toward the post office. Long Prairie Implement Company and the Lux and Borgman Implement were located on this corner in the 1920s. (Courtesy of TCHS.)

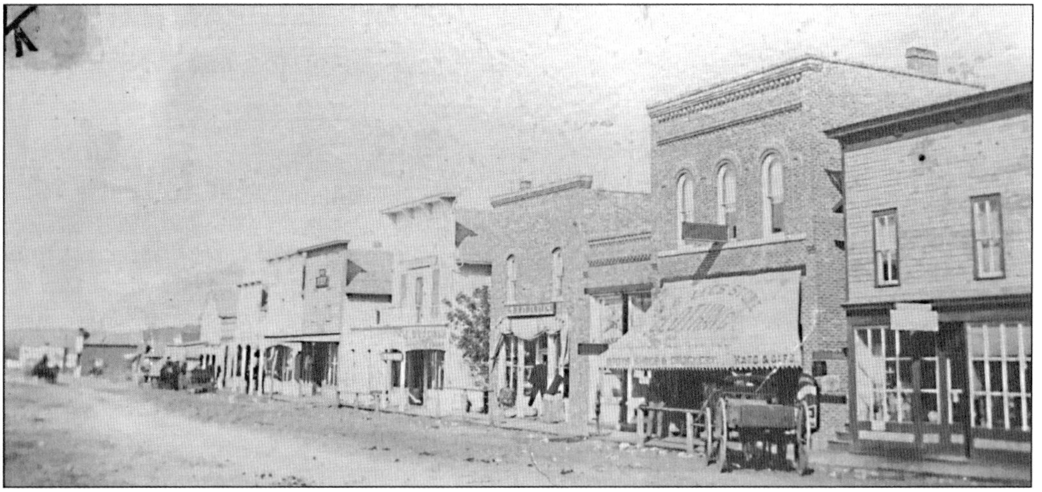

In this early photograph of Osakis Street (Central Avenue) taken about 1890, one may not immediately recognize the location of these buildings. With a view looking west, this photograph was taken in front of the Black Forest Thrift store. For reference, the second building from the right with the large awning and the small brick building to its left were incorporated into one building in 1903, becoming the Bank of Long Prairie, which, in most recent times, housed Michael's Café and then Mickey's Café. (Courtesy of TCHS.)

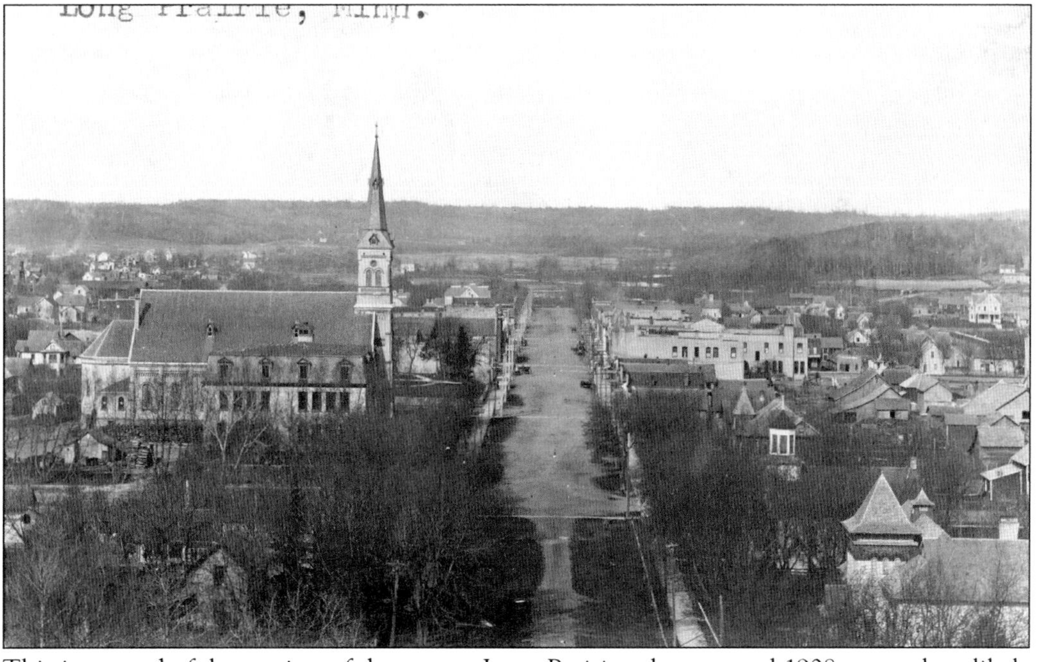

This is a wonderful overview of downtown Long Prairie taken around 1908, more than likely from atop the water tank at the eastern end of Central Avenue. This photograph was taken not long after the St. Mary's Catholic School and the Reichert Hotel had been built. (Courtesy of TCHS.)

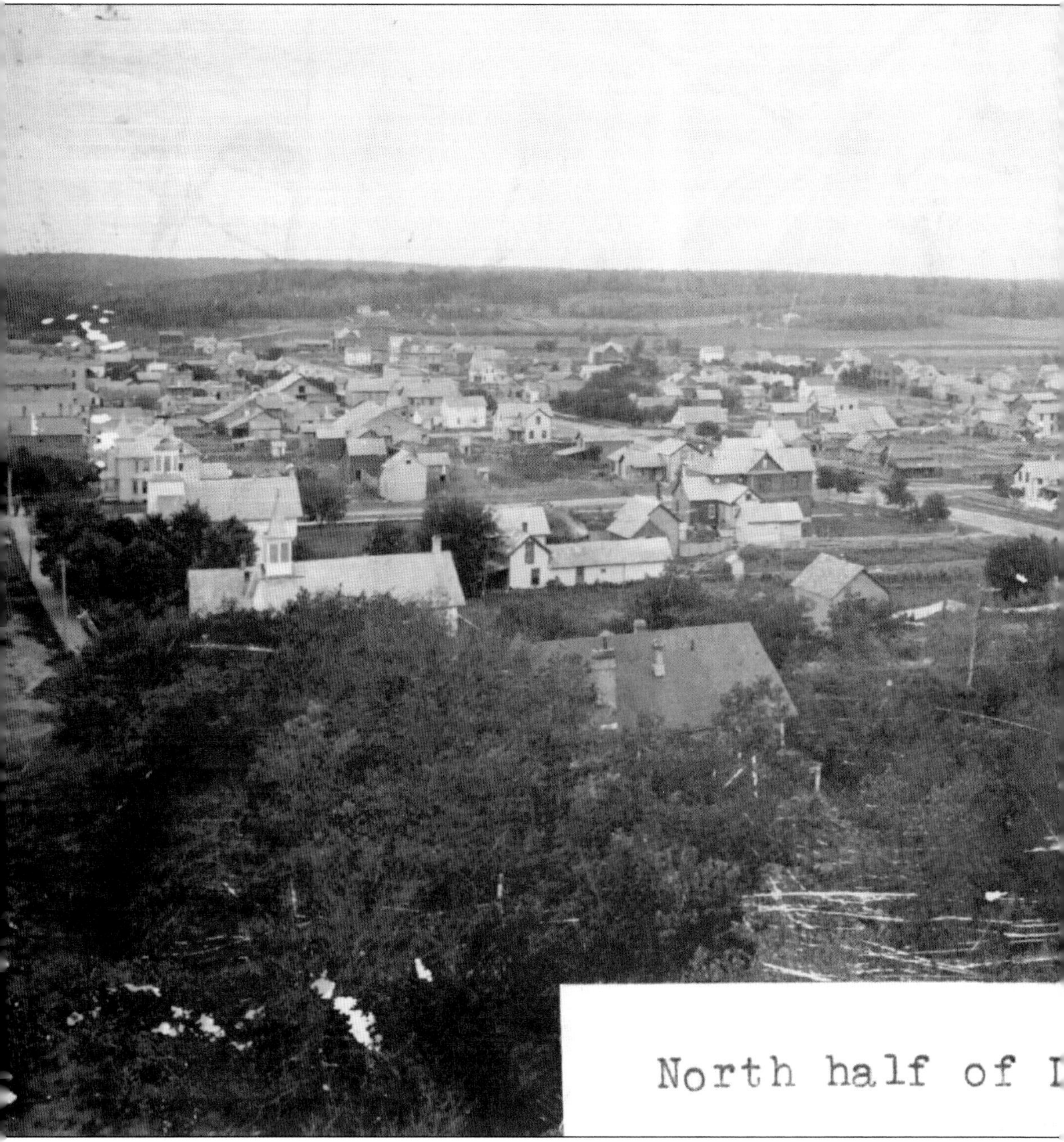

This photograph with a view looking northwest was taken from a location atop water tank hill on the east end of Central Avenue and captures the north half of Long Prairie in about 1900. Looking closely at the very right edge of the image, one will notice a larger square two-story building. This was the first modern high school in Long Prairie, which sat on the current location of Soldier Field.

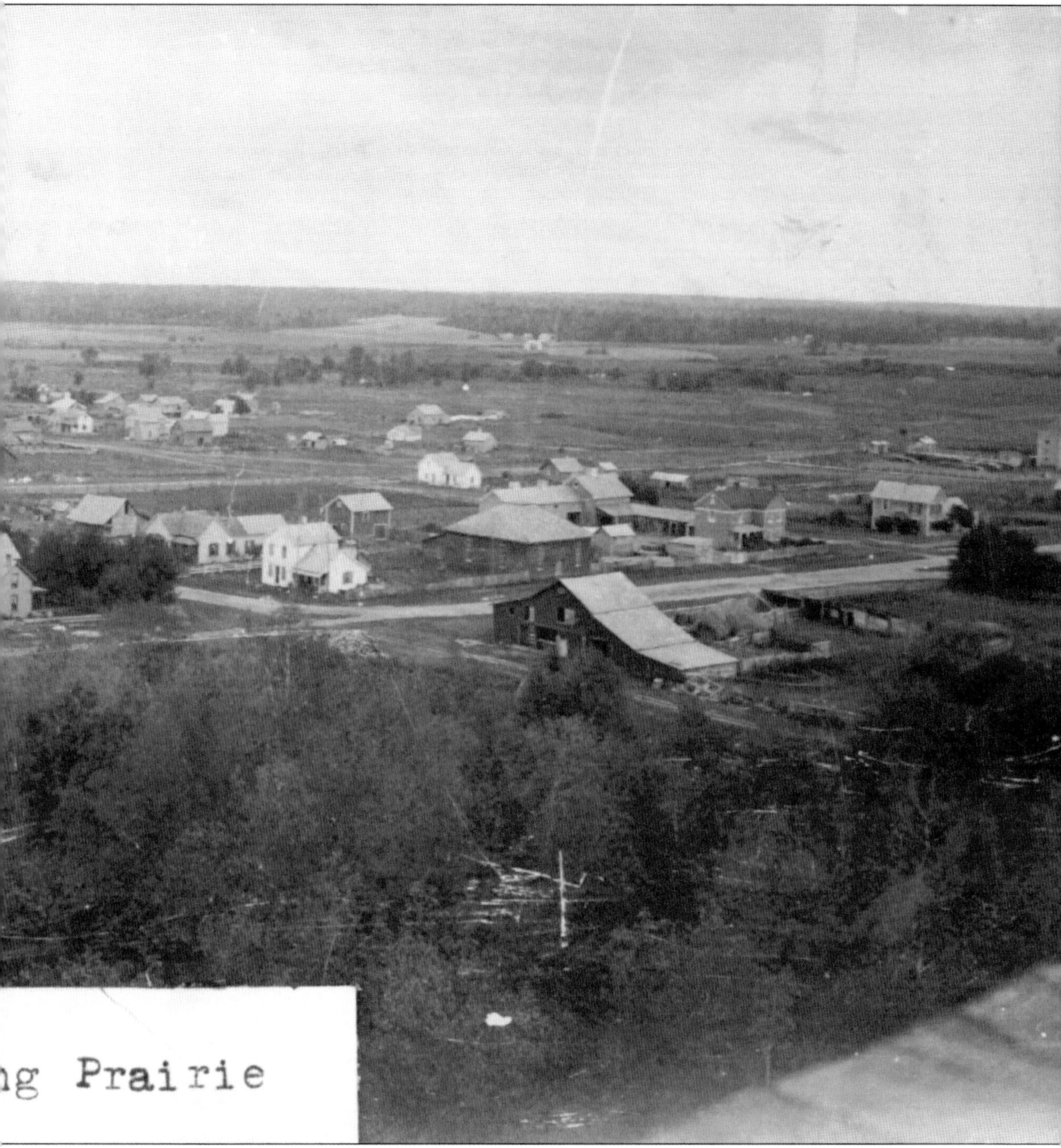

The two-story brick home, second building to the left of the school, is the Hartung home and livery stable. This redbrick house and livery stable still stand at 121 Sixth Street Northeast. The street running up the left edge of this photograph is Central Avenue. (Courtesy of TCHS.)

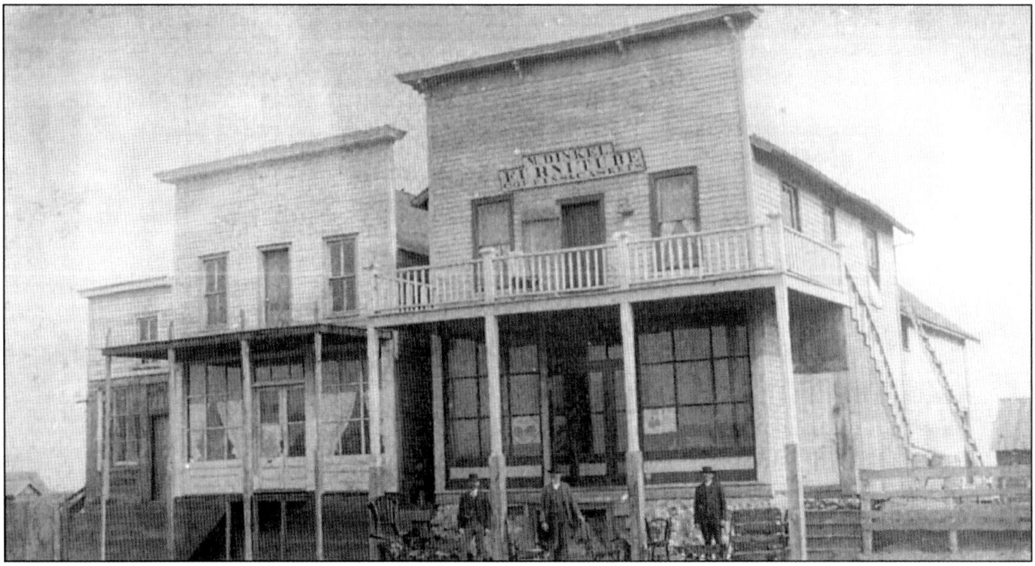

A veteran of the Civil War, Michael Dinkel arrived in Todd County in the spring of 1867. He was heavily involved in establishing Long Prairie as the county seat and erecting the first court house: a log structure. In 1873, he was elected sheriff of the county and served the duties well. Dinkel then established residence in Long Prairie, engaging in the operation of a general store. Always active in county, township, and school affairs, he likewise served on the town board of education. The above photograph shows evidence of the original Main Street having been shaved down, as the building is not level with the street. Below, this 1896 photograph shows Dinkel, and others, with an early fire apparatus in front of the construction site of St. Mary's Church. (Both, TCHS.)

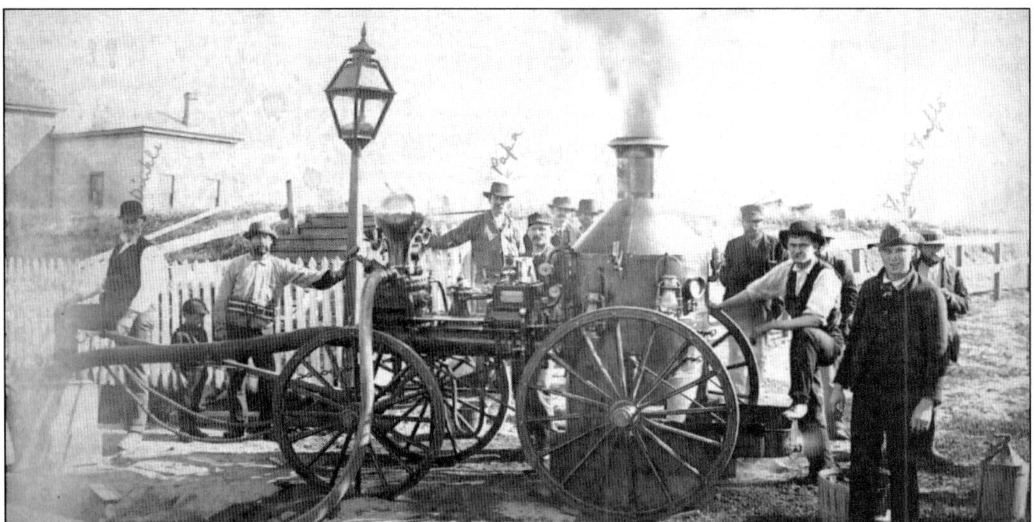

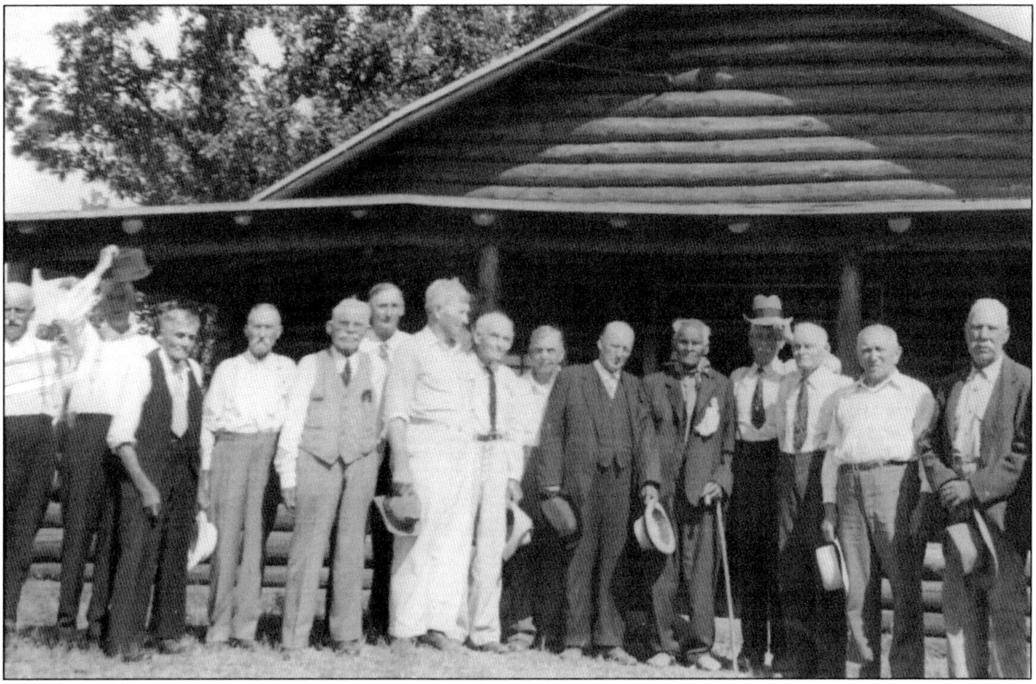

This photograph, taken in the 1930s, captures the members of the Old Settlers of Todd County. These men are, from left to right, Charley Debolt, Merton Gutches, Jud Newville, A.J. Gibson, A.H. Hendrickson, H.W. Reineke, Lambert Irsfeld, George Etzell Sr., Peter Webster, O.B. DeLaurier, Ralph Fowler, C.F. Miller, S.S. Sargeant, A.H. Macke, and W.W. Brooks. Some of these names are mentioned throughout this book. (Courtesy of TCHS.)

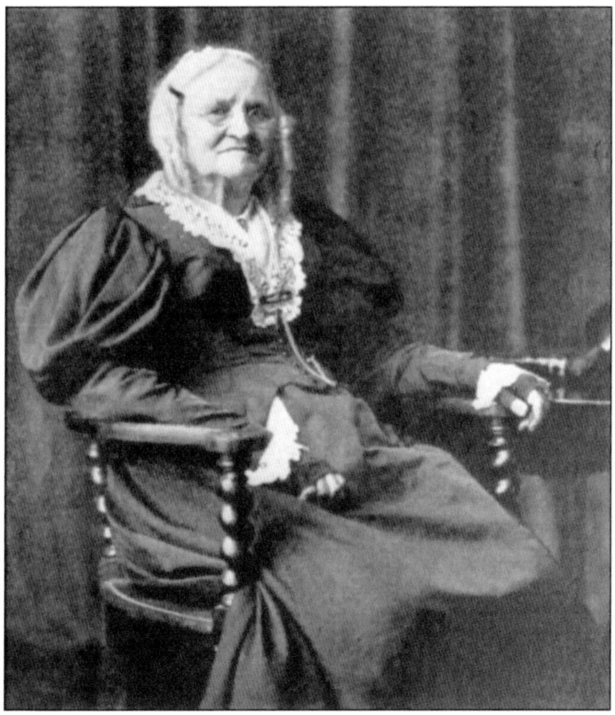

Charlotte Van Cleve arrived in Long Prairie with her family in 1856. The namesake of Lake Charlotte, she was the wife of the government land agent Gen. Horatio Van Cleve. In her book titled *Three Score Years and Ten*, she laments, "Long Prairie was our home for five years which though not unmixed with trial and sorrow, were happy years." She returned on occasion, delivering the commencement address to the first graduating class of Long Prairie High School in 1898. (Author's collection.)

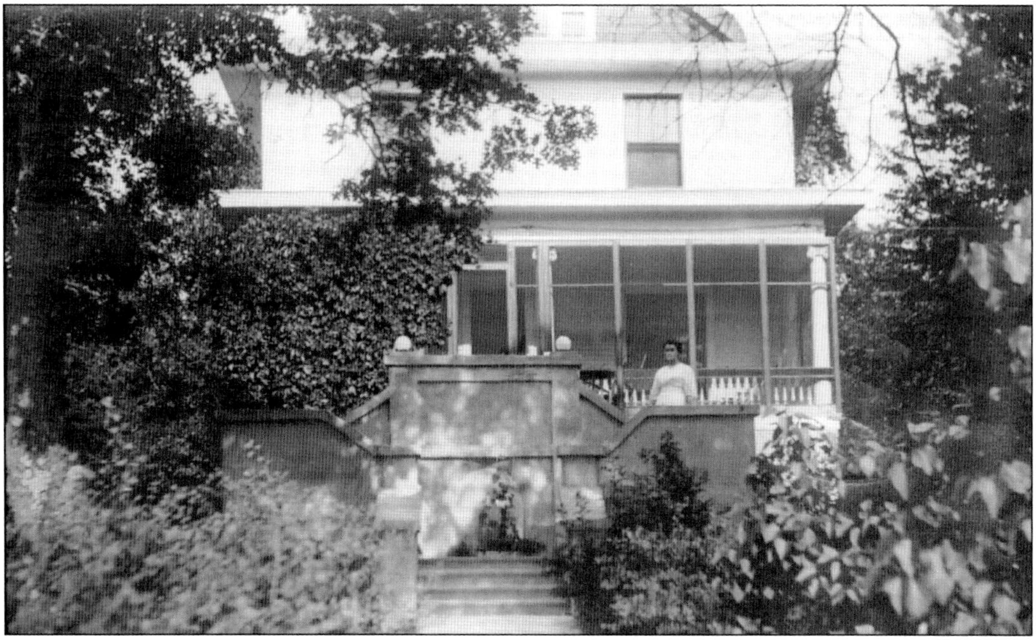

This home located at 16 Sixth Street Northeast was built by William E. Lee around 1896. Lee came to Long Prairie with his parents in 1858, making his home here until his death in 1920. In 1876, he married Eva Gibson, whose parents were also pioneers arriving at Long Prairie in 1857. Lee was prominent in county and state affairs. He was Speaker of the Minnesota House of Representatives in 1893. In 1914, he was the Republican nominee for governor. He founded the Bank of Long Prairie and donated the land for Lee Park. Upon his death, the funeral was held outdoors at this home with friends and family gathering on the lawn, with the casket lying at the bottom of the steps. All places of business, including the public schools, closed along with the banks of the county as a mark of respect to Lee's memory. (Above, courtesy of Guy Blaske; below, author's collection.)

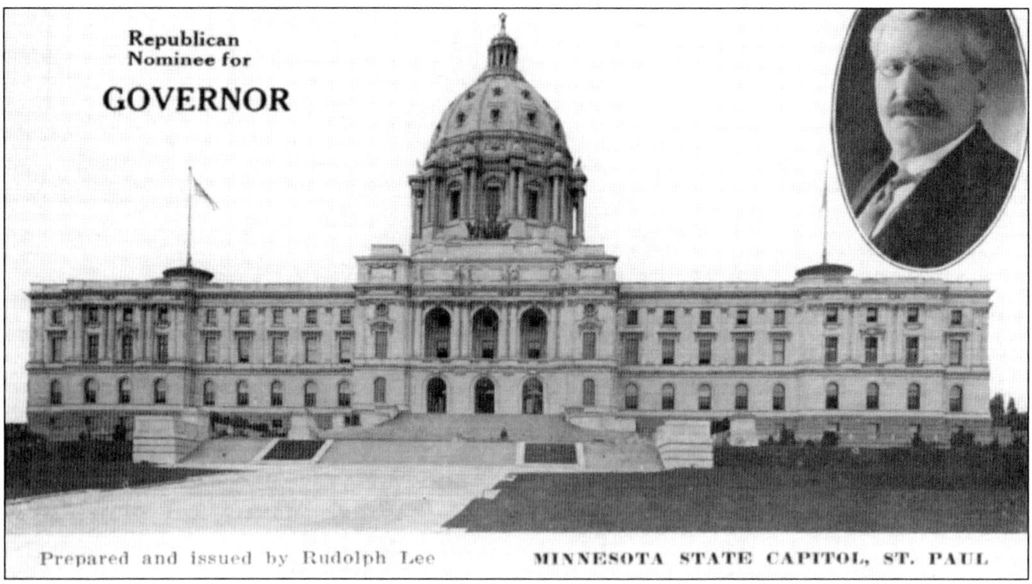

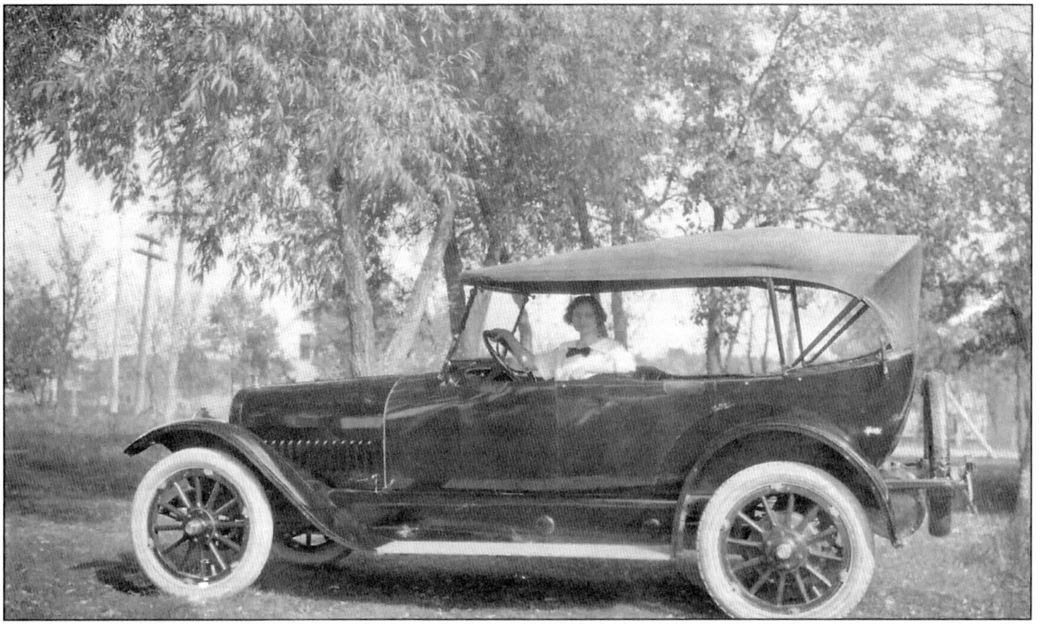

This 1916 photograph shows Kate Williams, wife of the slain city marshal George Williams. Her maiden name was Rohner, of the family that had a large brewery on the bank of Venewitz Creek. George Williams had a new Lincoln coupe in the garage when he was killed. Kate put it up on blocks and covered it with a tarp, never to be driven again. She would never sell the car. (Courtesy of Brian Cowdery.)

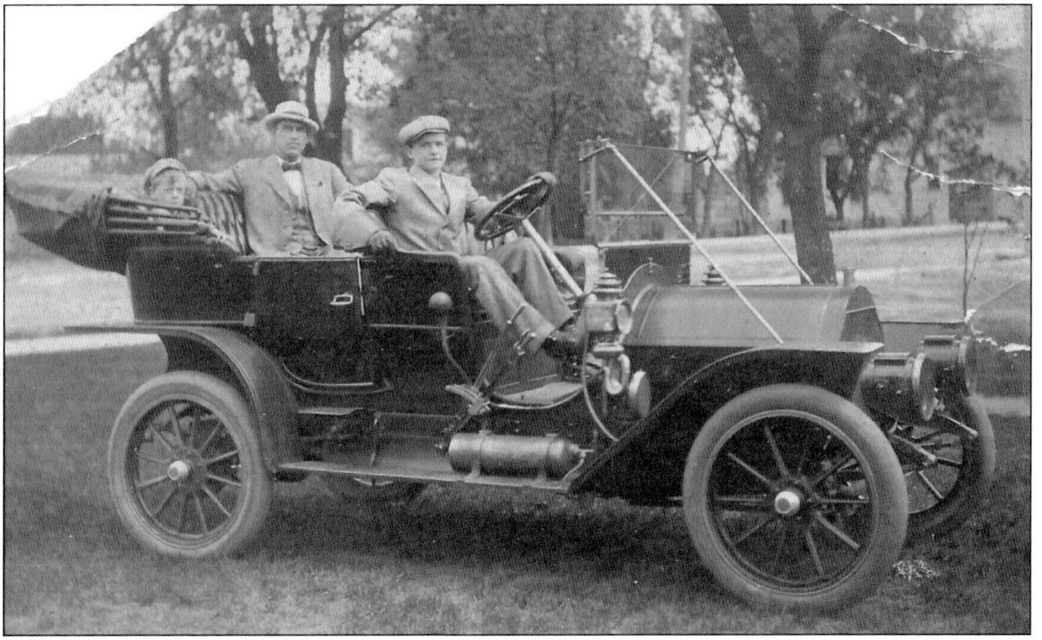

Seen here are Dr. George and Donny Christie (at the wheel) out for a ride in about 1910. Dr. George Christie came to Long Prairie to practice medicine in 1884 at the request of his friend Dr. Edwin Lewis (Sinclair Lewis's father) of Sauk Centre, Minnesota. House calls were common practice, and the doctor traveled by horse and buggy, by car, or on foot. (Author's collection.)

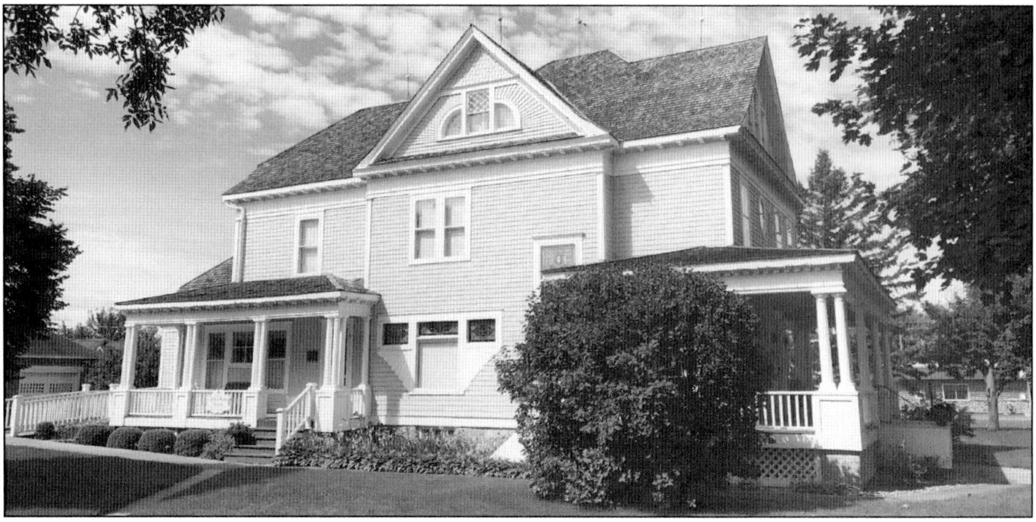

Founded in 1976, the Christie Home Historical Society is dedicated to the preservation and dissemination of knowledge pertaining to the Christie Home. The house, built in Queen Anne style in 1901, was home to Dr. George R. Christie Sr. and his family from 1901 to 1976, at which time Dr. Robert Christie, last resident of the home, passed away. The remaining family donated the home to the city, with the condition that it be maintained as a museum. The home was placed in the National Register of Historic Places in 2006. (Author's collection.)

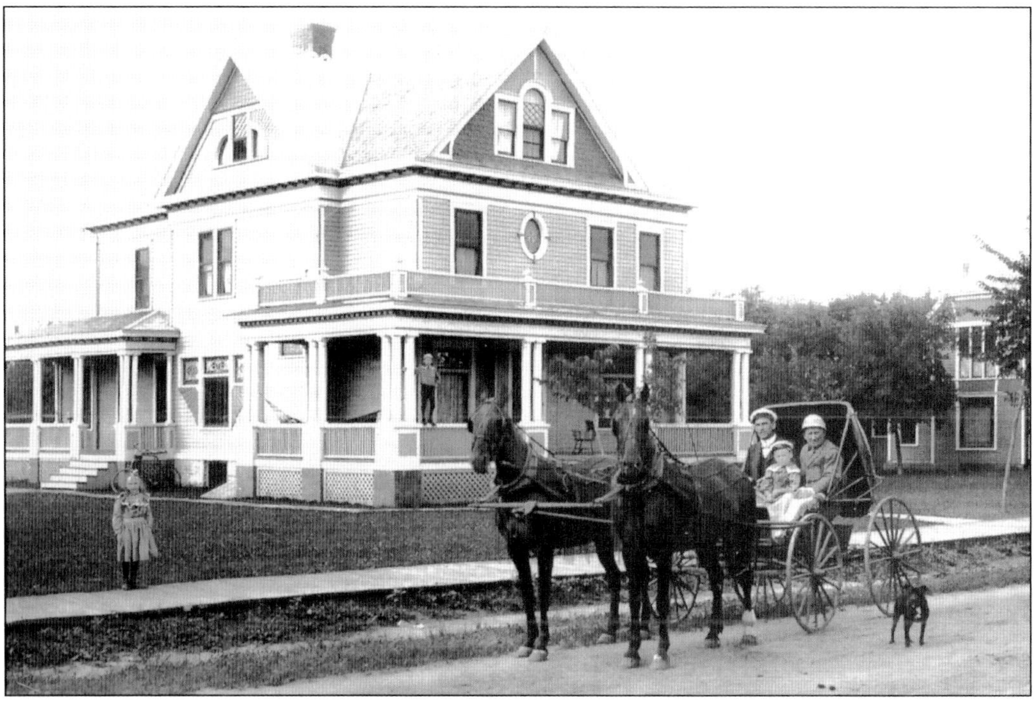

Today's Christie Home Museum has been lovingly restored and continues to improve every year. The museum hosts tours of the home and gatherings of vintage transportation clubs, offers private "after-hours" tours, and holds book signings by local authors. The museum also participate in community events such as citywide garage sales and is a stopping point on bike and trike rallies. (Courtesy of the Christie Home Historical Society.)

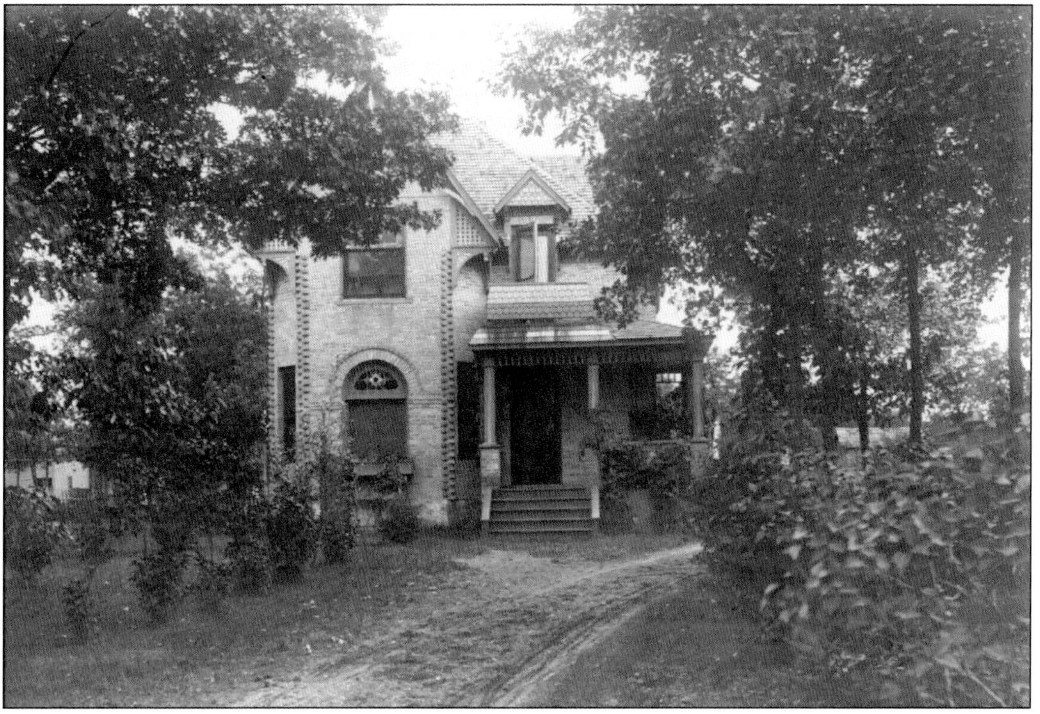

Built around 1903, this is one of the most recognizable homes in Long Prairie. The home was built by Ignatius Reichert, the first hotel proprietor and pioneer of Long Prairie. Reichert was born in 1838 in Germany. He came with his family to America at 10 years old. In 1869, he came to Long Prairie and built the first hotel with the help of lumberjacks and Chief Bad Boy, a local Native American. (Courtesy of TCHS.)

This large home was built by the Reichert family. The Reicherts owned the house for about 50 years, when it was purchased by the Norris family in the early 1940s when the war was still going on. A daughter of the Norrises' remembers celebrating the end of the war in the street out front of the home. The Norrises lived in the home another 50 years when it was purchased by the Robinson family, who have restored the home. (Author's collection.)

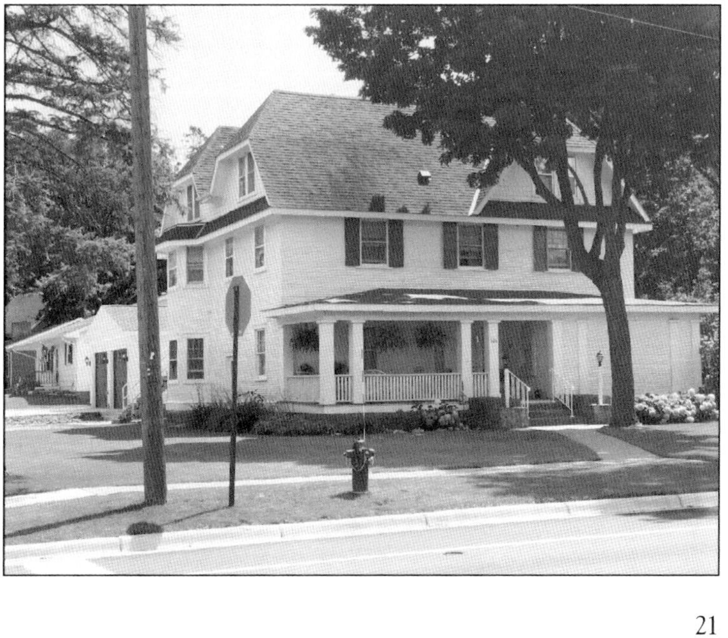

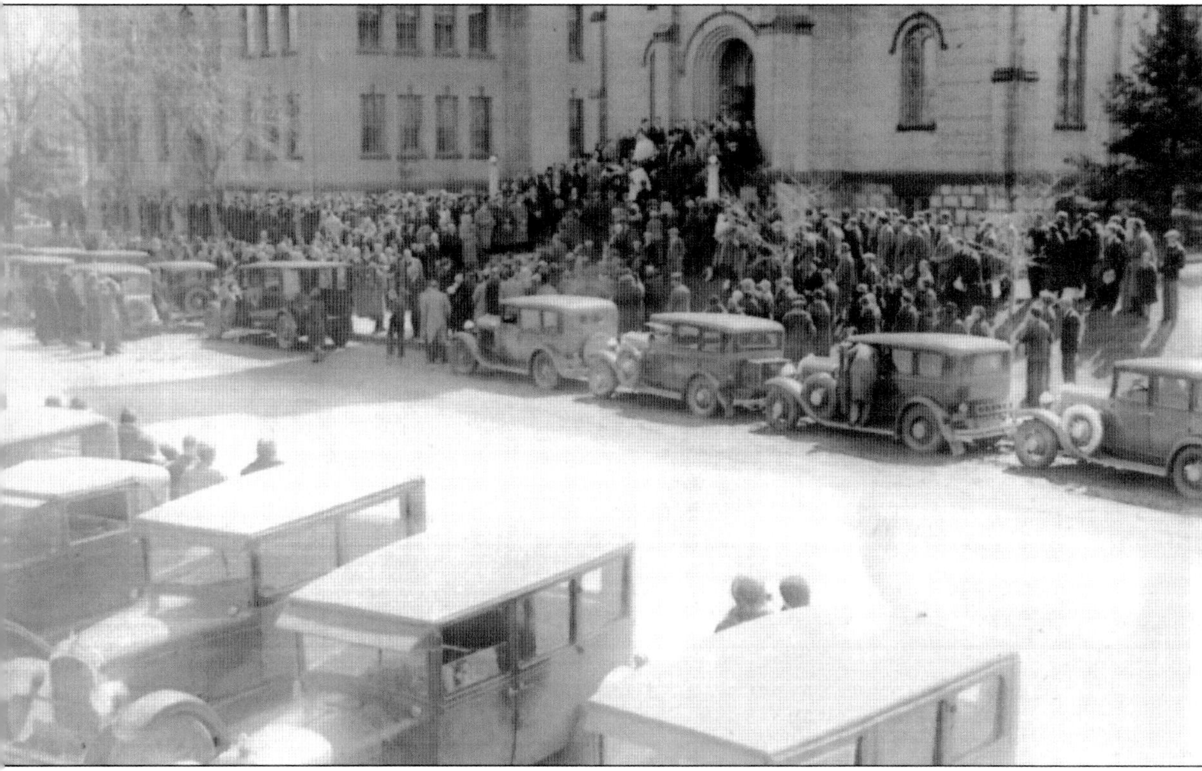

The Rev. Francis Britcher of St. Mary's Church died unexpectedly at the age of 64 on April 4, 1932. The funeral, conducted April 7, 1932, was one of the most impressive events ever experienced by the Long Prairie parish up to that time. It was attended by 66 priests and hundreds of relatives and parishioners; the church was packed to overflowing. The service was opened by the visiting priests chanting the office of the dead. The body was accompanied in procession by the Knights of Columbus honor guard and laid in state in the church until the final Solemn Requiem Mass the next morning. The Catholic school was closed during the week following Father Britcher's death. The funeral service attended by the schoolchildren was conducted by the Rev. Charles A. Mayer, who was a lifelong friend of Father Britcher's. Father Mayer was assisted by the Rev. John Guzdek of Browerville. Pallbearers were Steve Hansmeyer, E.A. Schenk, R.F. Knapp, Jake Siegle, William Koenig, George Oedbauer, John Wolf, and J.F. Chyba. (Courtesy of TCHS.)

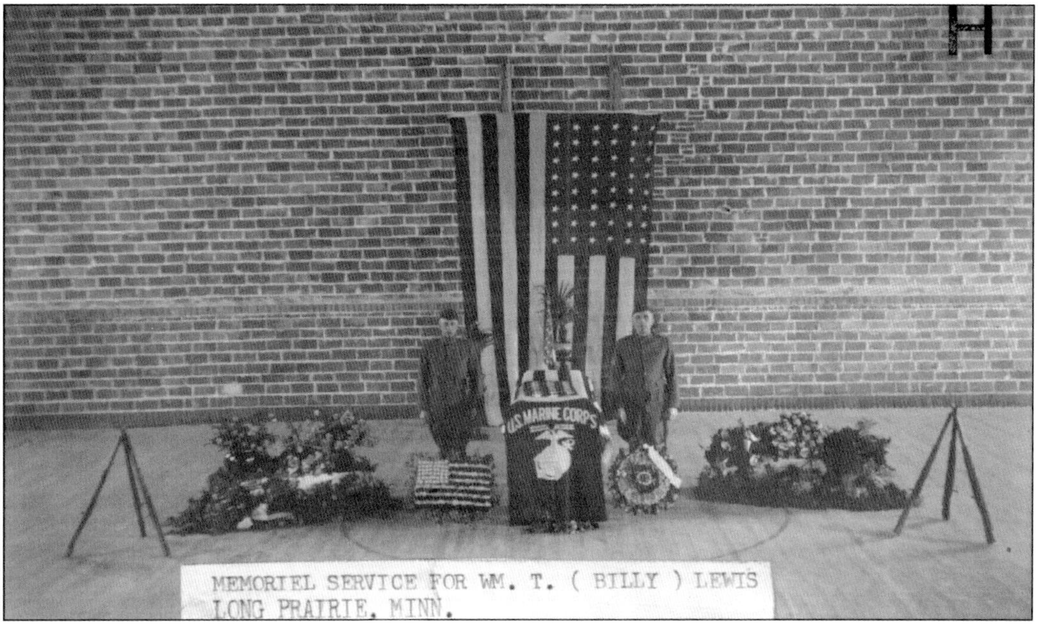

William Lewis, namesake of the William T. Lewis American Legion Post 12 in Long Prairie, was the first person from Todd County to be killed in France fighting under the American flag in World War I. He was killed in action on June 7, 1918, at the Battle of Château-Thierry. William was the brother of Joyce Lewis, a local Long Prairie lawyer who fought alongside his brother in the war. (Courtesy of TCHS.)

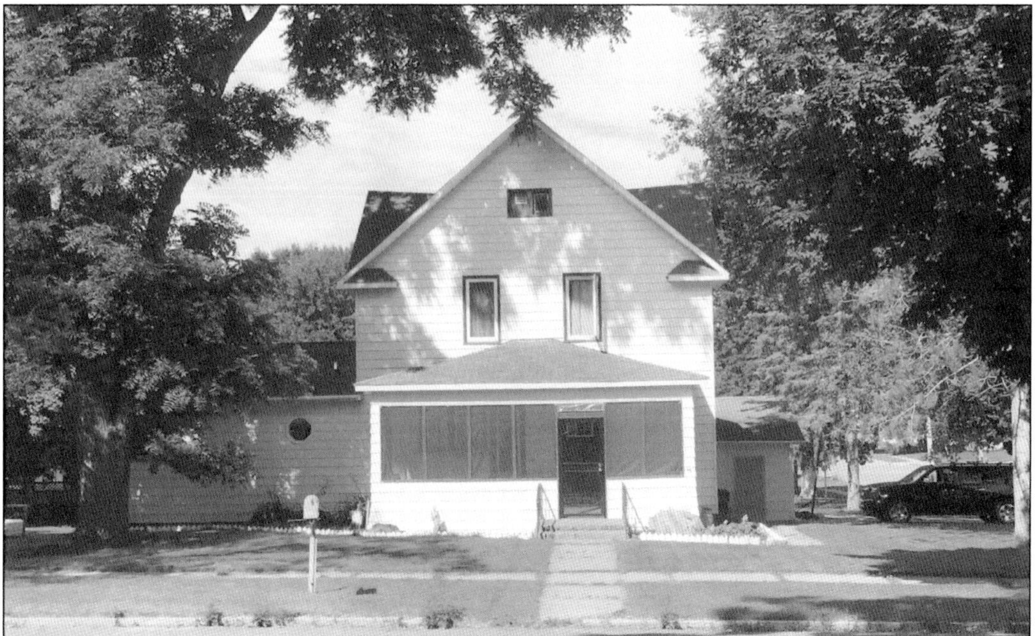

A walk down Todd Street takes one past many stately homes that were once occupied by many of the movers and shakers of Long Prairie. This home at 205 Todd Street South, built in 1914, was once the residence of Joyce Lewis, a local World War I hero. Lewis, who was severely injured and crippled in the war, went on to become a highly respected lawyer in Long Prairie. (Author's collection.)

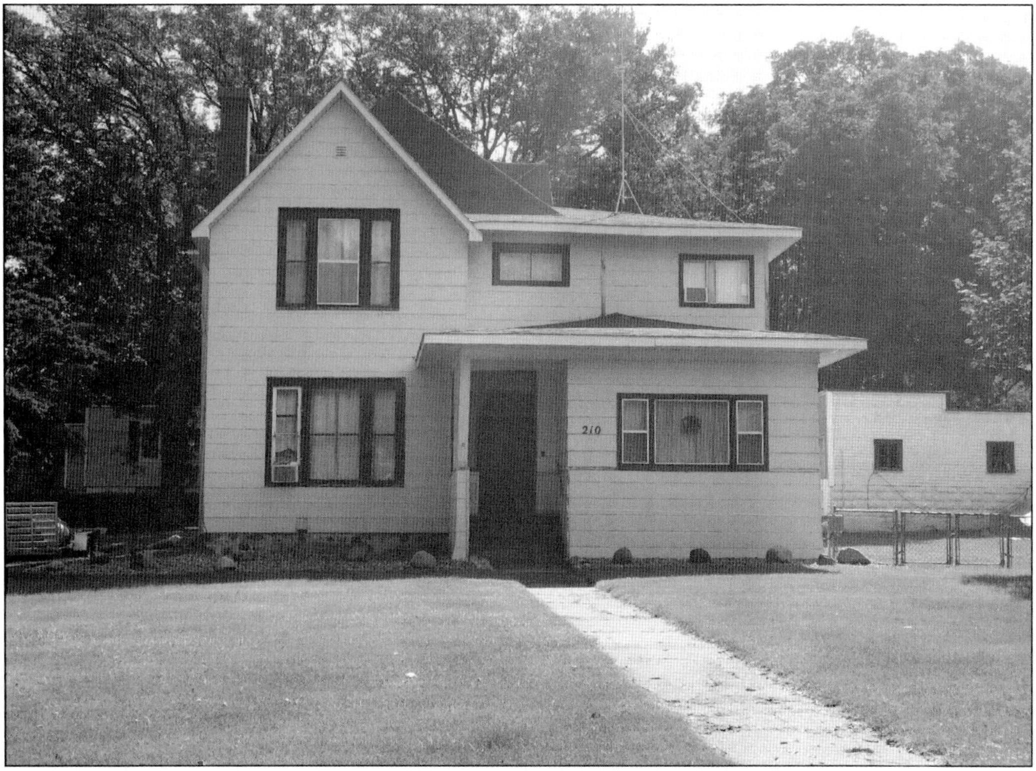

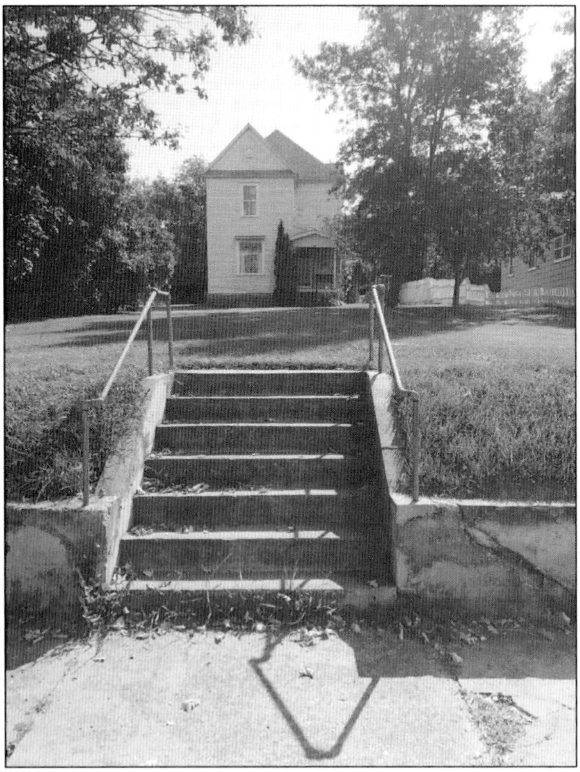

This home at 210 Todd Street South is a large, unique corner home for Todd Street. It has quite a large front yard, which stretches to the west. For a time in its life, this house was operated as the Westlawn Rest Home. It operated under this name from 1951 to 1968, and the last 11 of those years was owned and operated by the Mander family. (Author's collection.)

This home at 228 Todd Street South was owned for many years by John and Bertha Peterson. They had a son, Wally, who operated Peterson's Variety Store on Central Avenue. John worked for many years at Hart Press, and Bertha was a homemaker. They were charter members of the American Lutheran Church. Bertha died in 1974, and John followed in 1985. John lived at home until shortly before his death. Wally and his wife, Margaret, sold the house in 1986. (Author's collection.)

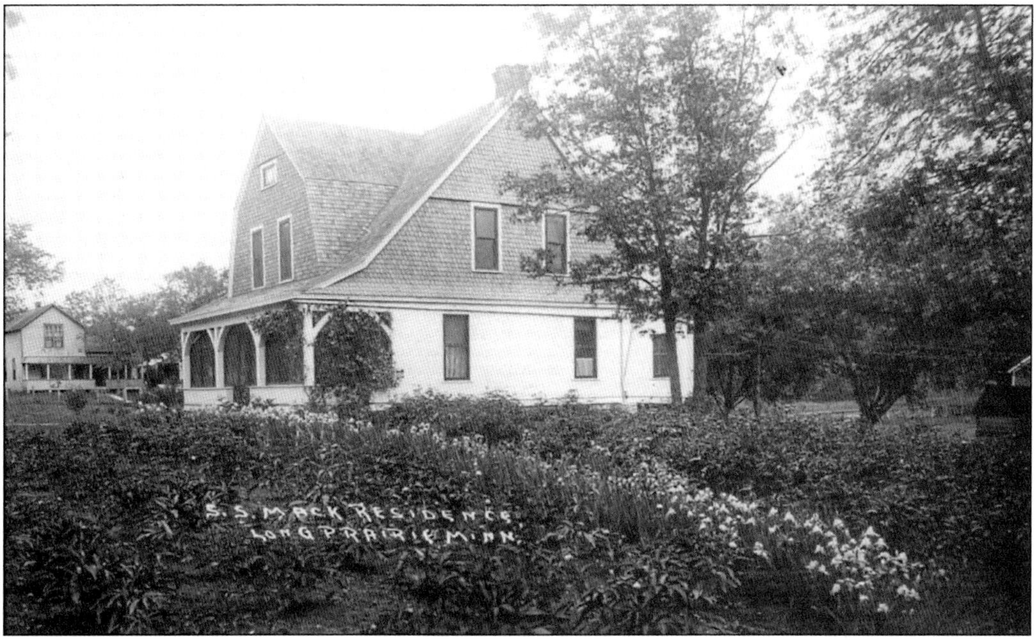

This home is located at 621 First Avenue Southeast. It was the residence of Sylvester "S.S." Mack. Not much is known about Mack. According to census information, he was a farmer in Decorah, Iowa, in 1870 and Round Prairie, Minnesota, in 1905. Shortly after that, he moved to Long Prairie and took up residence on Ford Street (First Avenue North). As of the 1930 census, he was still alive at the age of 82. (Author's collection.)

This home as seen today at 509 First Avenue Northeast was constructed in the 1890s by Arthur H. Sheets. Sheets was the publisher and owner of the *Todd County Argus* newspaper. The house was built for Sheets, his wife, Ella, and their 10 children. The residence was restored back to a single-family home in the late 1980s by Jerry and Marcy Caspers. (Author's collection.)

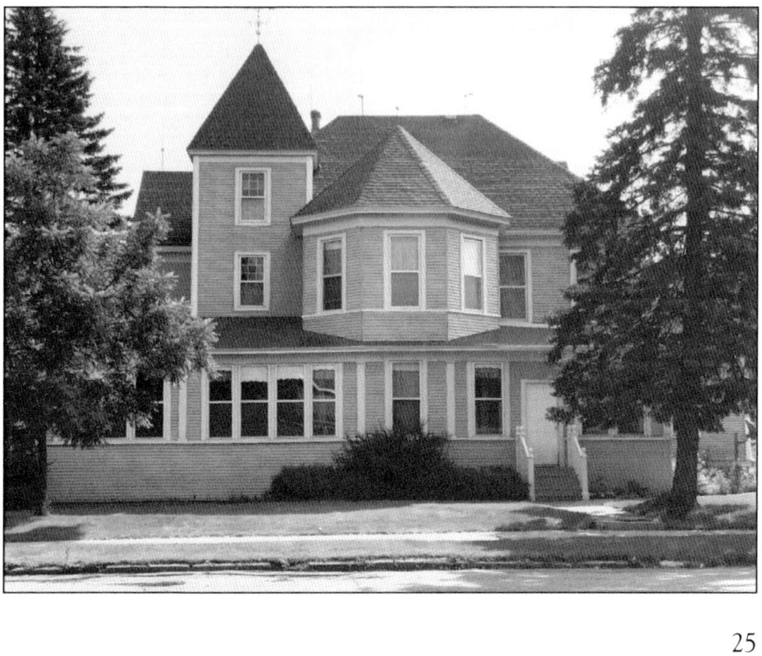

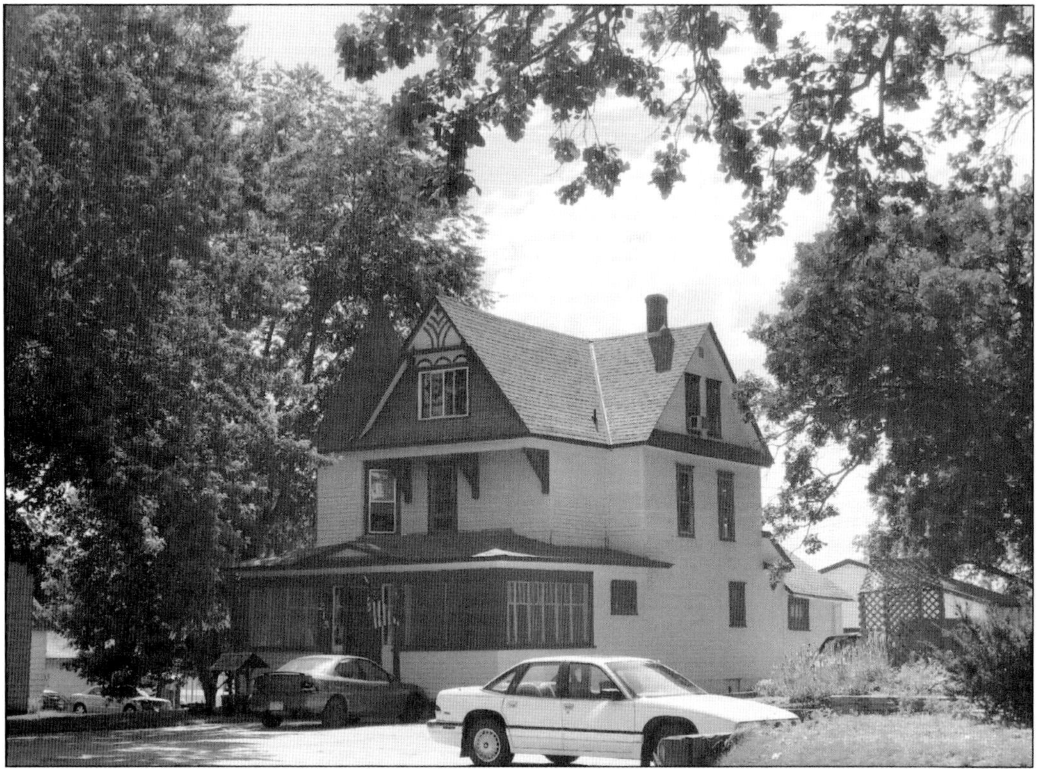

These two homes, known locally as the "Twin Houses," were constructed in 1895 by the Thiegs family. Soon after their construction, these homes became known as the Thiegs and Scow homes. Matt Scow and his third wife, Alberta, occupied the east house (above) from the late 1890s until their deaths. Matt passed away in 1944; Alberta, in 1968. Up until 1919, there was an electric generating plant that sat at about the location of 313 Second Avenue South, east of these homes. The homes along this block were heated by exhaust steam that came from the generating plant. Matt Scow came to Long Prairie because the town had a generating plant, as his interest was in milling, and he could utilize the plant's power. The Scow home is being lovingly restored by the current owner. (Both, author's collection.)

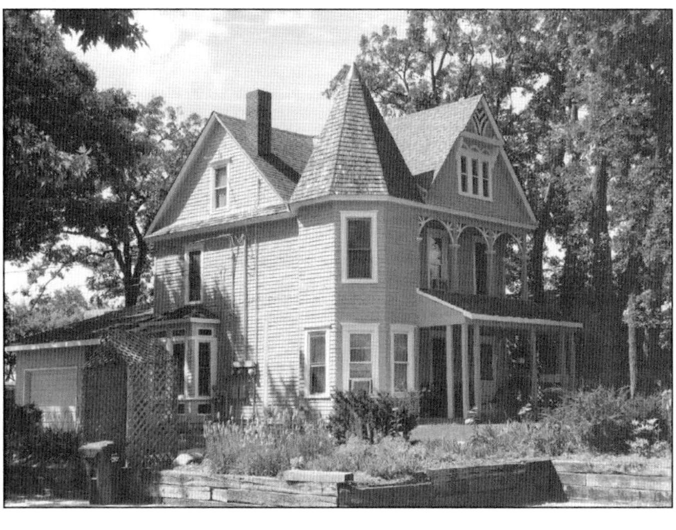

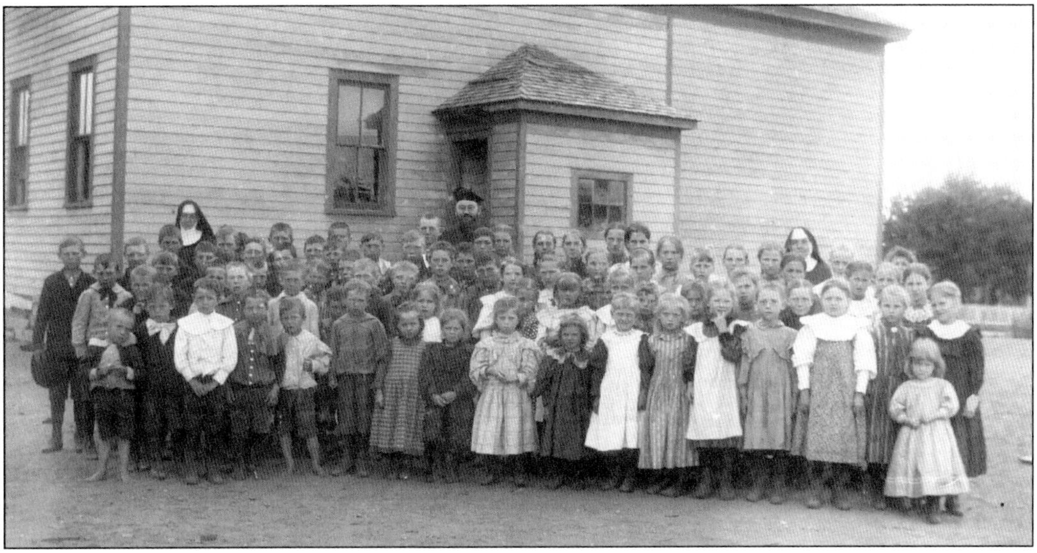

These photographs capture the children of St. Mary's Parochial School. The above image was captured in 1896. The wooden structure seen behind the children is the south side of the former St. Mary's Catholic Church before the current church was constructed. This church building sat where the current St. Mary's School, built in 1905, sits now. After the construction of the new church, this old church building was removed to the Todd County Fairgrounds, where it was used as an exhibit building for many years. These photographs were taken from nearly the exact same spot and facing nearly the same direction about 70 years apart. It would not be a stretch to think that some of the children in the above image could be grandparents to children in the below photograph. The picture below was taken in the mid-1960s. (Both, courtesy of St. Benedict Monastery.)

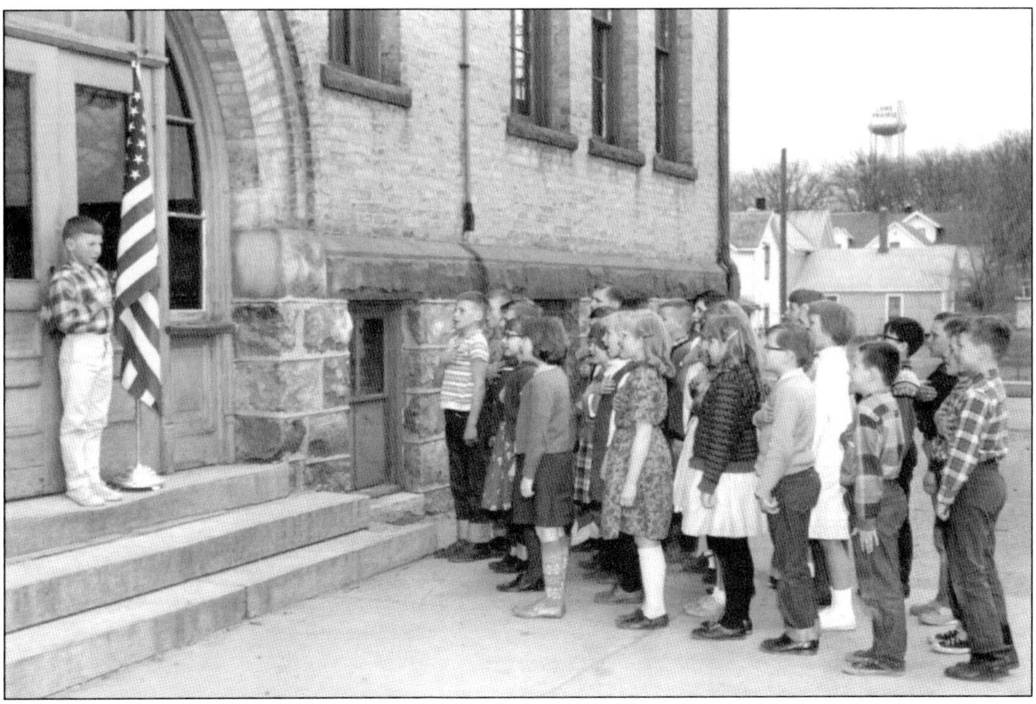

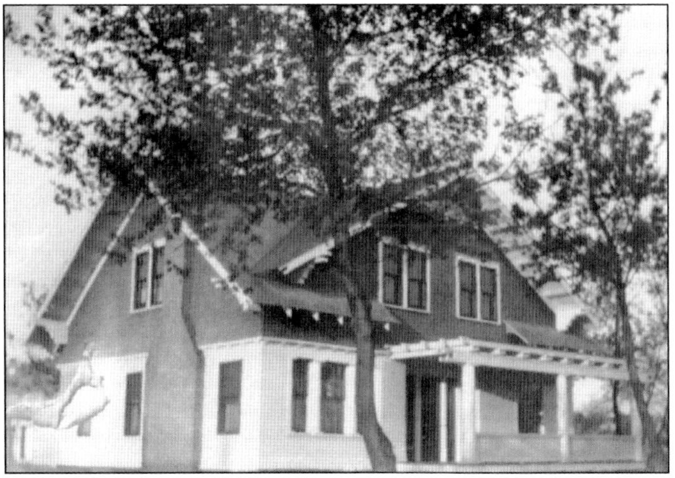

This home still stands at 315 Second Avenue North in Long Prairie. It was built by August Stephan, father of Myron Stephan, who was the town mortician for many years. Frank King, a lawyer, and his wife, Kay, lived in this home during the 1960s. The family of Bob Bauer lived in the home during the 1970s and 1980s, and Jerry Ruda purchased the home in the late 1980s. (Courtesy of Harold Connelly and Valley View Estates.)

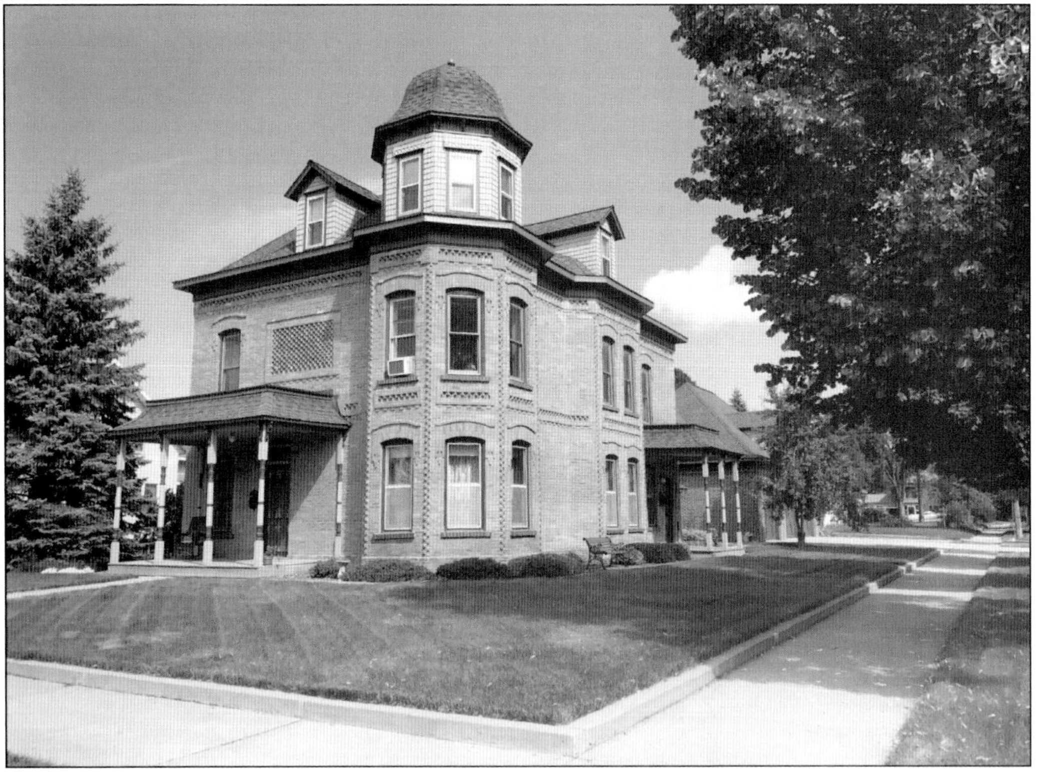

This three-story brick residence known as the Fisher House was built in 1884. The walls are constructed with two layers of brick, which were manufactured at the Schroeder Brick Yard east of Long Prairie. Shortly after the house was completed, it was purchased by a Dr. Fisher, a veteran of the Civil War. In the early 1980s, a fire destroyed much of the fine woodwork; however, an elaborate wooden staircase has been preserved. The house was purchased in 1987 by Orv and Rita Dahlen, who are restoring the home. (Author's collection.)

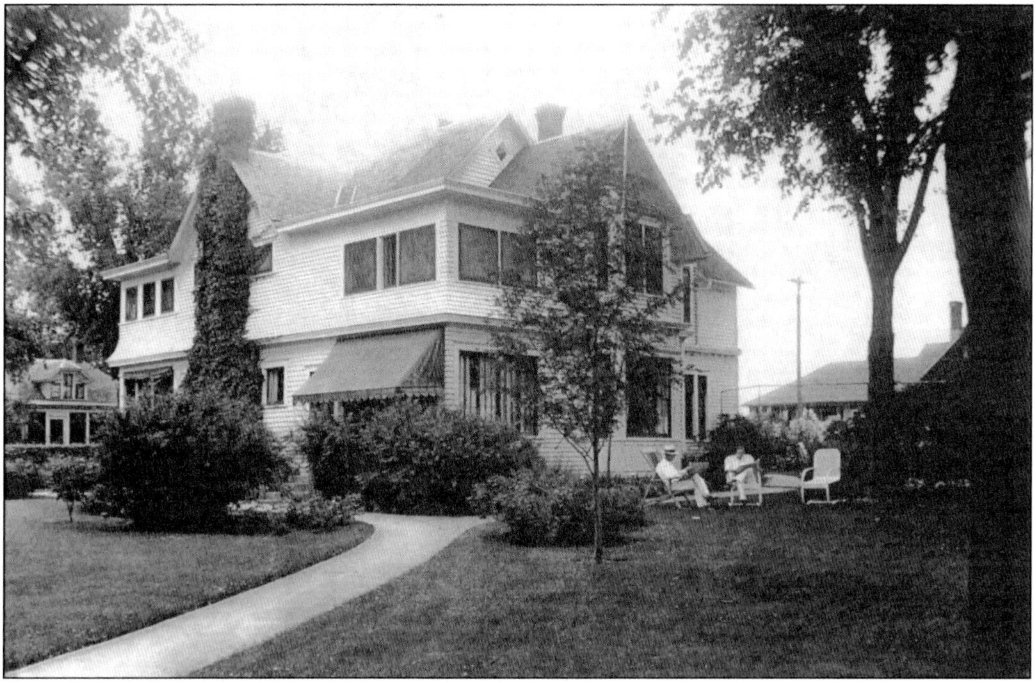

Located at 224 Second Avenue North, the C.F. Miller house was built in 1890. Miller was one of the prime movers and shakers in Long Prairie, becoming a prominent implement and automobile dealer. This home originally had open porches on the first and second levels. The hardwood floors consist of maple and dark oak with an alternating pattern. The home was owned by Dr. Kintop, a local chiropractor, and in recent years, it operated as a bed-and-breakfast named Crabtree Corners. (Courtesy of TCHS.)

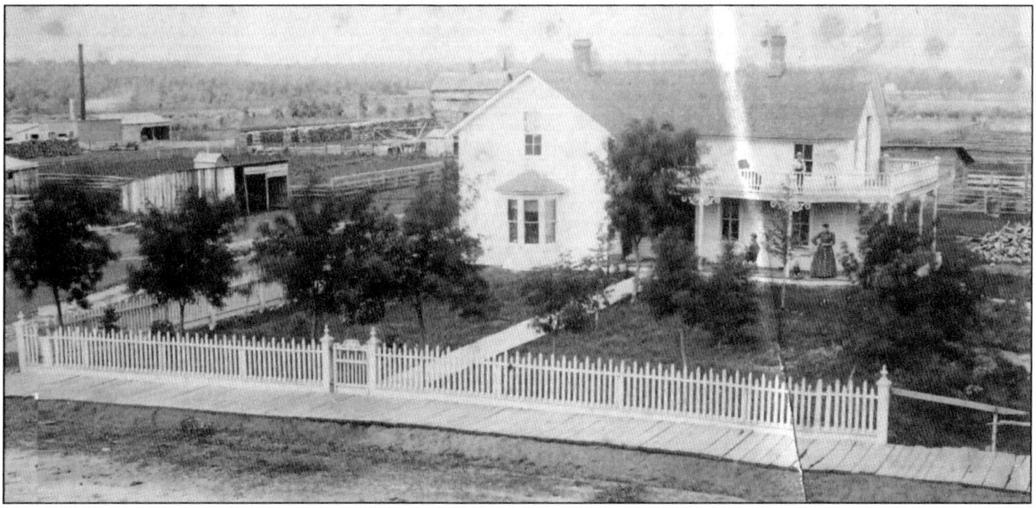

This 1888 photograph is of the Swan Thornquist home. The Thornquists lived here from 1888 to 1892. Swan operated a small apartment building where the present-day post office is located and just to the west of where a small newspaper plant at one time published the *Long Prairie Democrat*. This home sat on the corner kitty-corner across Central Avenue from the Christie Home. The S.S. Sargeant family then lived here. Mundry (Mundri) Mill is in the background. (Courtesy of the Christie Home Museum.)

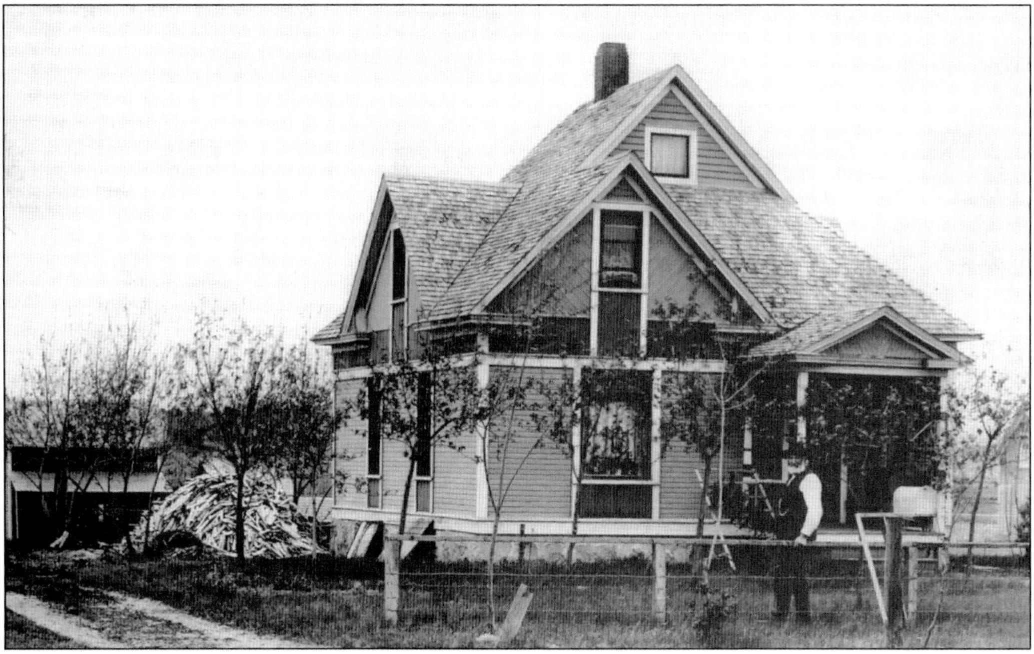

This home is located at 529 Lake Street South. As depicted in these photographs, the overall appearance of this home, built in 1901, has changed very little over the years. Joshua McCay, seen here in front of this house, purchased the home in 1902 and lived here until 1919. McCay, a Civil War veteran who fought in Arizona, was taken prisoner, returned to the Union, again fought in Chancellorsville, Fredericksburg, and Gettysburg, and came to Todd County in 1869. He was a farmer and county commissioner, playing a part in establishing the Great Northern Railroad in this county. The home was purchased by August Minke in 1919 and transferred to Robert and Ella Minke in 1938. Ella sold the home to Franklin and Kathleen Bertzyk in 1981. In 1990, Vanguard Insurance purchased the house. (Above, courtesy of TCHS; below, author's collection.)

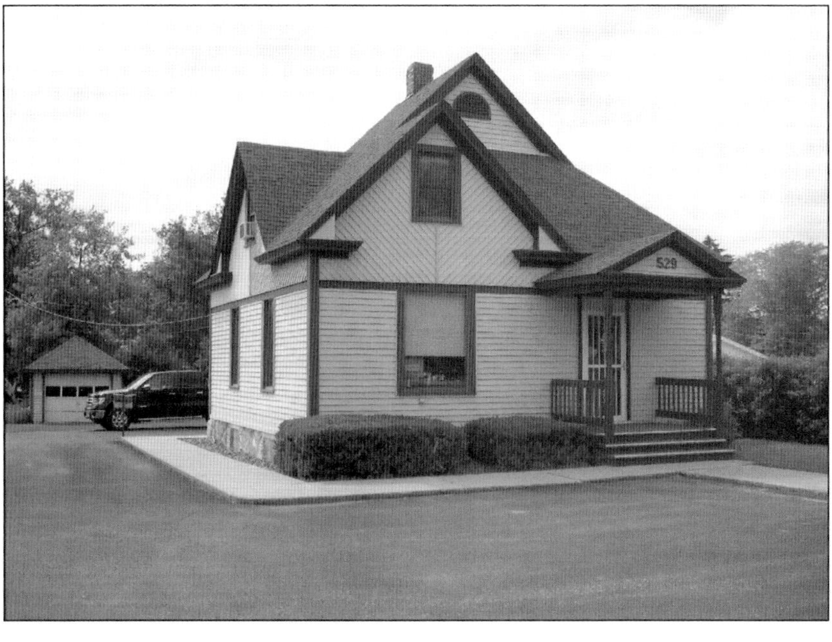

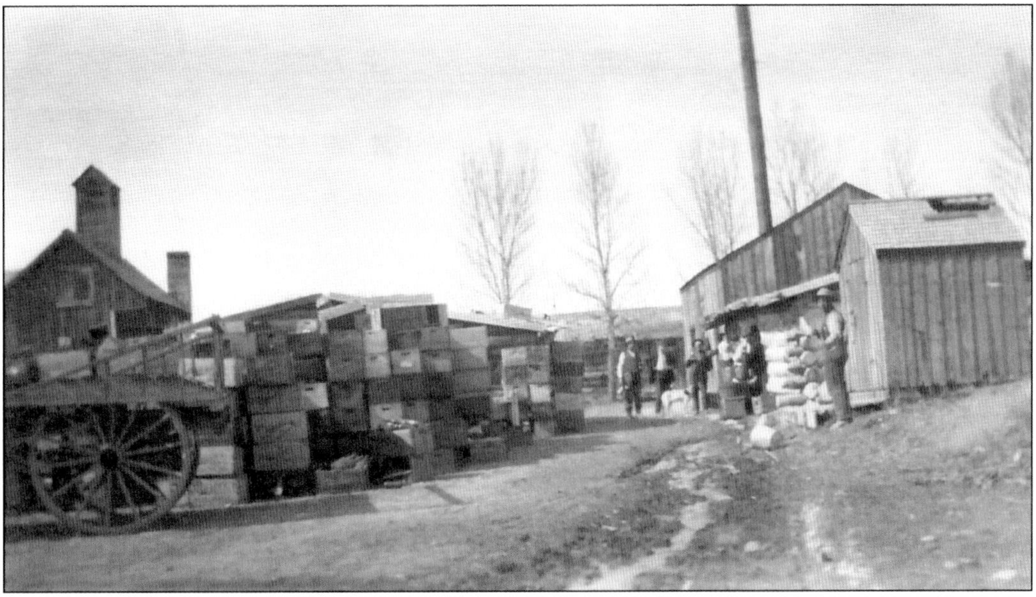

The Long Prairie Brewing Company was established in 1874 by Geppert Rohner. In 1906, it was sold to C.F. Hirth and Joe Niedermair. The brewery was located on the west side of Venewitz Creek in Long Prairie in the area of 405 First Street Southwest. The Rohner home has recently been restored and still stands at 324 First Street Southwest. Joe Rohner was the son of Geppert, seen below in 1906 during the construction of his home located at 544 First Street South. The home still stands at that location today. The Rohners also had an "ice barn" that sat directly west of the Joe Rohner residence. The Rohners would cut the ice out of Lake Charlotte and store it in the ice barn, supplying ice to the residents of the village. (Both, courtesy of Brian Cowdery.)

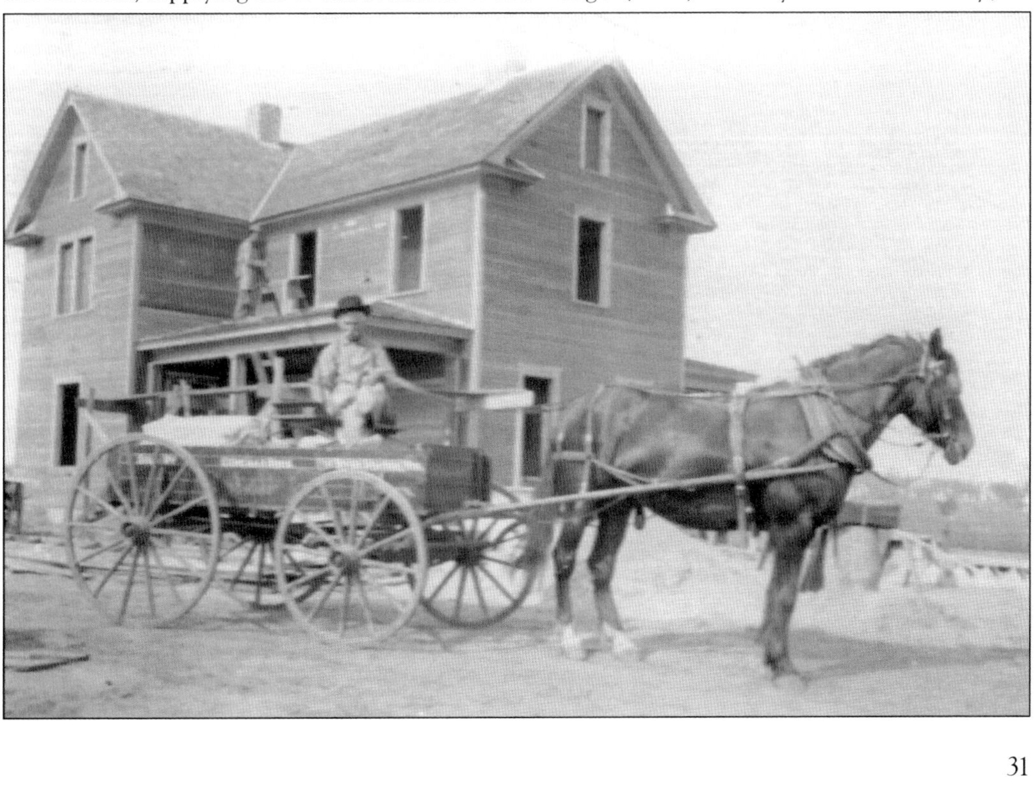

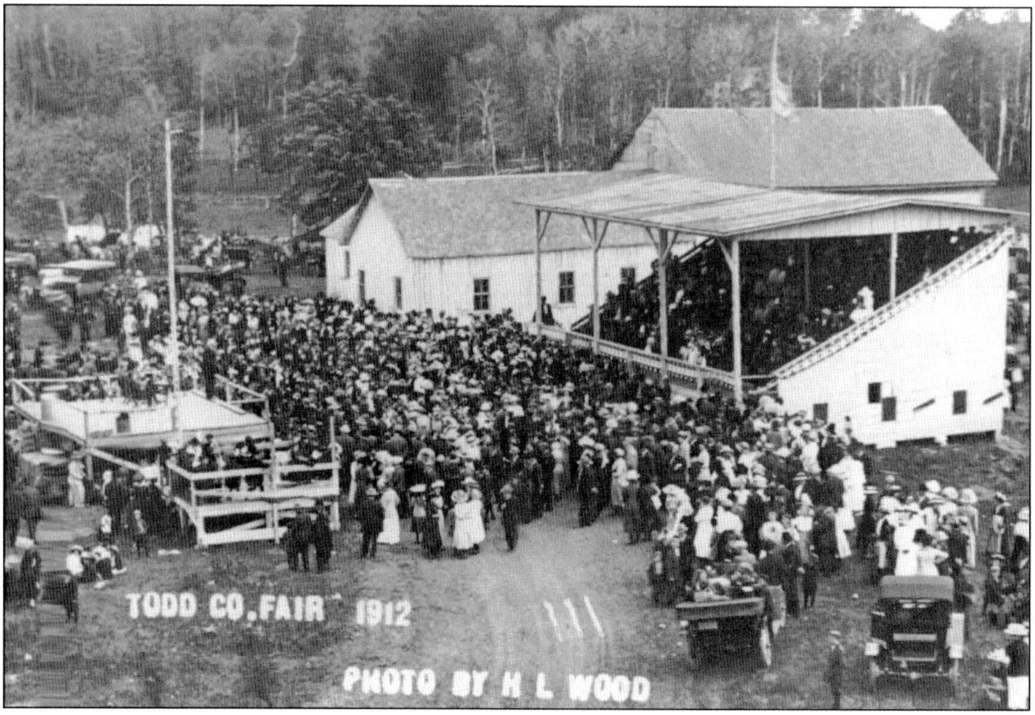

The photograph above of the 1912 Todd County Fair captures the building layout and grandstand of the fairgrounds back in those days. This small wooden grandstand was used for many years prior to the construction of the current grandstand in 1940. This wooden grandstand was located about where the sandstone "Senior High School" sign leading into the current high school parking lot stands now. It faced west. Taken in 1910, the photograph below shows a football game between Long Prairie and Sauk Centre. The football field was at the fairgrounds. In the background is a larger building to the left of the large tent. That building is just to the side of the grandstand in the above photograph. The grandstand had not been built yet in 1910. By the way, Long Prairie won, 49–0, per the information on the back of the image. (Above, courtesy of the Christie Home Museum; below, author's collection.)

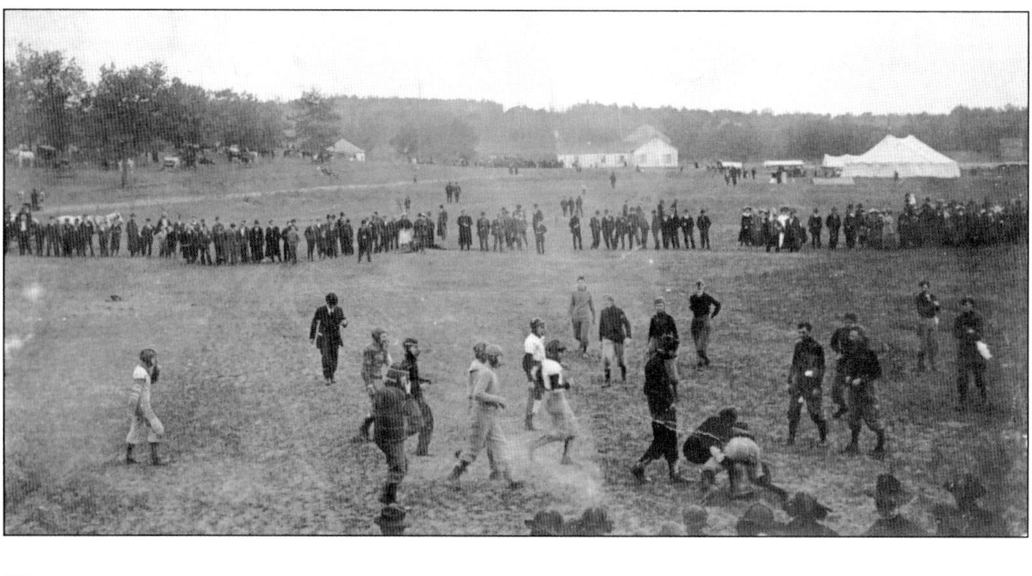

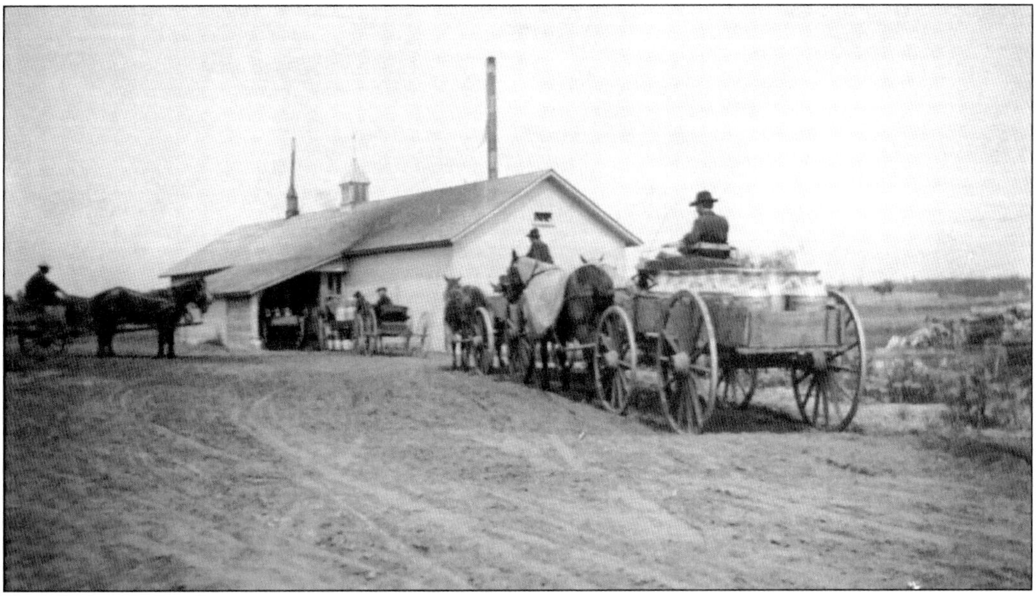

Located in the area of 111 Fairview Avenue Northwest, the first creamery in Long Prairie was operated in 1891 by Ward and Scow, seen here. It failed and was later owned by G. Karlen. This creamery was discontinued when the Todd County Co-operative Creamery was organized in Long Prairie. That creamery was located along the river on the north side of town, where the former outdoor skating and hockey rink was located. (Courtesy of TCHS.)

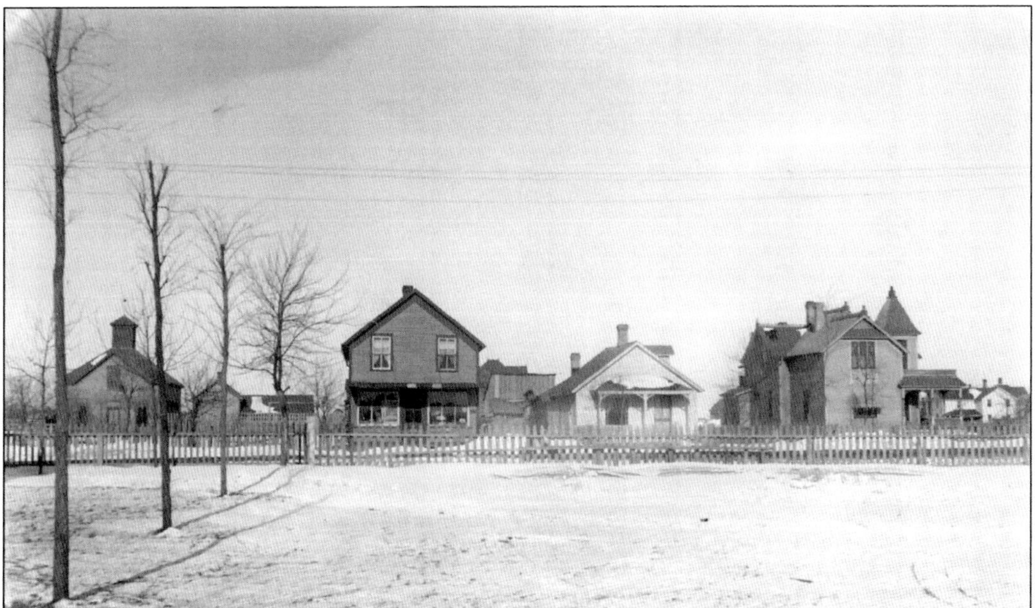

With a view looking north, this undated photograph was taken from a location about where the current Countryside Restaurant stands. The homes seen here were located on the north side of Central Avenue; they no longer stand. The large home on the right was the residence of E.A. Leidl, a local dentist. It stood on the corner currently occupied by Everybody's Market. The middle home with the two second-floor windows was the childhood home of local resident Rich Wall; it stood at 20 Central Avenue. (Courtesy of the Christie Home Historical Society.)

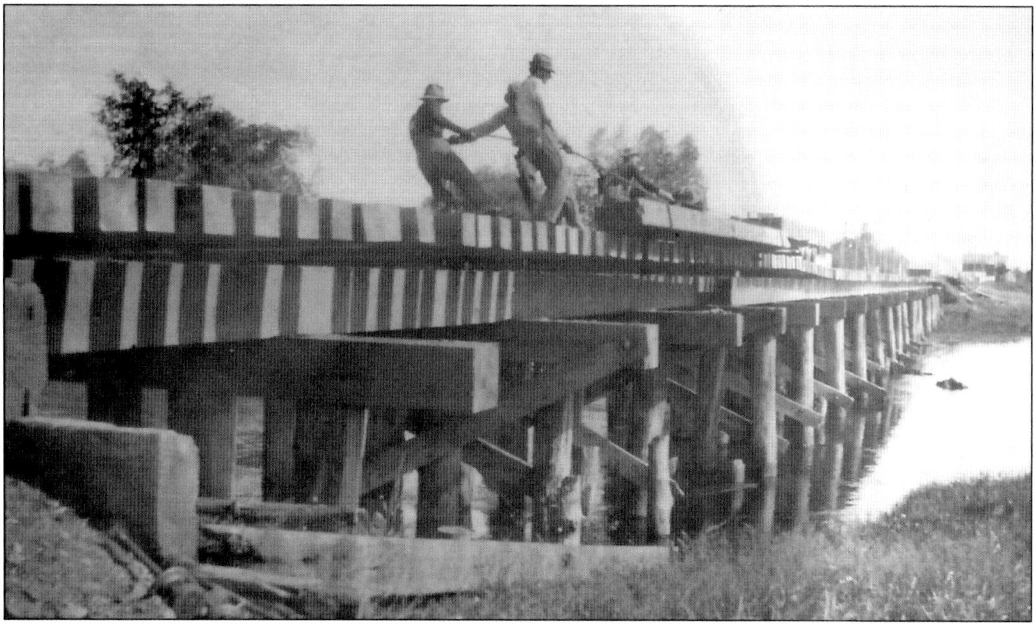

The railroad was built through Long Prairie in 1880 by the Sauk Center and Northern. Almost immediately, it was purchased by the St. Paul, Minneapolis, & Manitoba Railway. In 1907, it became part of the Great Northern Railway, and in 1970, it was merged into the Burlington Northern, which abandoned the line in Long Prairie in 1983. With a view looking south down the line, this undated photograph was taken from the north end of the Long Prairie River railroad bridge. (Author's collection.)

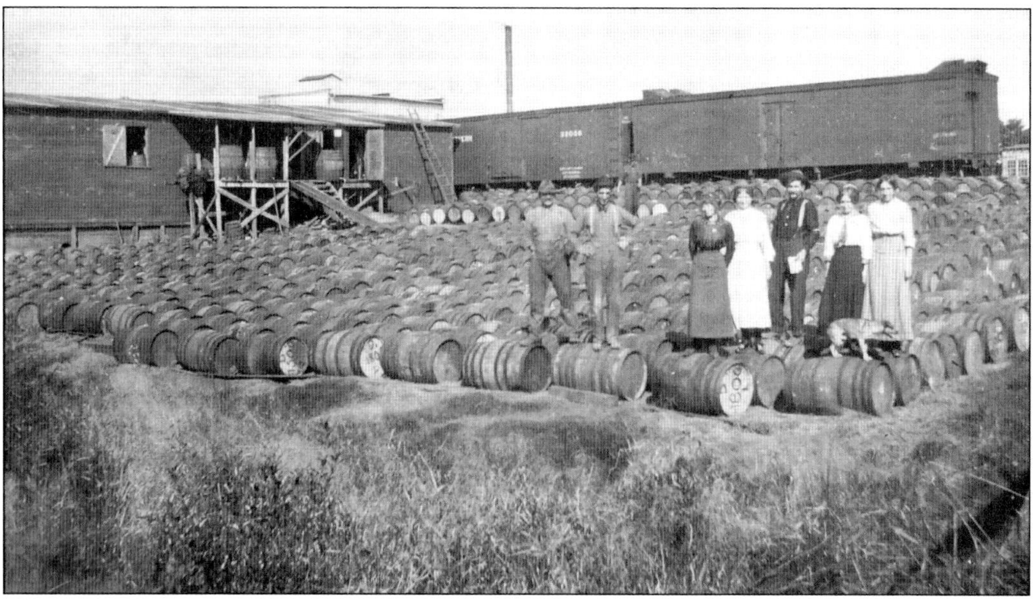

The Hansmann pickle factory in Long Prairie was established around 1913 and located between the east bank of Venewitz Creek and the railroad tracks, about where the storage garages currently stand. The factory was opened due to the large numbers of farmers that were growing pickles at the time. The pickles were packaged in barrels and transported to locations far and wide to supply retailers. (Author's collection.)

Two

Downtown

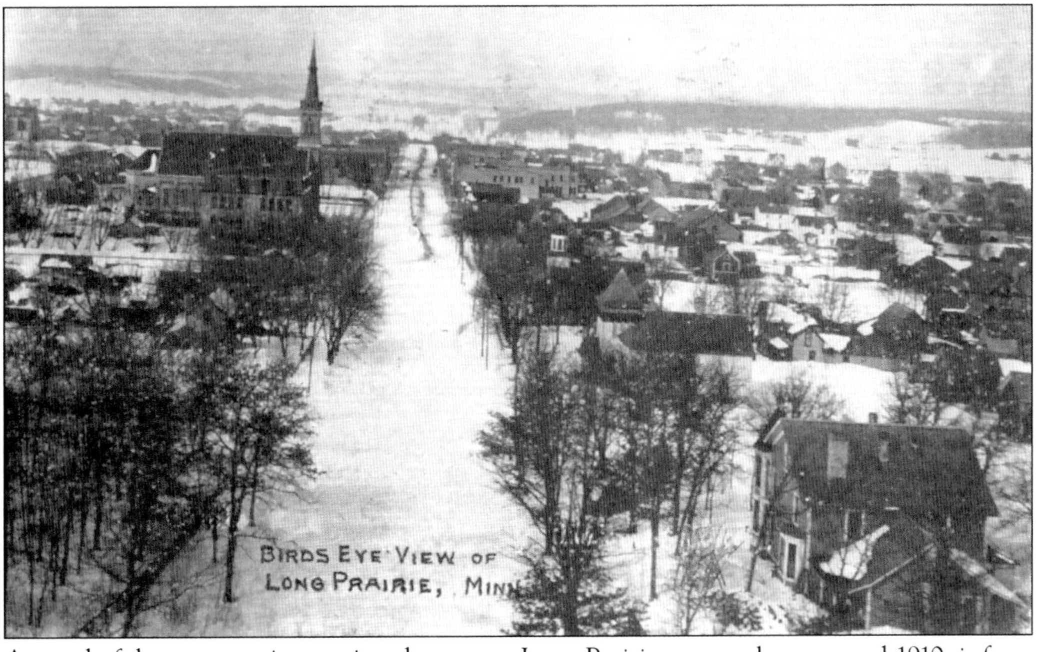

A wonderful vantage point to view downtown Long Prairie, as seen here around 1910, is from "Water Tank Hill." In 1896, a large water tank was erected on the hill in the eastern part of the village. Some 10 or 12 years after this tank was erected, the hoops gave way and the tank collapsed. A replacement tank was built on the same steel structure. One morning in April 1912, a terrific explosion destroyed the tank and the steel structure. (Author's collection.)

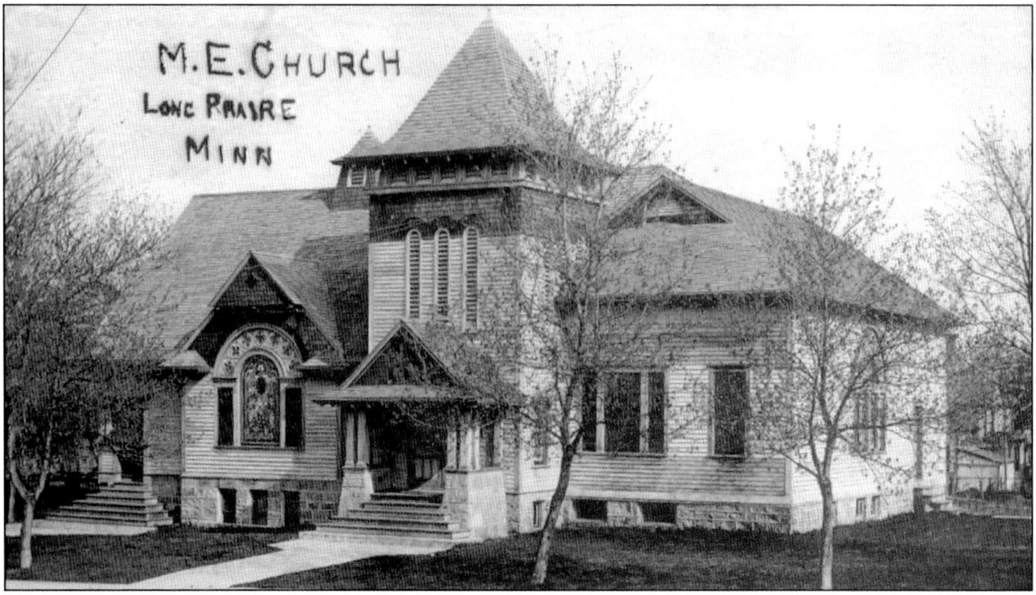

On March 20, 1876, a Methodist church in Long Prairie was organized. The estate and property of the Methodist church was established with the name St. Peter's Methodist Church. This location of the Methodist church was deeded on May 23, 1876. The church in this undated photograph, constructed in 1900, sat in the parking lot of the current church at 524 Central Avenue. This church burned down in about 1941, in what was believed to be arson. (Author's collection.)

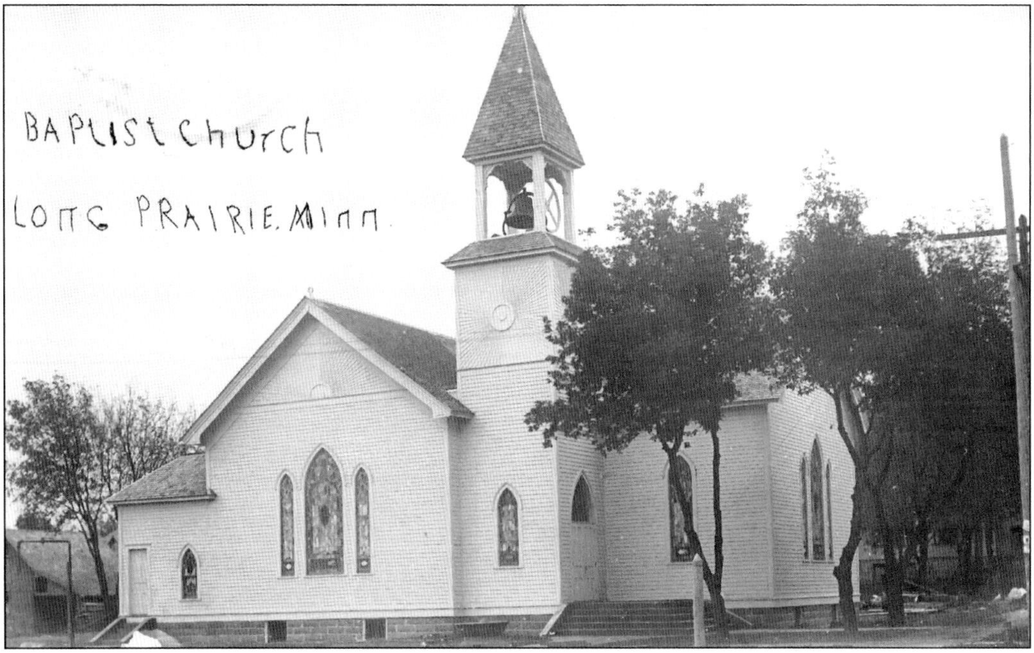

In 1910, the original First Baptist Church was moved 50 feet to the west and additions were made to two sides to enlarge the structure as seen here in 1911. At this time, the stained-glass windows were added at a total cost of $300. In 1967, this building was dismantled when the new church was built on the corner of Fourth Street and Fourth Avenue Southeast. (Author's collection.)

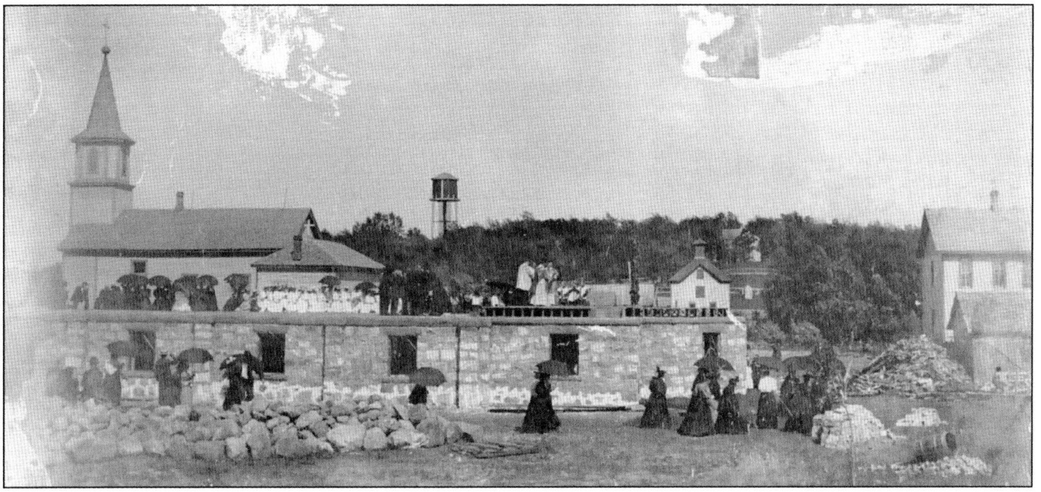

The Long Prairie congregation of St. Mary's had its first service in May 1869 in the home of a Mr. Venewitz. In the fall of that same year, a log church was constructed. The St. Mary's Catholic Church was constructed in 1896. Prior to the building of the current church, located on the site of the current St. Mary's School, a small wooden structure was used as a church. These photographs capture the event of the present-day St. Mary's Catholic Church cornerstone dedication in 1896. Nearly the entire congregation attended this momentous event. (Both, courtesy of TCHS.)

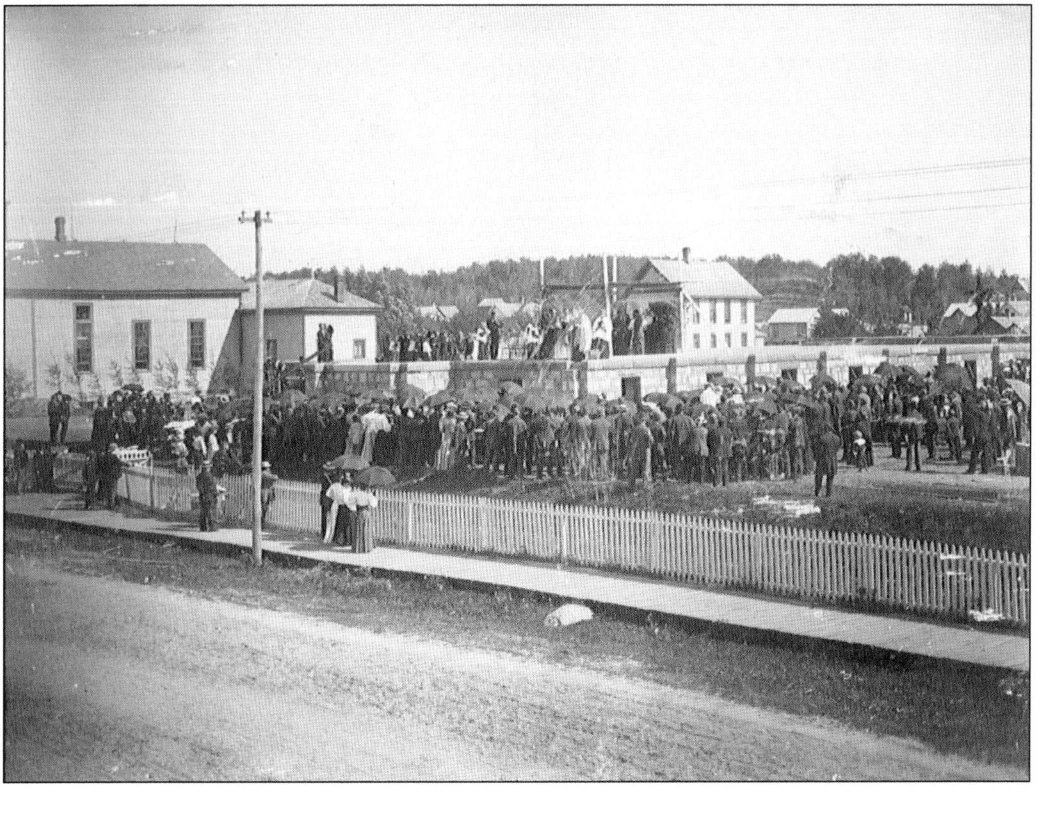

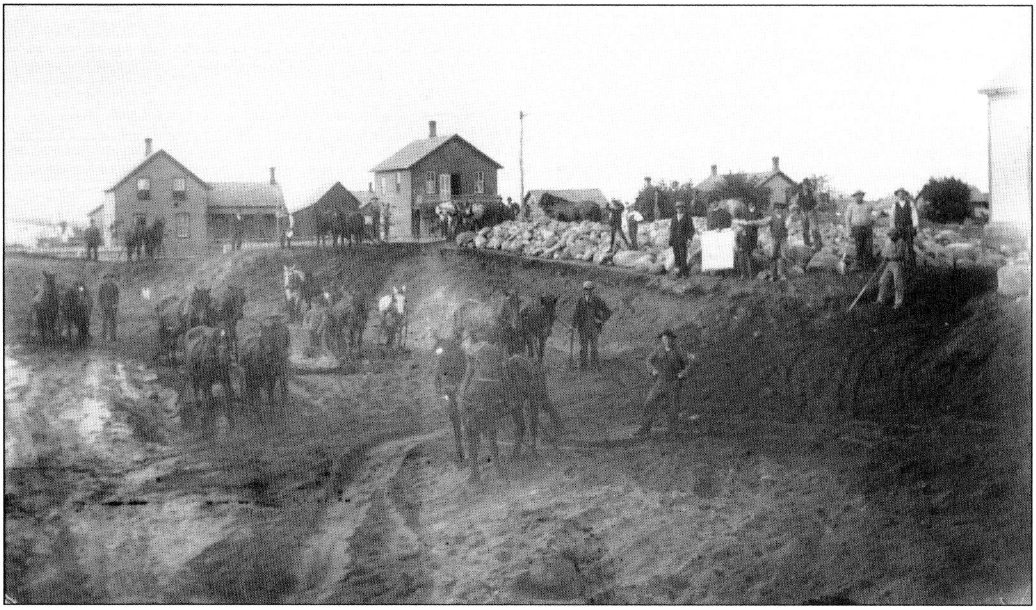

John Alfs, who conducted a small shoe repair and shoe retail store, came to Long Prairie in 1883. After some 10 years on a farm, he moved into the village and engaged in the shoe sales and repair trade until his death in 1931. His store was located directly across Central Avenue from St. Mary's Church. The photograph above is showing the digging out of the St. Mary's Catholic Church basement in 1896. In this image, one can pick out the Alfs home, as shown below in 1971. The Alfs residence was located next door to the repair shop. The shoe repair shop and the residence no longer stand. The home sat on the current site of Hats Off Coffee. (Above, courtesy of St. Benedict Monastery; below, courtesy of Harold Connelly and Valley View Estates.)

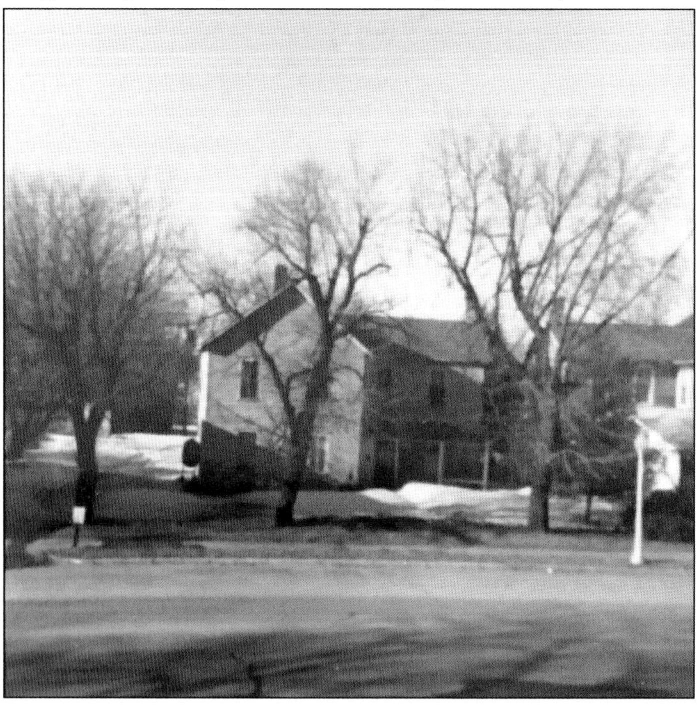

This 1970 photograph is of John Alfs shoe repair and shoe retail store. Alfs was a grandfather of the late Harold Connelly, a well-known and beloved man of Long Prairie. Just like his maternal grandfather, Harold was a quiet, friendly man and was highly esteemed by all who knew him. (Courtesy of Harold Connelly and Valley View Estates.)

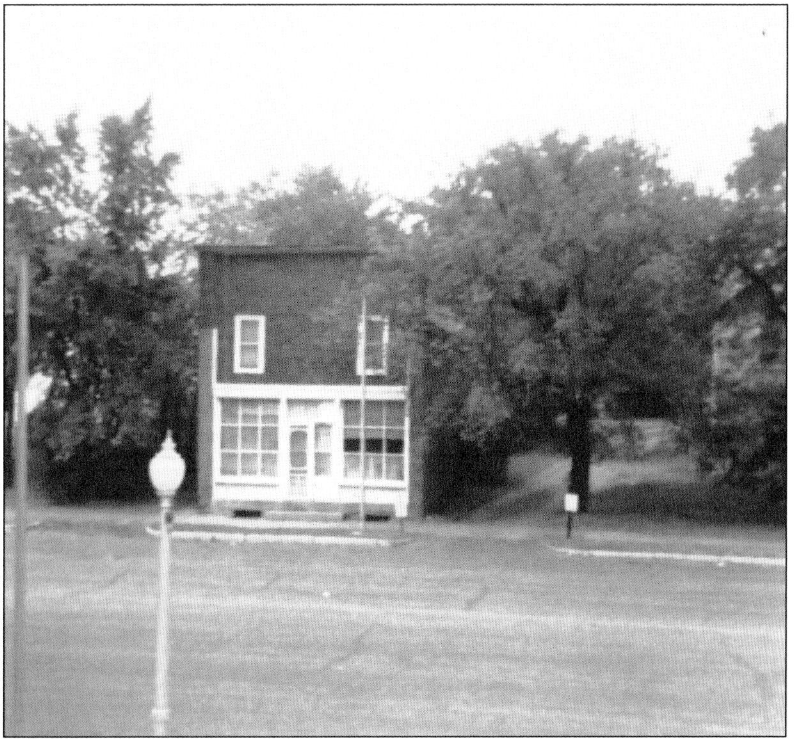

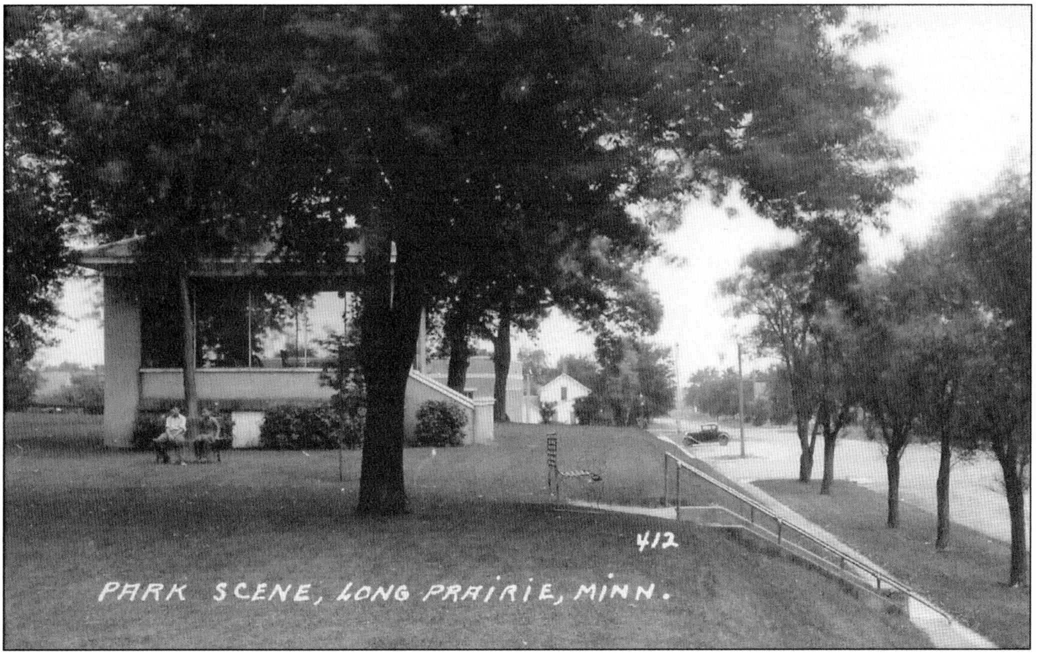

One of only two city parks original platted in Long Prairie, Lee Park was named after William Lee. This old landmark of the village was elevated from four to ten feet above street level. The view in this 1941 photograph is looking north towards the post office. (Courtesy of Barb Hamel.)

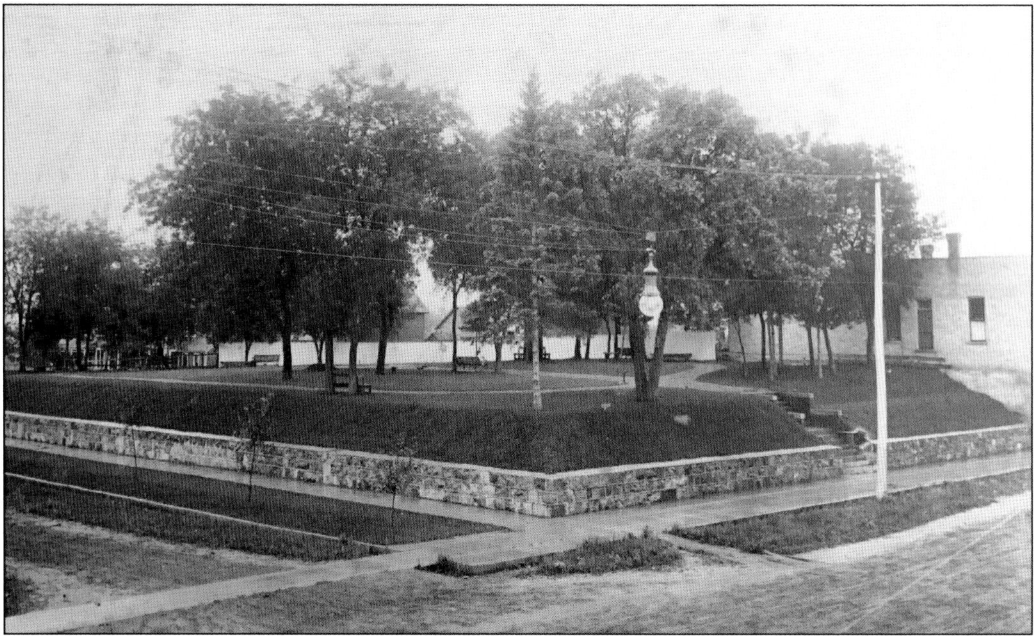

This location that was Lee Park (seen above) may easily be argued as the birthplace of Long Prairie, as the agency house sat here during the Winnebago Agency days. The park was used as a tourist park years ago and for band concerts by local bands. The entire park was abandoned and removed by the city in 1950. The fill was purchased and used to make a new athletic field for the high school, and the bandstand was moved out to the swimming beach at Lake Charlotte. Coincidentally, the Todd County Historical Society (pictured below) sits on this birth site of Long Prairie. (Both, author's collection.)

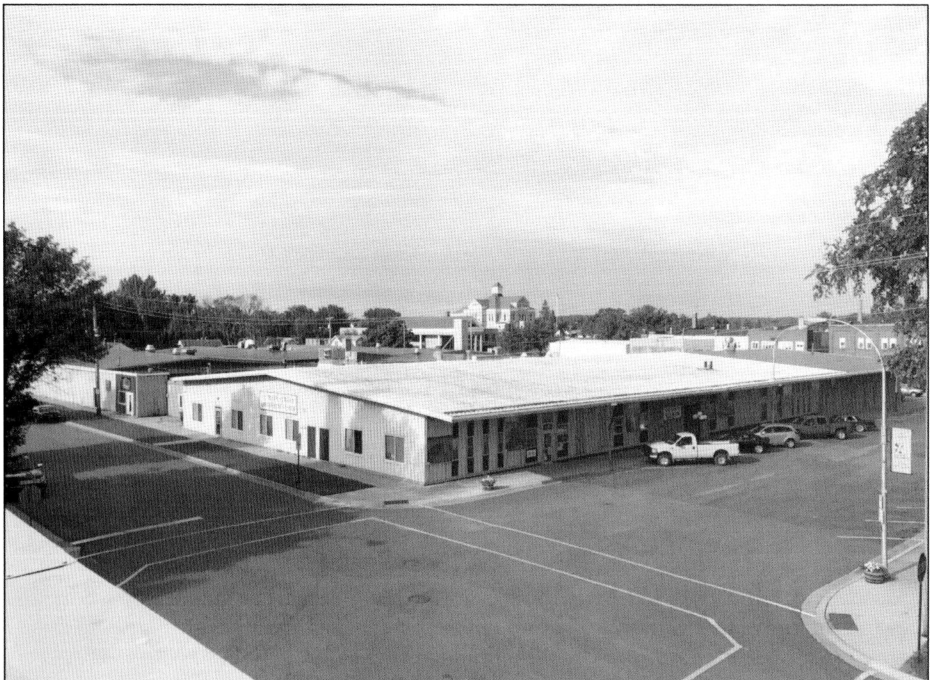

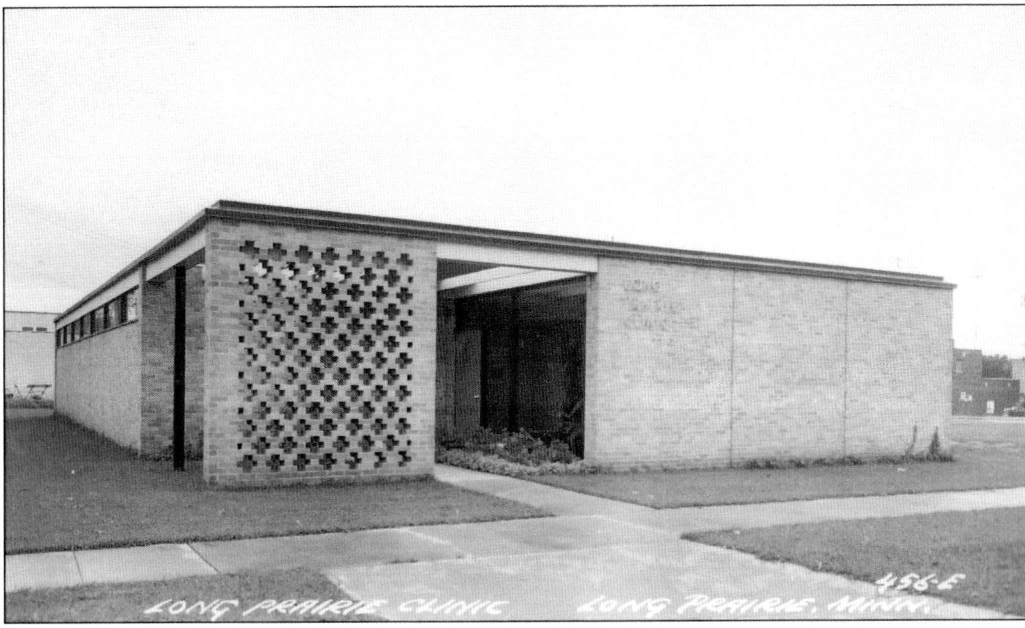

After the abandonment and removal of Lee Park by the city in 1950, this section of the block became home to the Long Prairie Clinic (seen here in about 1956), the Palmgren and Clavin residences, and eventually the Hart Press. Currently occupying a major section of the former Hart Press building and former clinic building, Krain Creek Fabrication is the builder of construction trailers. (Author's collection.)

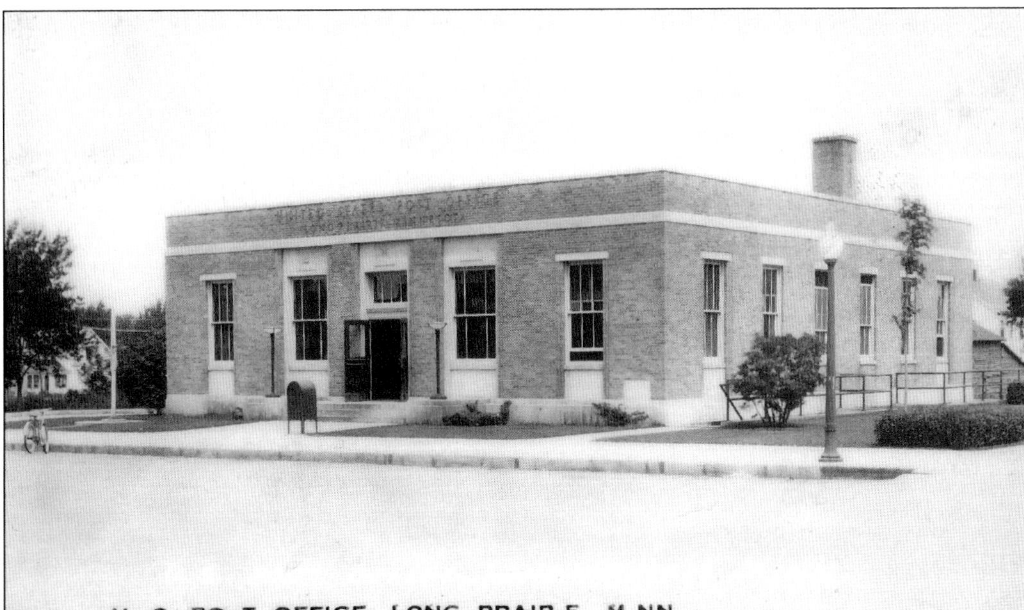

The current post office in Long Prairie was constructed in 1936. It has had some interior alterations throughout the years, but remains largely unchanged as viewed from the outside. The east lobby wall of the post office boasts a fresco painted by Sister Lucia Wiley titled *Indians Gathering Wild Rice*, commissioned by the Works Progress Administration in 1939. (Author's collection.)

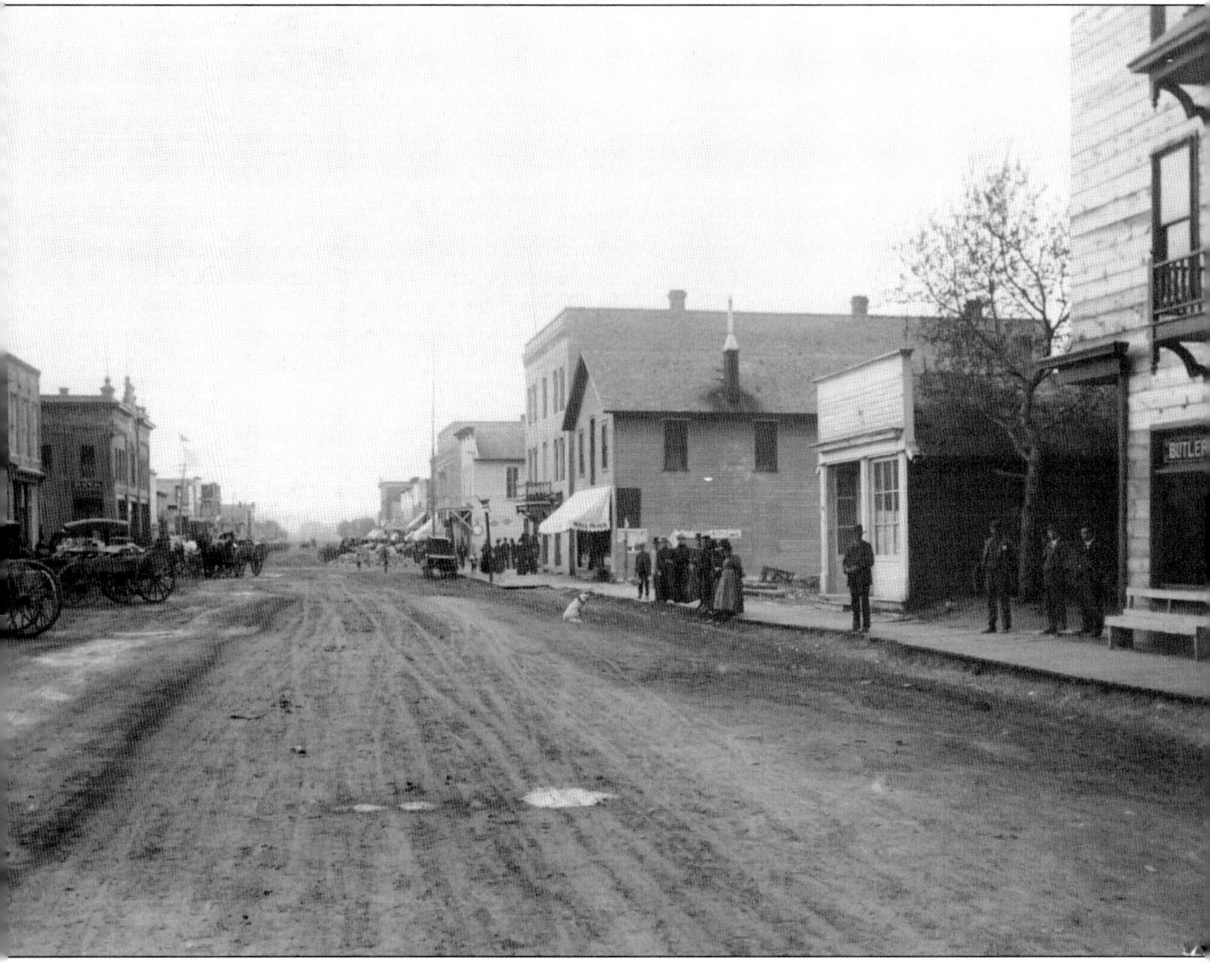

This photograph from about around 1900 was taken from the vantage point in front of the current post office; the view is looking west down Central Avenue, then known as Osakis Street. The Butler's Hotel, on the far right edge of the photograph, stood just west of where the post office stands today. The hotel was built by Walter "Bob" Butler. He first worked in the American Hotel, which stood on the corner directly south of the Reichert Hotel building on Central Avenue during the late 1800s. When Butler struck out on his own, he first opened a restaurant that became so successful, he turned it into the hotel seen in this image. The hotel seemed to be doing very well when it was destroyed by fire in 1902. The hotel was not rebuilt. Traces of the old foundation of the hotel could be seen up through the 1940s. The large three-story building three doors down the street is the Reichert Hotel, which stood on the same corner as today's Reichert. (Courtesy of TCHS.)

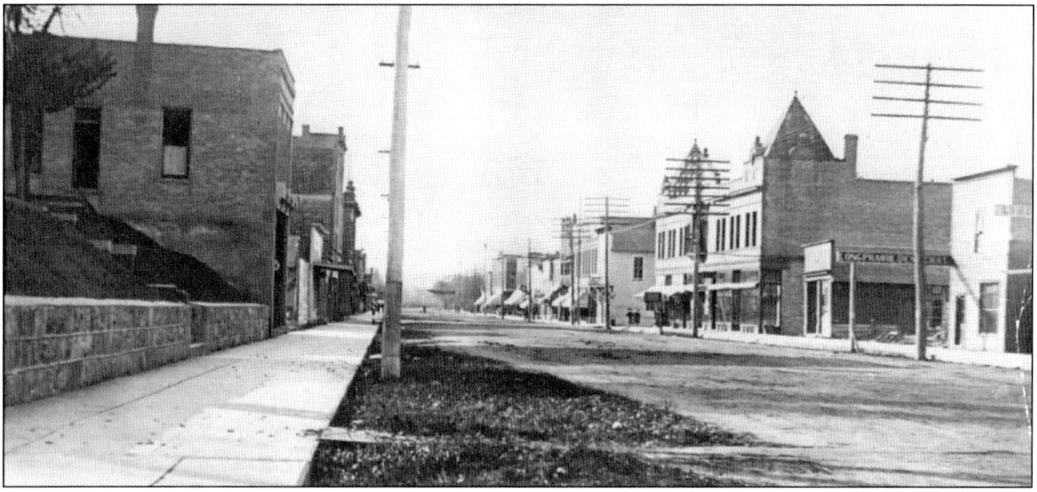

As with many small towns, the Main Street has seen many changes. Long Prairie's Main Street was original named Osakis Street before it was renamed Central Avenue. The original street, which rose sharply to the east, was "shaved down" in 1881, with the excavated material used to fill in the low spots on its west end. This photograph captures Osakis Street in the 1920s. (Author's collection.)

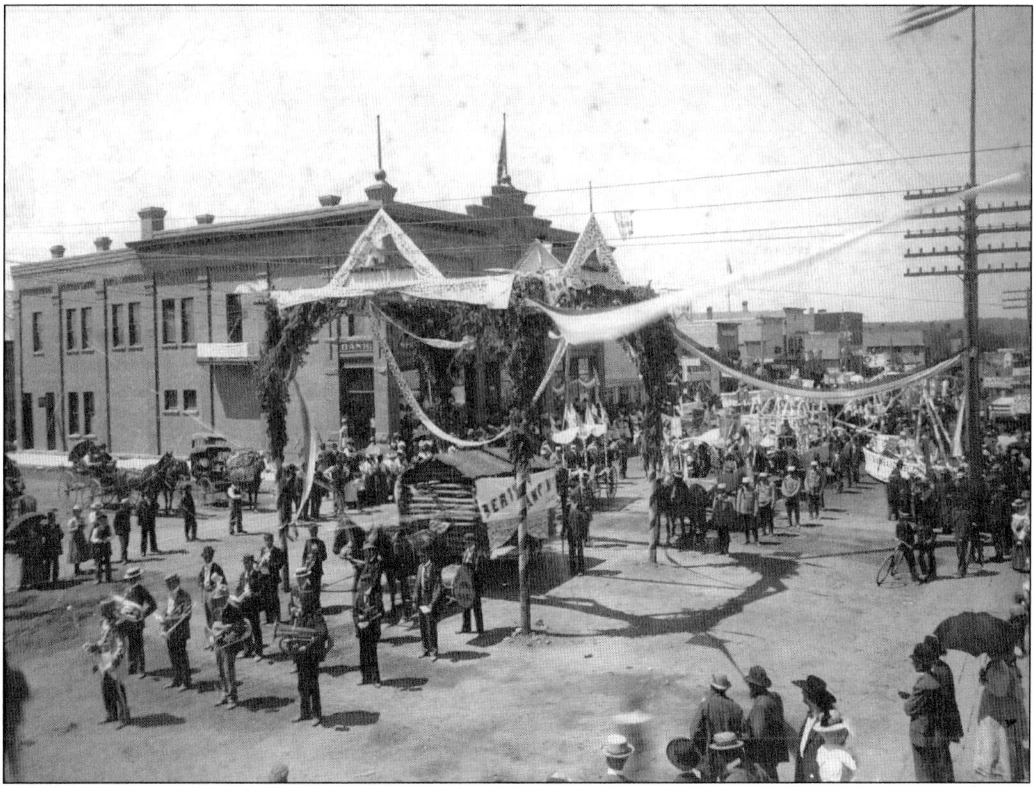

As with any small town in America, generations of residents in Long Prairie spared no expense utilizing their Main Street as a backdrop for celebrations. This 1904 photograph of the Fourth of July celebration and parade in Long Prairie undoubtedly captures this town pride. (Courtesy of TCHS.)

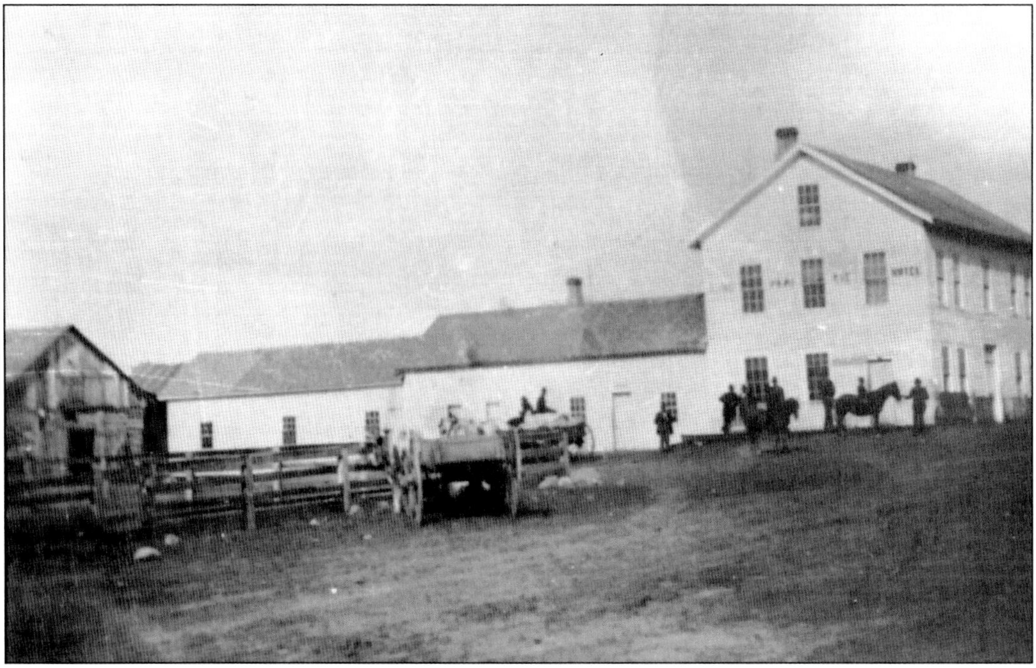

The Reichert Hotel property was founded by Ignatius Reichert in 1869. Up to this time, there were five different hotel buildings on this corner, starting with a small log building. Pictured above is the third hotel property, named the Long Prairie House. A number of these buildings were destroyed by fire. The last fire took place in March 1902 and completely destroyed the fourth property, also known as the Long Prairie House, seen below, and the drugstore on the east side of the hotel building occupied by Reichert and Schenk Drug company. At the time of the fire in 1902, the fire department had a hard time putting out the blaze, as firefighters could not locate the new fire hydrant wrenches for some time to get water on the fire. (Both, courtesy of TCHS.)

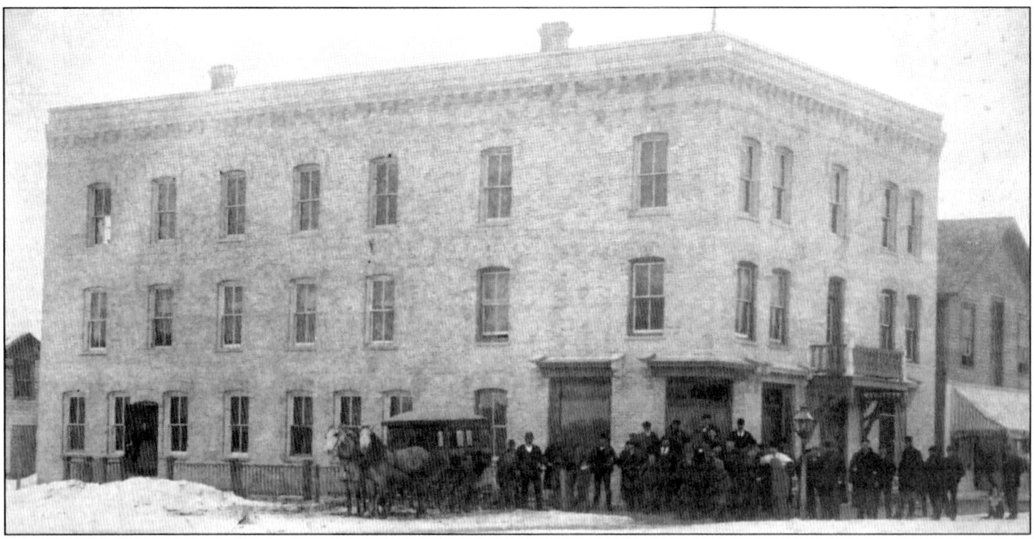

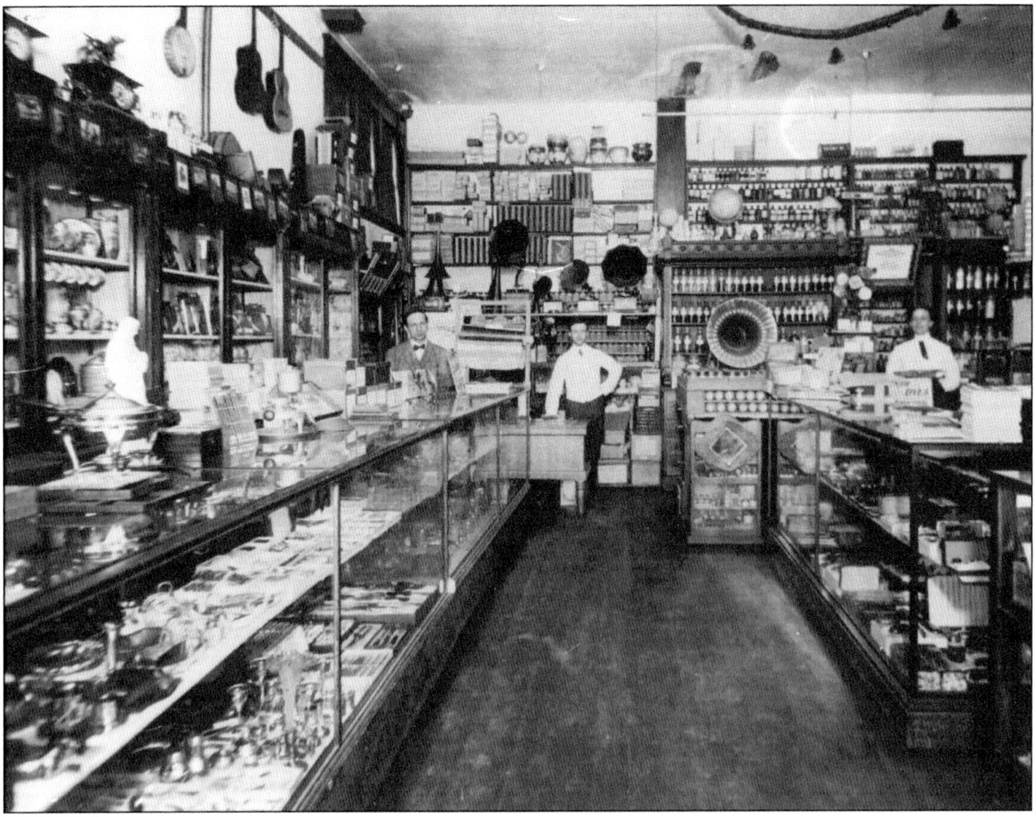

These early-1900s photographs show Eddy and Amalia Schenk inside the "new" Reichert & Schenk store located in the fifth Reichert Hotel building to occupy this location. The first Reichert & Schenk drugstore was started in 1891 in a modest frame building that sat just east of the current Reichert building. This first building burned down in the Long Prairie House fire in March 1902. The business moved into the new Reichert Hotel and occupied the southwest room of the ground floor. At one time, this Reichert & Schenk drugstore bought pianos by the carload and conducted a retail piano business, along with Edison and Victor photographs for a number of years (as seen in the photographs), as well as offering pretty much all necessities of life. (Both, courtesy of Rich and Marge Wall.)

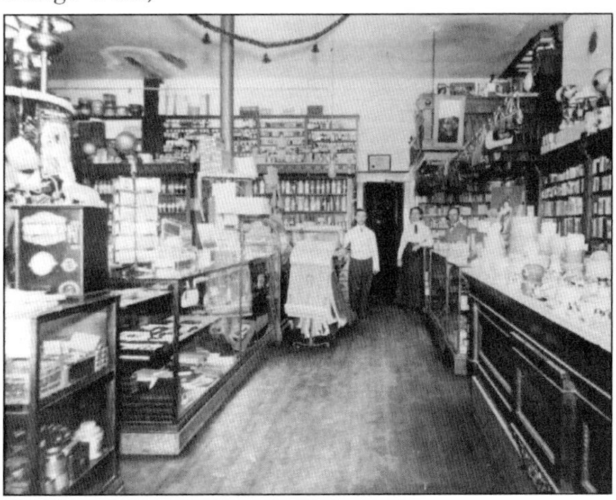

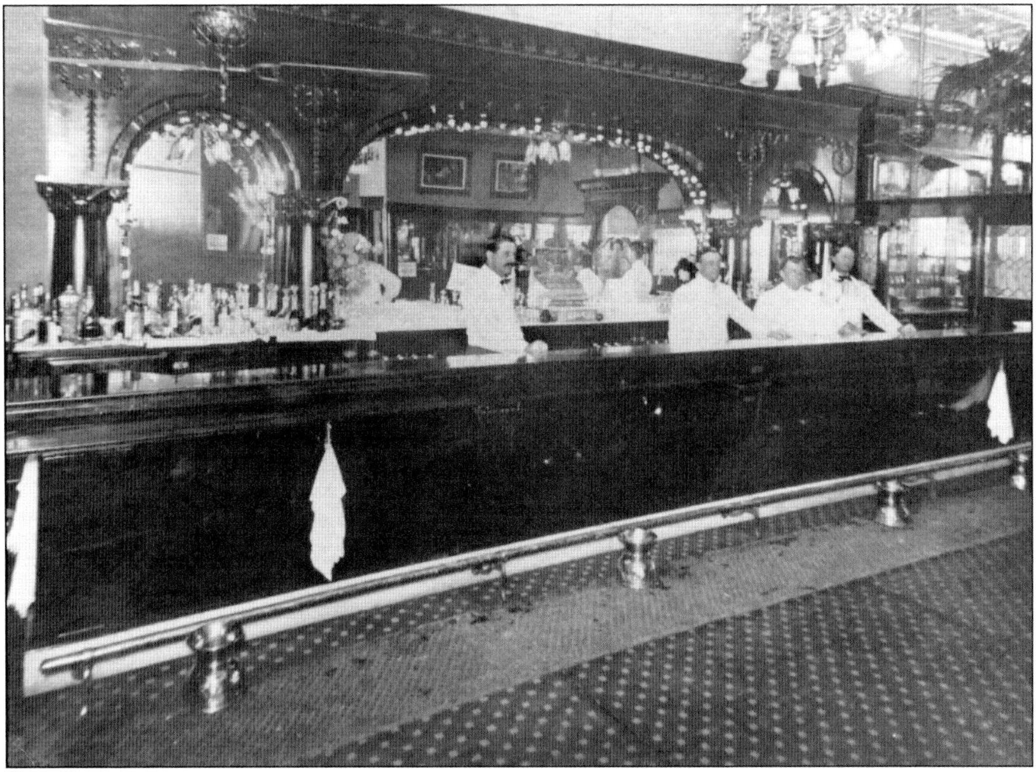

It seemed no expense was spared in the construction of the new Reichert Hotel. This grand bar was welcoming to the travelers of the day. The towels hanging off the bar were used to wipe the foam off of the men's beards. The formal opening of the hotel took place on February 23, 1903. A testimonial ball and banquet was given to the Reichert Improvement Company by the citizens of Long Prairie. (Courtesy of Rich and Marge Wall.)

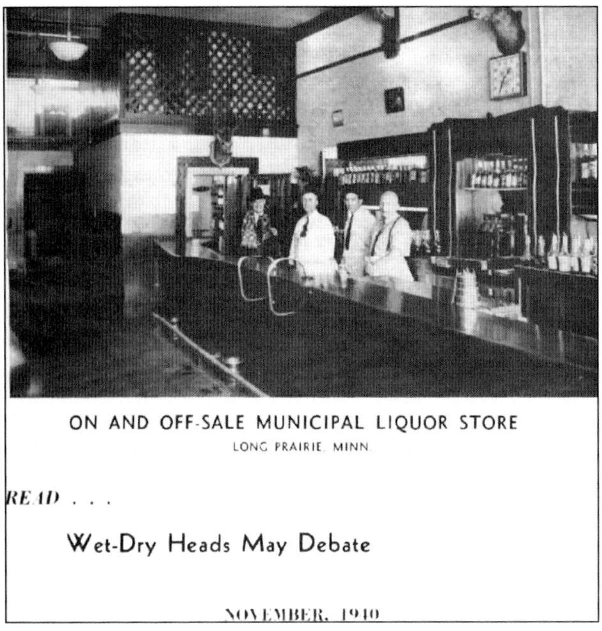

The Long Prairie Municipal Liquor Store has had different homes throughout its existence. It was located in the northwest corner of the Reichert Hotel building in the 1940s, 1950s, and 1960s. From there, it moved into a new building just north of that location, where the city library and chamber of commerce offices are now. (Courtesy of TCHS.)

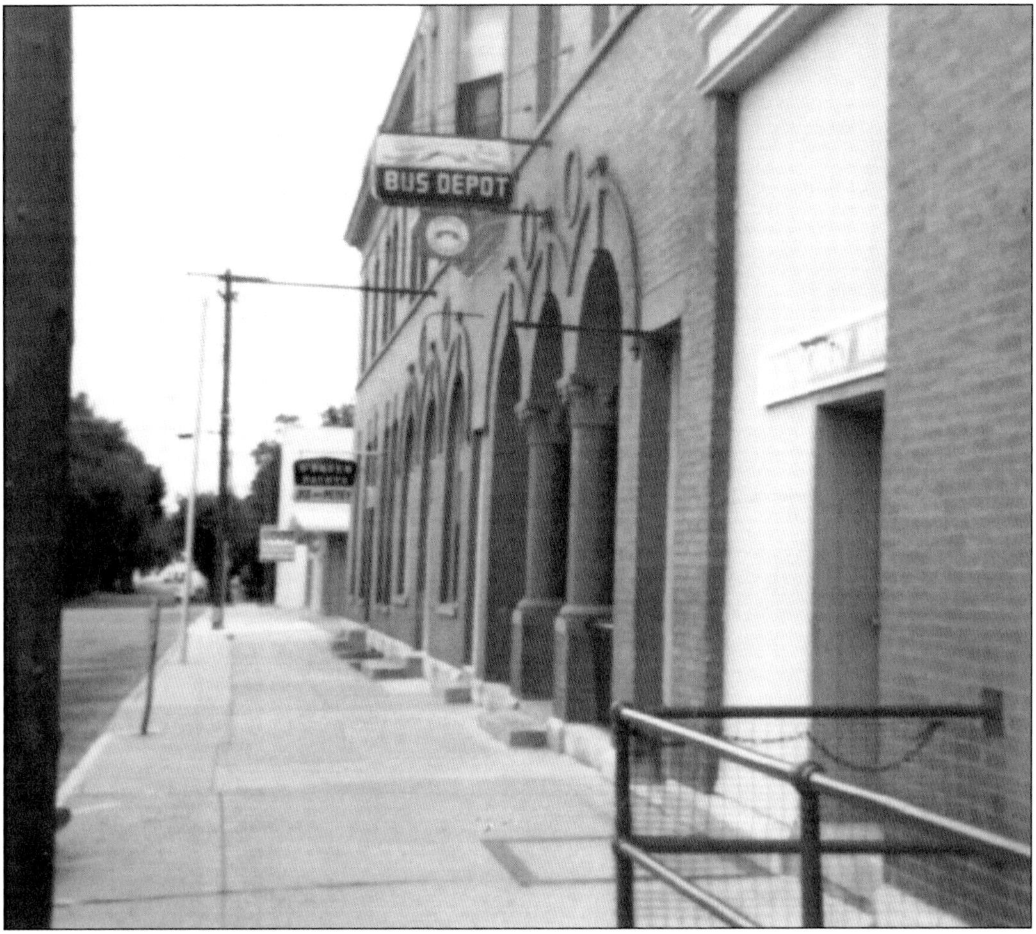

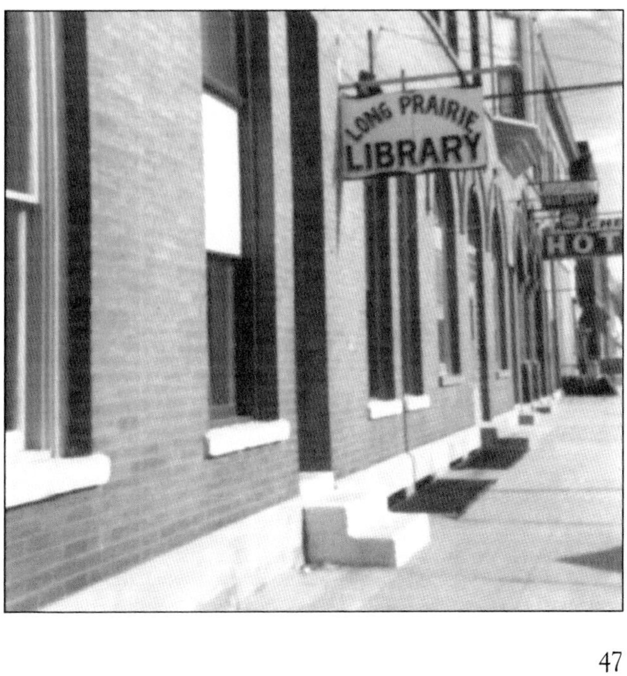

The Reichert Hotel building has held many tenants throughout its lifetime. In these photographs from the early 1970s, one will notice the different signs that directed the residents and visitors to the Reichert. As seen above, Jes and Petey (a paint store owned by Jes and Petey Peterson), the Greyhound bus depot, and Montgomery Ward's catalog store called the Reichert Hotel building home. At right, the Long Prairie Library was in the Reichert for a time. Pine Cone Ceramics also called the west side of the Reichert Hotel building home for a time. Golden Gloves boxing club had a ring in the basement during the 1980s. (Both, courtesy of Harold Connelly and Valley View Estates.)

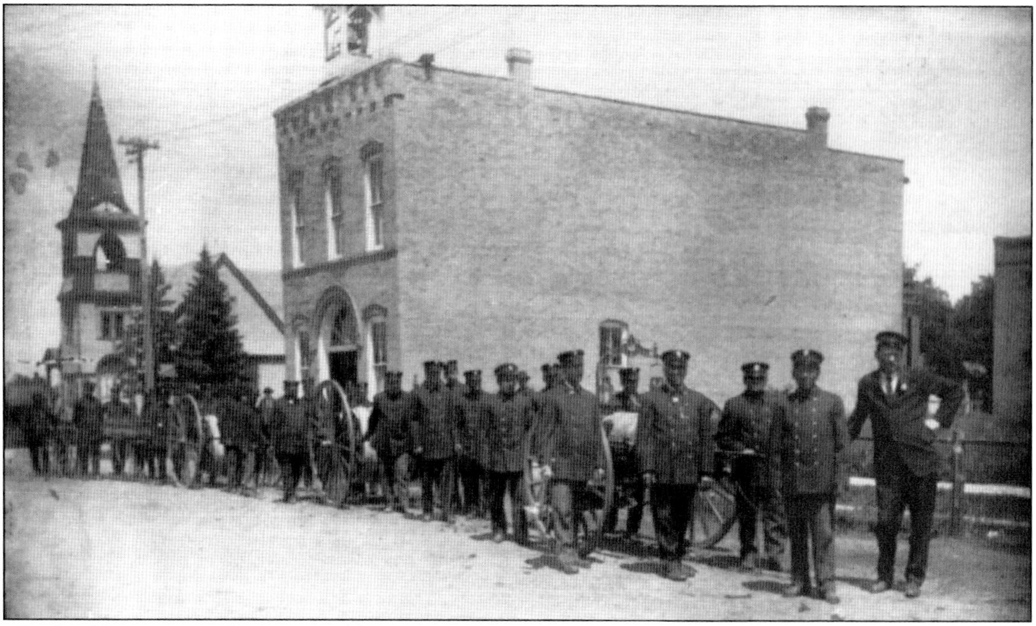

The building currently occupied by the Senior Citizens Day Center has been in city ownership for many years. In its lifetime since the late 1880s, the building housed the village hall, library, fire department (above), and city lock-up. The building was also used by the American Lutheran Church in 1936, not long after the denomination first organized in Long Prairie. In this photograph taken in 1971 (below), this building has been extensively altered over the years to include a full front-entrance remodel, added windows on the south side of the building, and the removal of the fire bell tower. This fire bell, which rang the warning to call the firemen to muster, currently sits on display at city hall. However, the most noticeable change to this building was when the second floor was removed by the city in 1983. (Above, courtesy of TCHS; below, courtesy of Harold Connelly and Valley View Estates.)

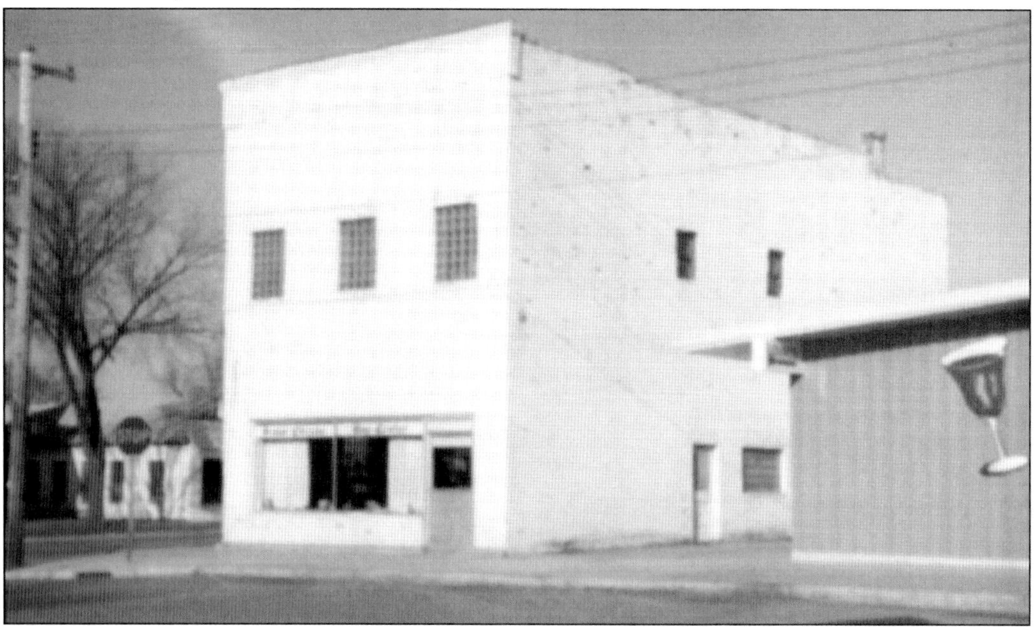

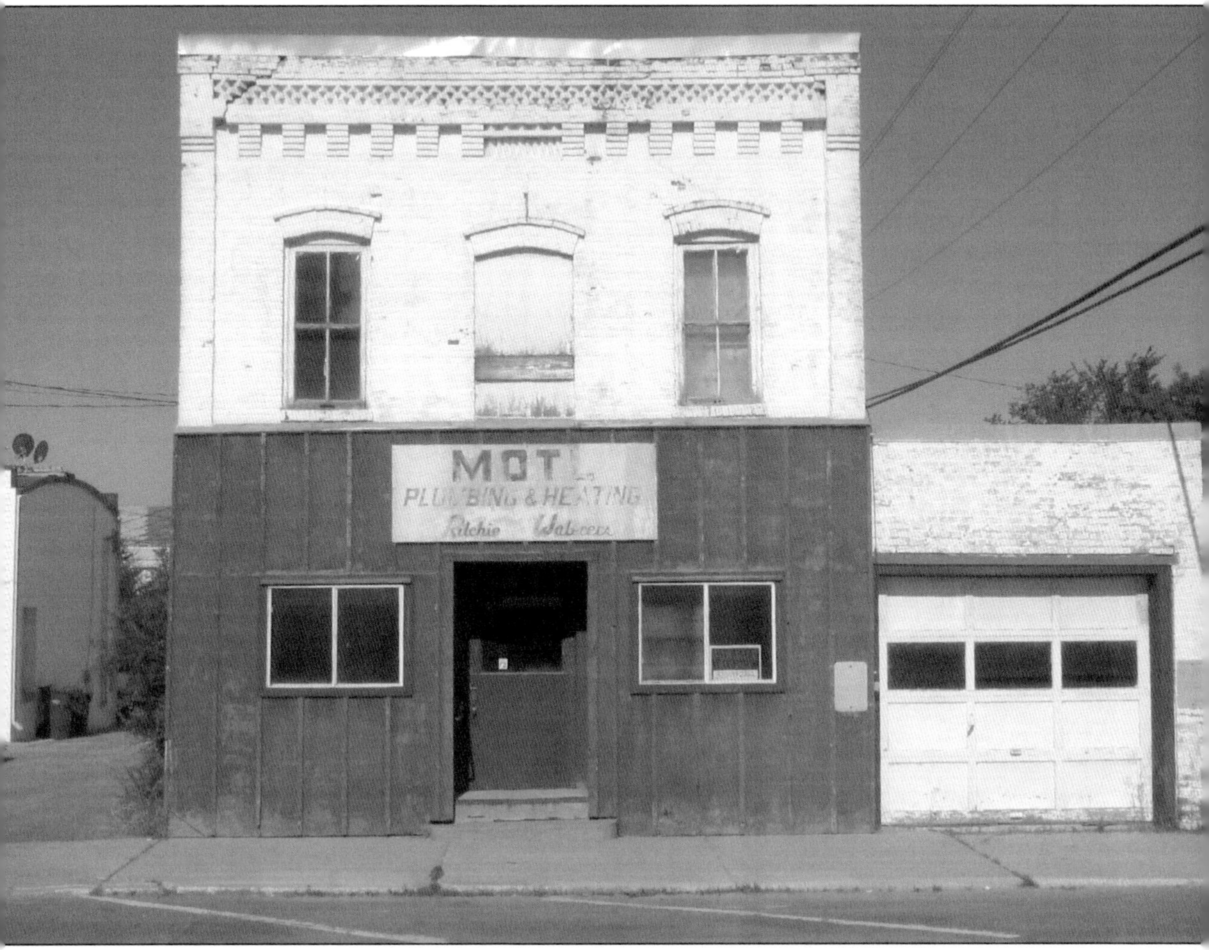

This building at 15 Third Street North was built and owned by a Mr. Francke, who conducted a jewelry and gun business here. His wife, Catherine Franke, died in Long Prairie in 1920 and left no known relatives. She donated one of the bells in the Catholic church tower. Mr. Francke taught the watch repair business to Fred Fortmann, the father of Henry Fortmann, who operated the Fortmann Jewelry Store on Main Street in Long Prairie. North of the Motl Building was a small blacksmith shop operated by Fred Abeling, one of the pioneer businessmen of Long Prairie. Frank Minette and his sons John and Tony operated a furniture and auction business in the building for a number of years. Tom Shinabarger purchased the structure in 1962 and operated a plumbing and heating shop here. It became Motl Plumbing and heating in 1962. Lilah (Motl) Gripne and her husband purchased the business from her parents in 1972 and retired in June 2010. Lilah holds the distinction of being the first licensed master plumber in Minnesota. (Courtesy of TCHS.)

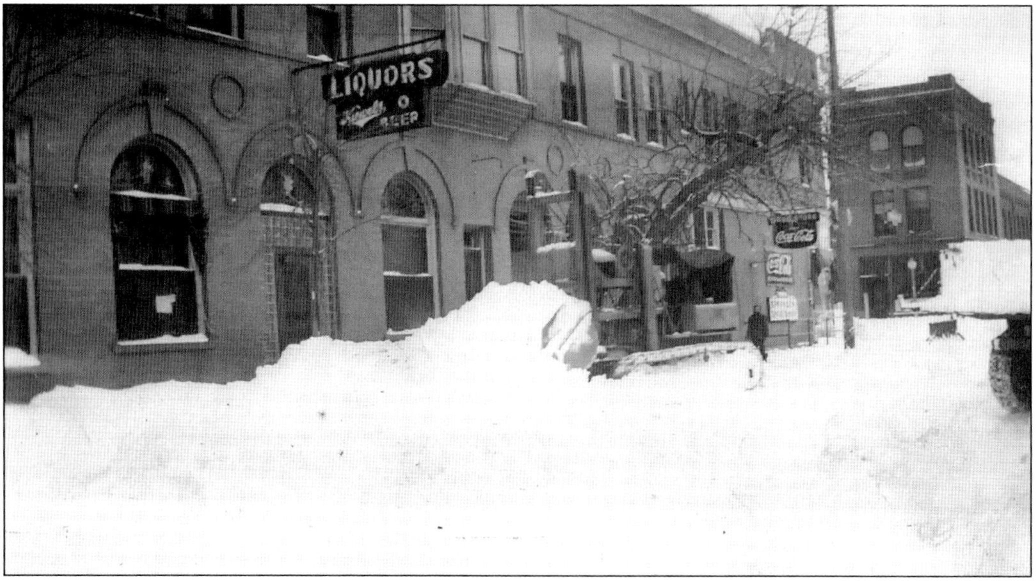

The basement of the Reichert Hotel building has been occupied by many businesses. Manny Reichert had a pool hall in the basement in the 1920s. In 1939, the Works Progress Administration (WPA) opened the Long Prairie WPA sewing shop in this space. As seen in this image, Simonson Shoe Shop was in the basement. Anton Clasemann also operated a shoe business here from 1949 to 1951. (Courtesy of TCHS.)

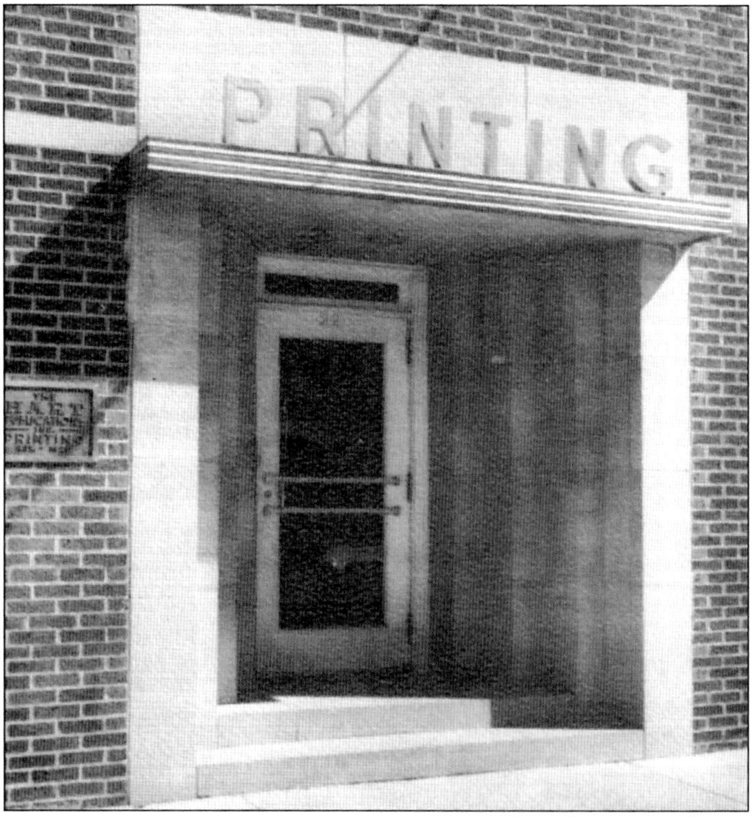

Harvey Elmer Hart, the eldest son of James Hart, was the driving force behind the establishment of Hart Publications in 1920. Along with his brother Charles, Harvey Elmer had the foresight to establish the *Hart Rinkles* advertisement circular for the Hart Store in Long Prairie. This move proved quite useful, as other firms noticed its potential and became interested in this type of advertising. From this, Hart Publications was born. (Courtesy of TCHS.)

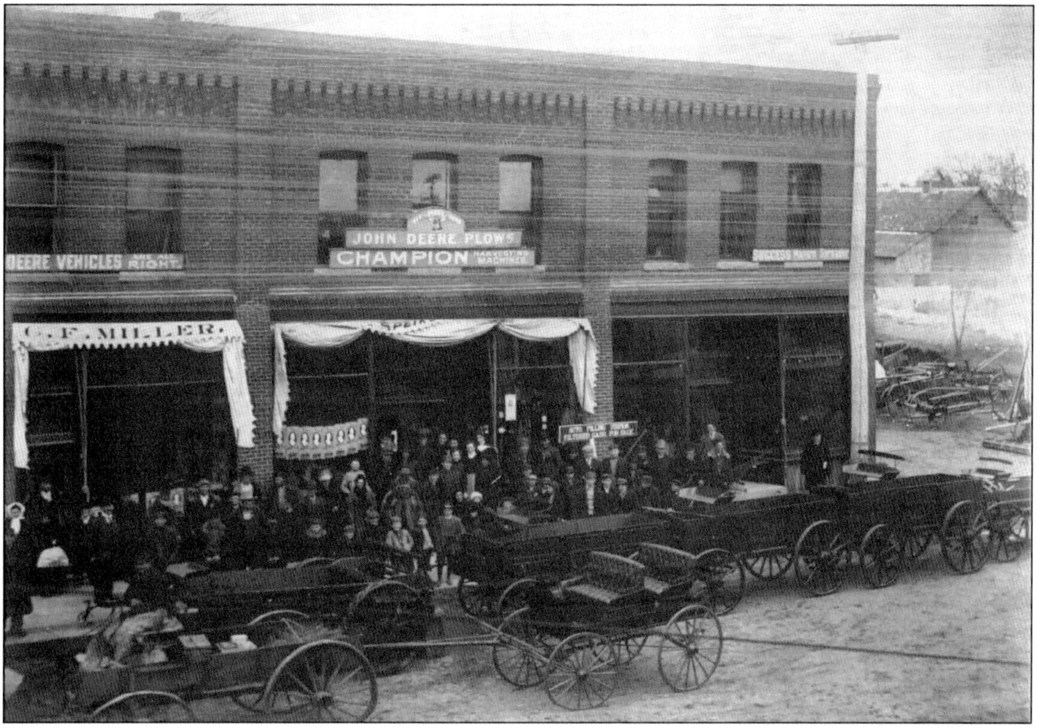

These photographs capture the inside and outside of the C.F. Miller Implement building that was built and owned by C.F. Miller. Miller operated this farm machine business, grocery store, and feed store. The building was located across the street from the *Leader* newspaper office. Later, it was used by Hart Press (formerly Hart Publications) as the shipping/receiving department, with the second floor being converted to apartments. In 1911, Miller branched out into the automobile business with the Ford and Overland agencies. Miller Motor continued in the automobile business, remodeling and moving into a building on Central Avenue right around the corner from this one. Miller had an agency at one time for Chrysler automobiles, followed by Chevrolet, Pontiac, and Buick. These buildings were removed in 1989. (Both, courtesy of Becky Hillig.)

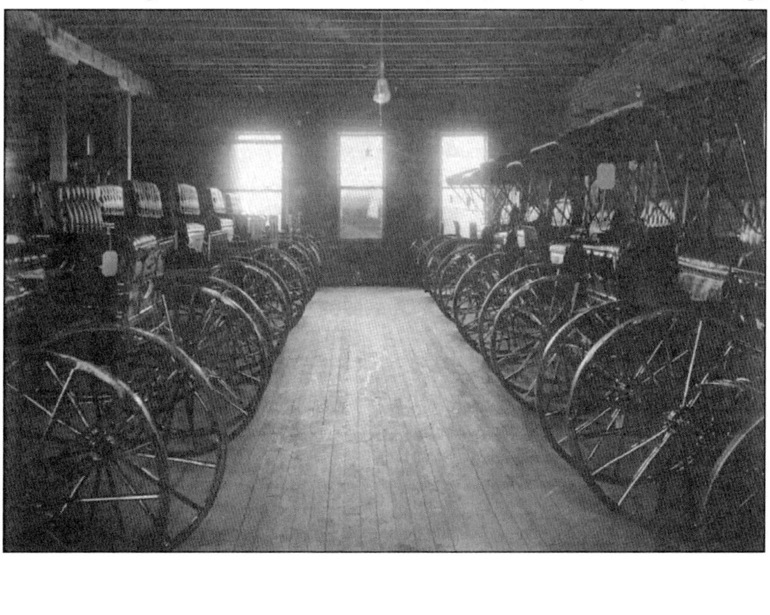

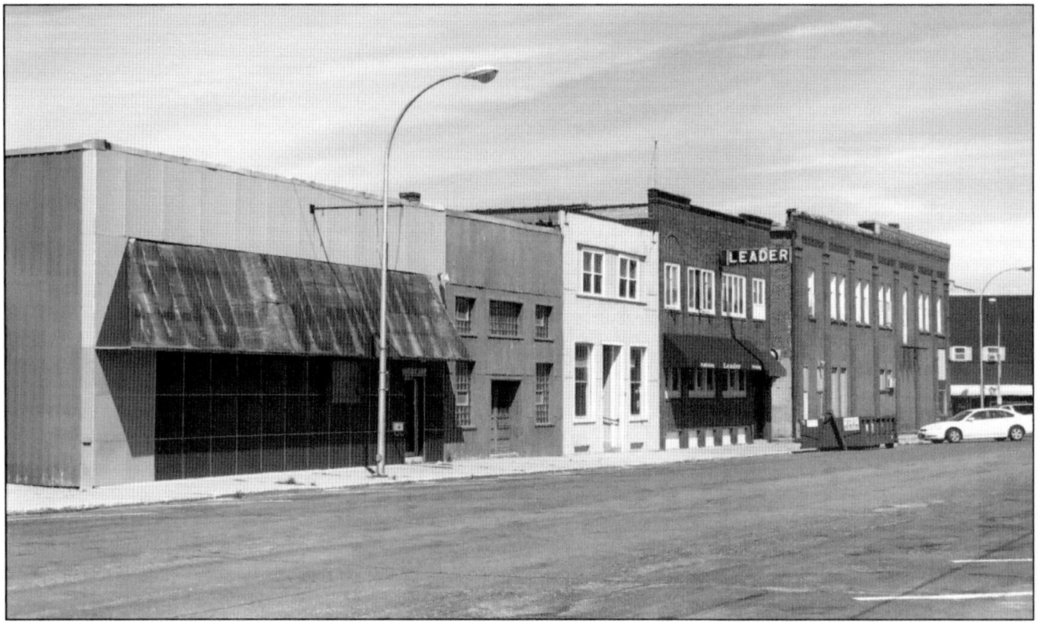

The west side of Third Street South is home to one of the longest-running business in Todd County. Founded in 1883, the *Long Prairie Leader* is the largest-circulating and longest-serving newspaper in the county. The building south of the *Leader* office was constructed in 1910 by Dr. Leidl, DDS, and Dr. Van Valkenburg, MD, and it was later purchased by lawyer Logan Scow. (Author's collection.)

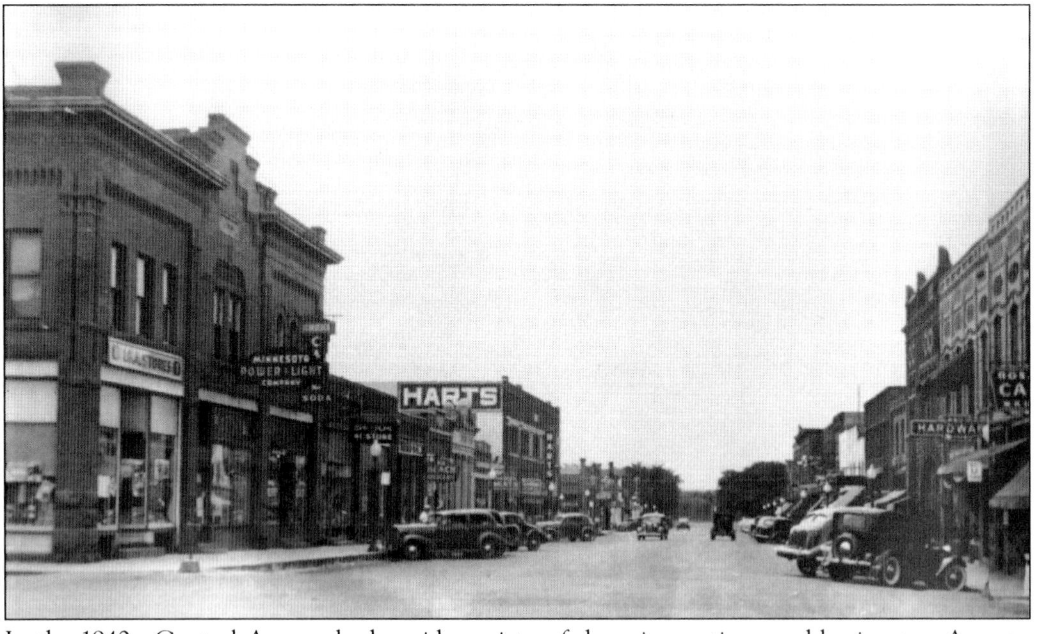

In the 1940s, Central Avenue had a wide variety of shopping options and businesses. As seen in the Arcade Building on the left of the photograph, a grocery store occupied the east room. The middle room was occupied by Minnesota Power and Light prior to its move west on Central Avenue in the 1950s, to the corner next door to Irish's place. Schroeder Café occupied the west room. (Courtesy of TCHS.)

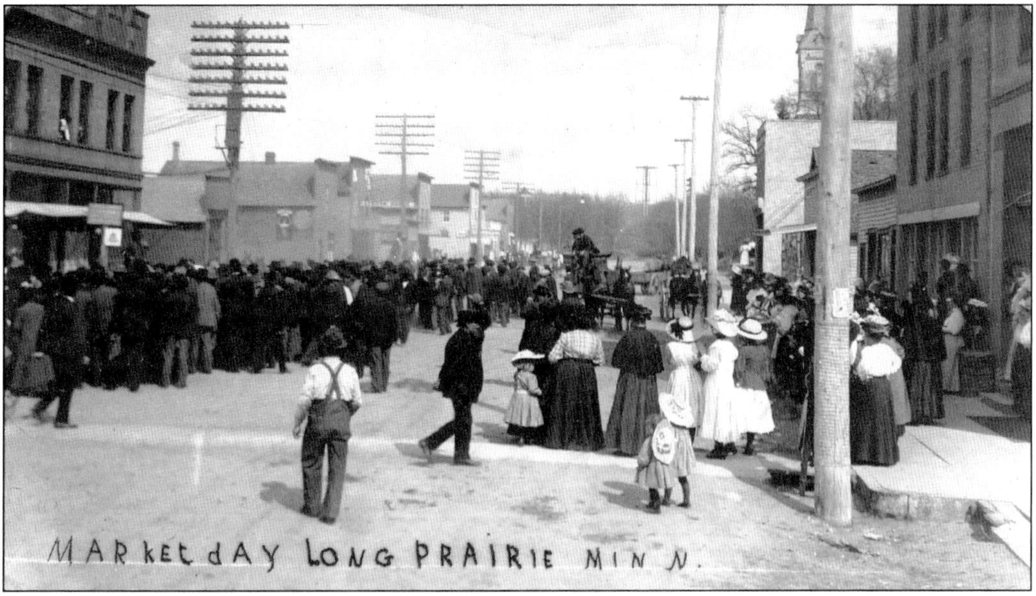

Downtown Long Prairie has been a central meeting place for this village from the beginning. Events, parades, and community celebrations brought all residents to congregate and visit with one another while supporting the local businesses. Stores stayed open past 8:00 p.m., welcoming all comers to view their wares or just tell stories. This photograph from about 1910 has a view looking east up Central Avenue from the intersection of Central Avenue and Third Street. (Author's collection.)

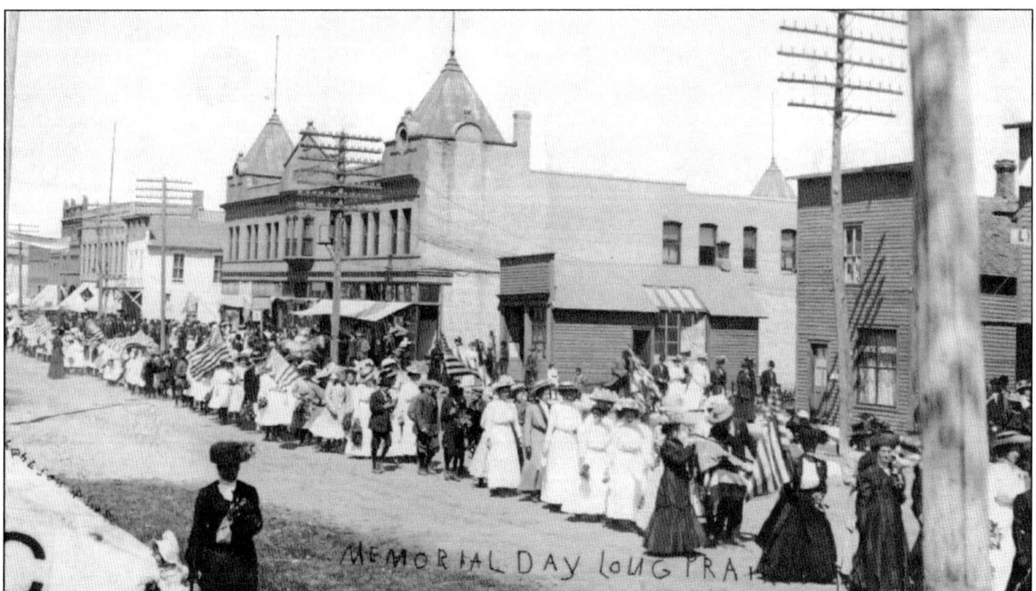

In this 1914 photograph of the Memorial Day parade moving down Central Avenue, look at the Reichert Hotel building. One will notice that the "pyramids" on the top corners no longer exist on the building today. It is unclear when these were removed. The wooden structure next to the hotel was occupied by the *Long Prairie Democrat* newspaper that ran for only a few years. For a time, it was also occupied by Moses Prentice, who operated a small restaurant. (Author's collection.)

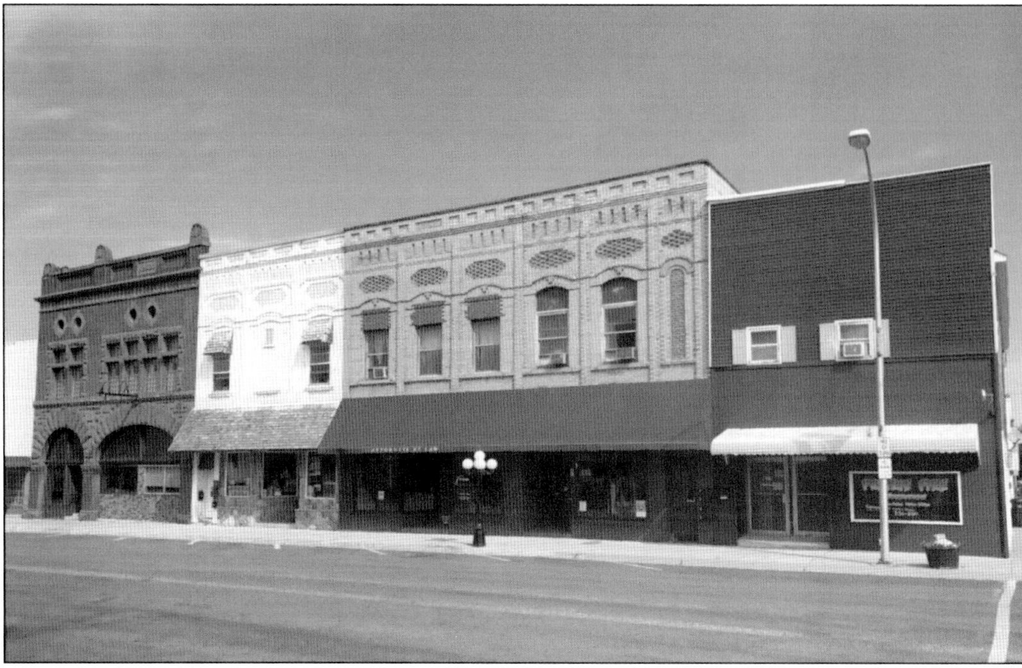

The red-painted corner building on Central Avenue and Third Street North (above, on the right) was built in 1882 by Henry Williams, one of the pioneers of Long Prairie. This building, the oldest on Central Avenue, was owned by the Williams family, who operated a saloon here, as seen below. The building was then occupied by William Dodds Confectionery and Ice Cream Parlor, and for many years, a café was operated here by various owners. During Prohibition, the town marshal was publicly challenged by the village council to find out who was visiting the saloon illegally, based on complaints by the village residents. When the marshal reported at the next meeting that he observed the village council members coming and going from this saloon at odd hours, the inquisition was dropped by the council. (Above, author's collection; below, courtesy of TCHS.)

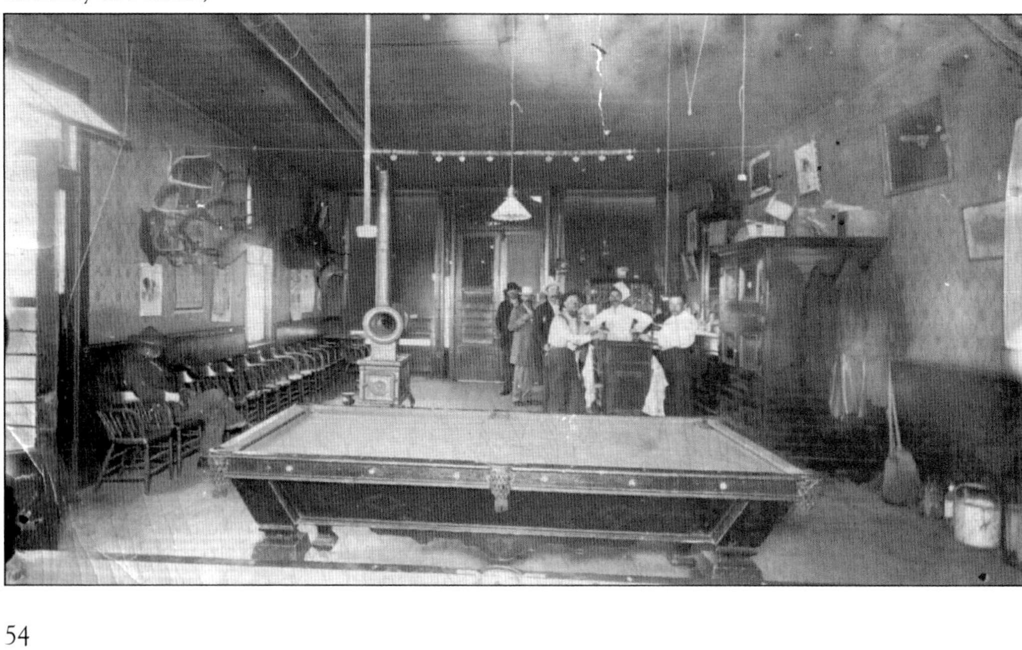

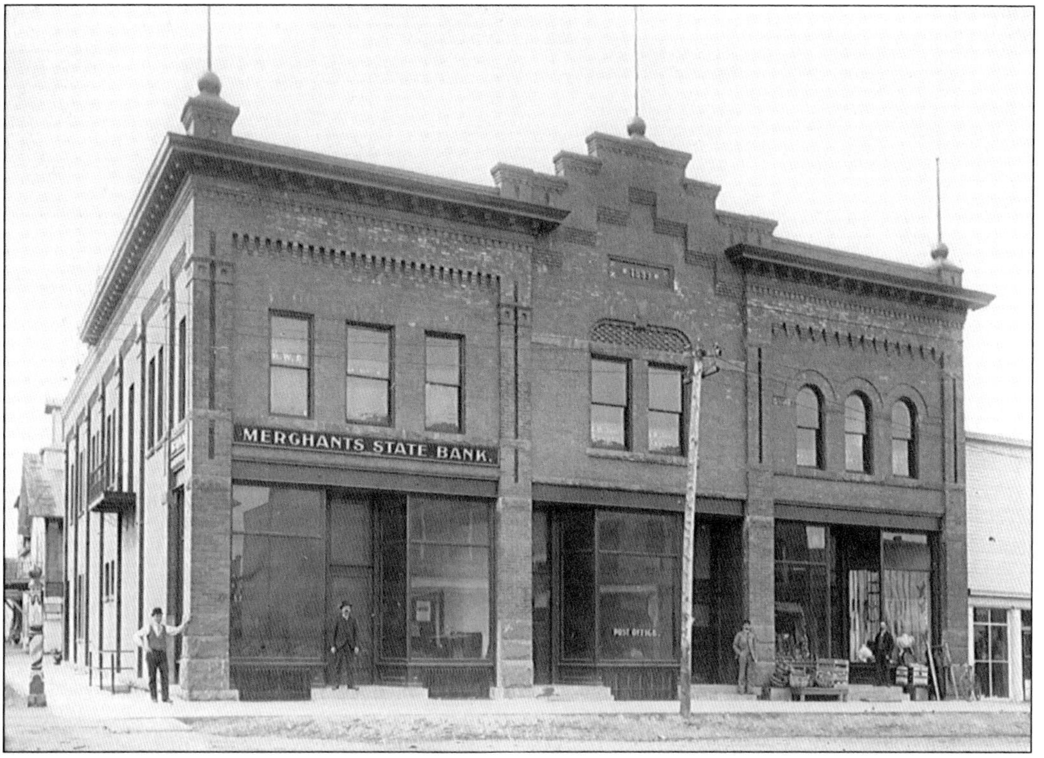

Seen here, then and now, is one of the most recognized buildings on Long Prairie's "Main Street"—the Arcade Building, constructed in 1899. This building has had many tenants throughout the years: Walls Jewelry, Peterson Variety Store, Klemenhagen Barber Shop, Minnesota Power & Light Company, and many cafés, including the Green Parrot, the Grille, and the Snack Shack, to name a few. This building was twice gutted by fire—once in 1906 and again in 1926. The upper floor housed the city opera house, which served as the entertainment center of the community. There were also spaces on the second floor occupied by medical offices. Today's Arcade Building continues to serve as a place where the town residents can gather for a great meal. It is now home to the Taqueria Chavez Mexican Restaurant, whose owners have combined the center and west rooms of the lower floor. The upper floor serves as apartments. (Both, author's collection.)

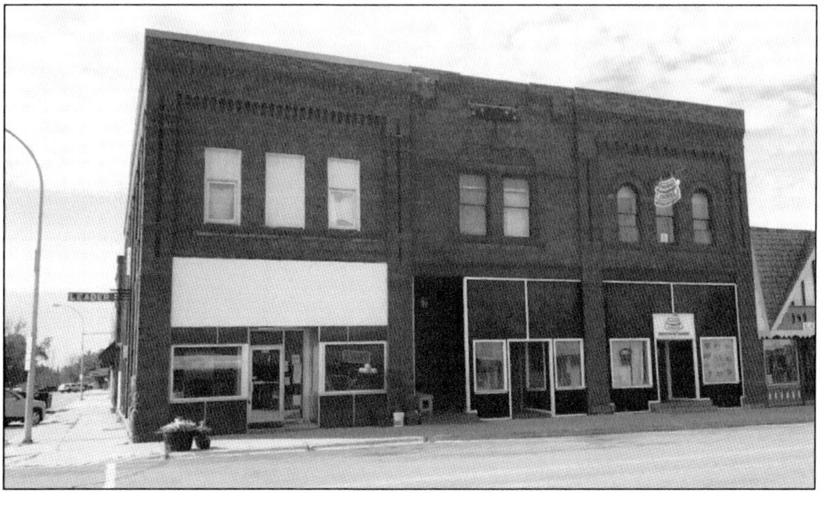

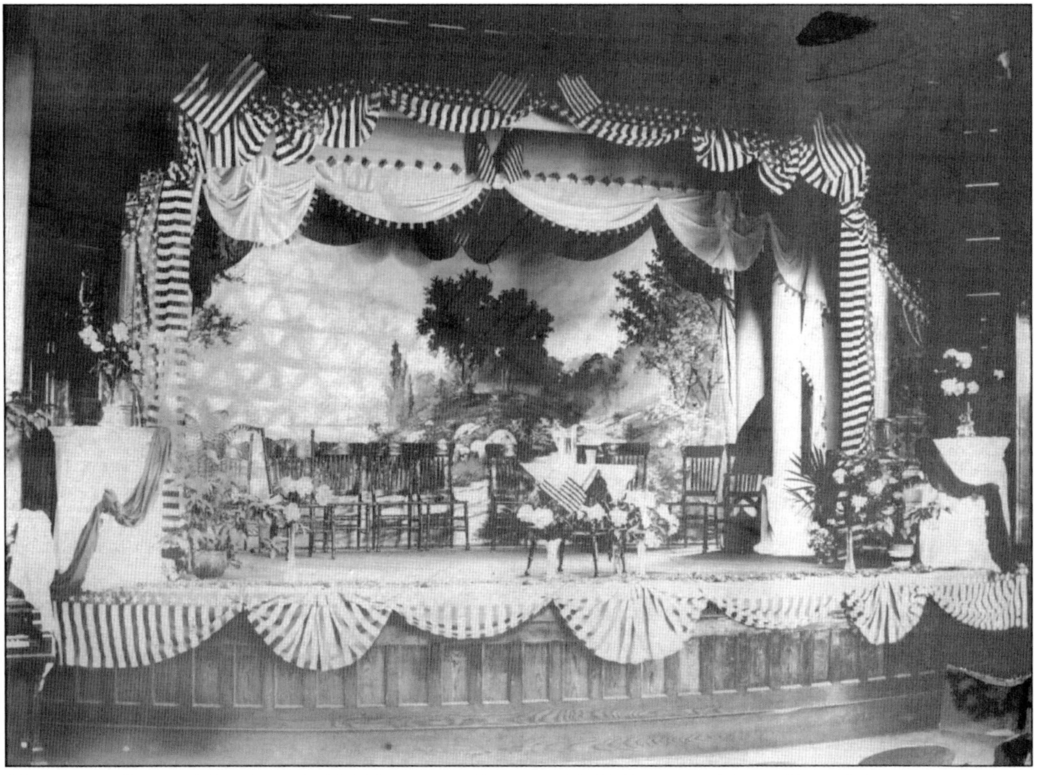

The upper floor of the Arcade Building, seen here in 1900 decorated for a Grand Army gathering, housed the city opera house, or Arcade Hall, which served as the entertainment center of the community in the early mid-1900s. There were many traveling show companies and dance bands that played here. In 1914, the first big moving picture to be shown in Long Prairie, *The Spoilers*, was shown in this hall. The Knights of Columbus and the Masons also used this hall as a meeting place. (Courtesy of TCHS.)

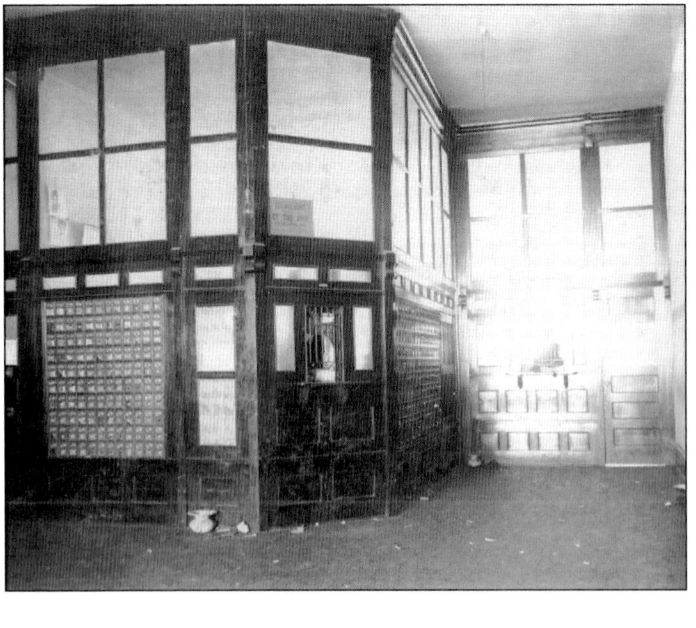

The Long Prairie Post Office saw a few different locations around town prior to its current home. It was in the Reichert Hotel during the 1920s. In the late 1800s, it was located on the "post office corner" in a wood-frame structure where the Arcade Building stands now. When the Arcade Building was completed in 1899, the post office moved into the middle room of this building. This undated and unlabeled photograph found in the Todd County museum shows quite possibly this Arcade Building post office location. (Courtesy of TCHS.)

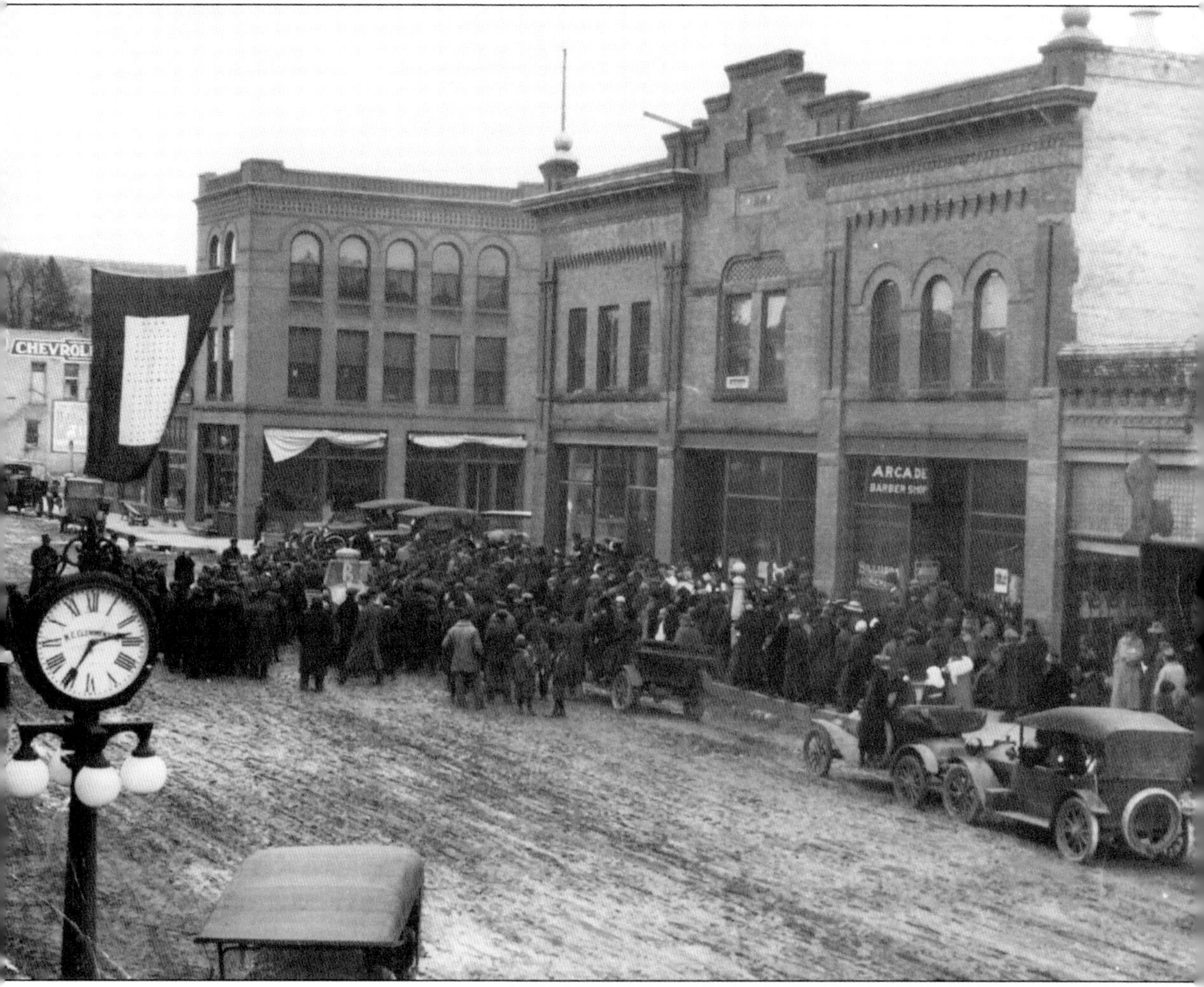

In this 1917 photograph of a World War I gathering in front of the Arcade Building, one will notice the small storefront of the Martin Cech Shoe Store next door to the right. This small brick building with the silhouette shoe sign hanging off the front, dwarfed by its neighbor, is the replacement for the first store at this location, which burned down in 1910. Cech sold this store in 1923 to Anton Johnson who, with his son, operated the Model Shoe Store for a number of years. It was then sold to Robert Beery, who operated a grocery store at this location. Clem Mieszkowski operated Clem's Shoe Store here also. In the 1970s and 1980s, Sears had a catalog store in this location. Jim Chyba III and his wife, Marge, owned and operated this Sears store from 1974 to 1984. The storefront has been greatly altered in recent years, and it is currently home of the Black Forest Thrift Store. (Courtesy of TCHS.)

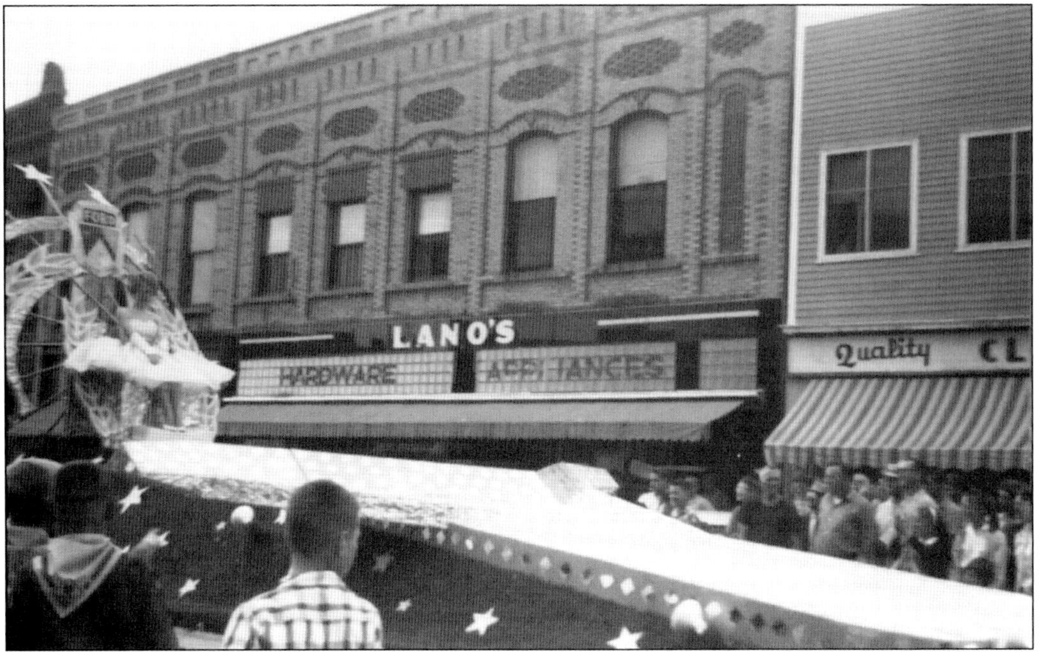

The building located at 274 Central Avenue, seen above in 1961, was built by Henry Williams in 1895. This building also housed various business enterprises until 1912, when Lano's Hardware moved to this location. This hardware business, going by the name Lano & Deuhs for a time, was owned and operated by Frank Lano beginning in 1891. Later, the business was continued by his sons I.F. "Neats" Lano (below behind the till) and T.J. Lano. In 1936, the business was taken over by T.J., who continued the business with his son Frank Lano until the time of T.J.'s death in 1964. This store was the oldest business establishment in Long Prairie continuing under the same name, for a period of 78 years. Today, the building is owned by Greg and Diane Peters. (Above, author's collection; below, courtesy of TCHS.)

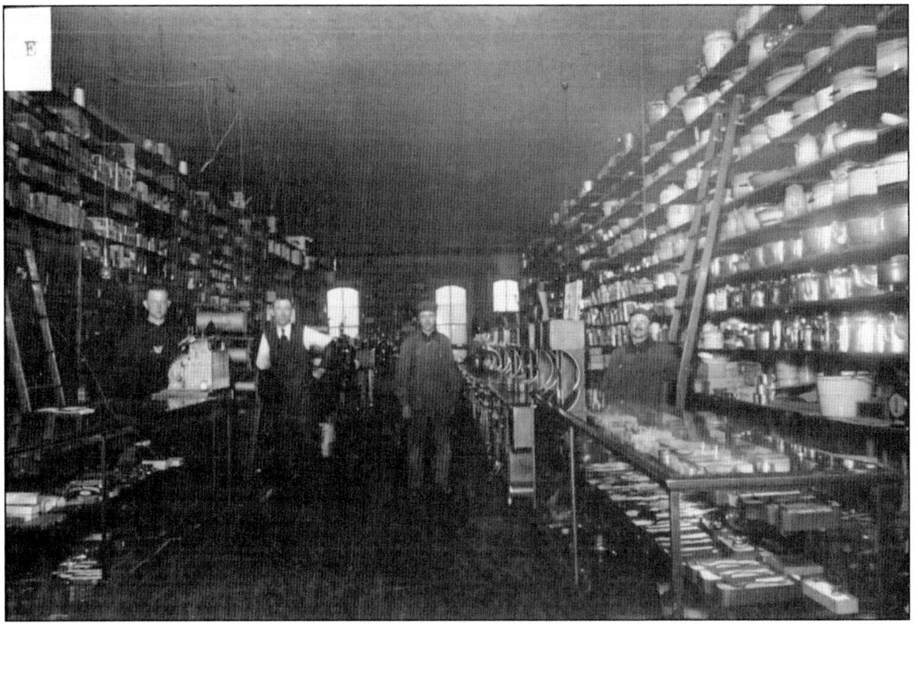

This is an undated photograph of a confectionery building that sat at 270 Central Avenue, the current location of Nobedades Bronco. It is unknown who owned it, but the structure provides an idea of the buildings that occupied downtown Long Prairie in the early days. This structure was replaced by the Christie Building, now painted white, which had been owned by the Seelhammer Department Store, Victor Clothing, and for many years, C.O. Anderson and Company. (Courtesy of TCHS.)

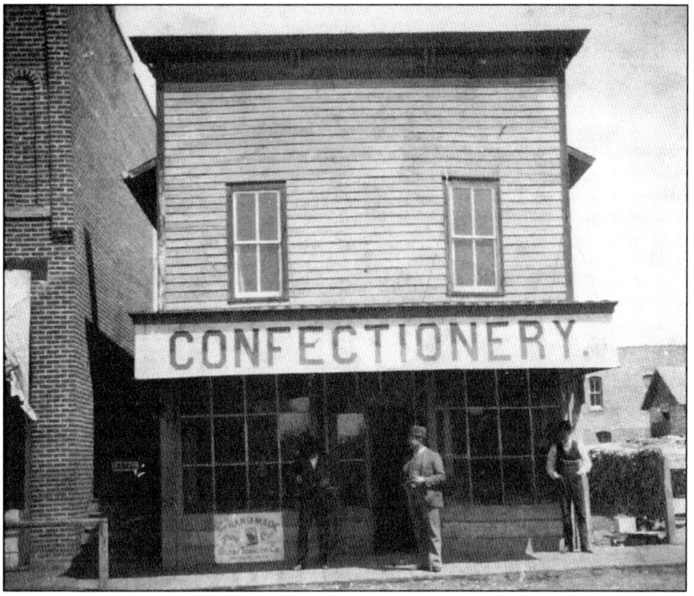

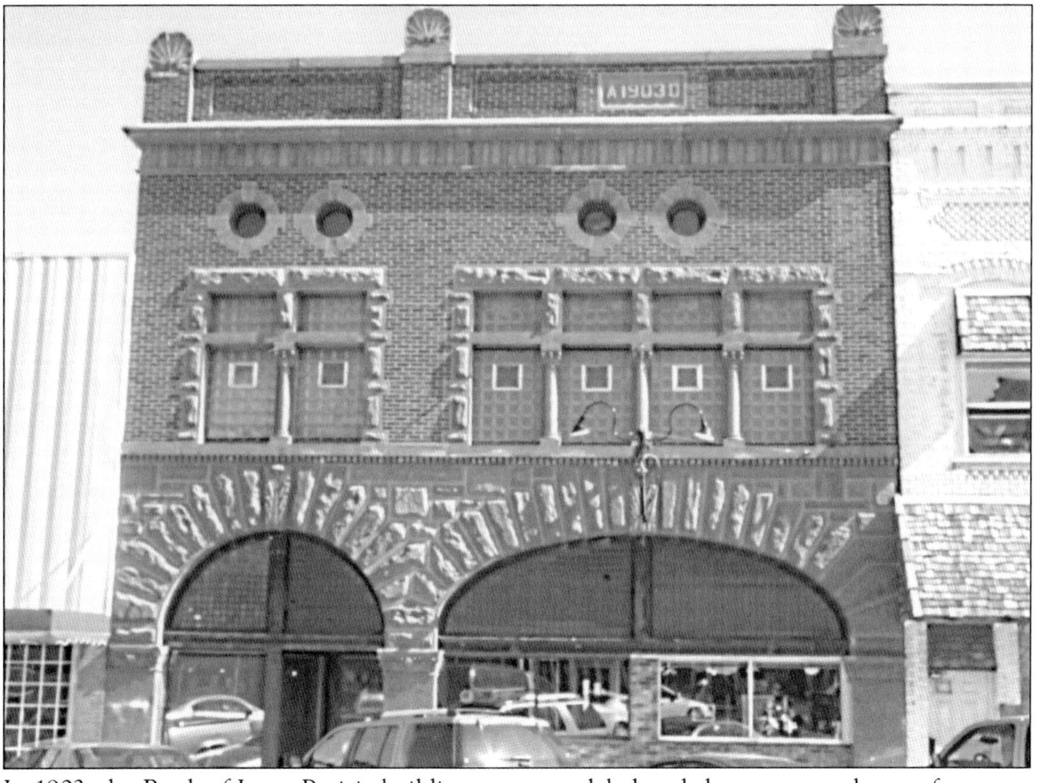

In 1903, the Bank of Long Prairie building was remodeled and the present red-stone front was installed. The former store quarters were converted into new banking quarters. The old banking quarters of the west room were then rented to H.C. Clemmensen jewelry store until Clemmensen's retirement, when Wall's Jewelry took over. This bank was owned by William E. Lee, who established a bank here in 1860. The bank continued doing business in this location until it sold out to the Peoples National Bank In 1947. (Author's collection.)

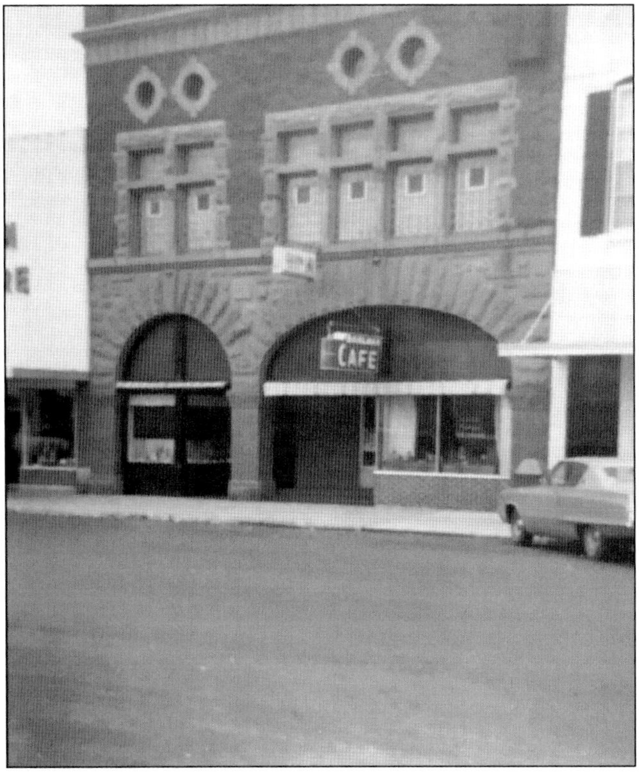

Today's Bank of Long Prairie building is showing signs of neglect. Post-banking days, the building was converted into a café, operated under various names including Dahlman Café (left), Marie's Café, Michael's Café, and most recently, Mikey's. The years ahead for this iconic town landmark are unclear, with the best wishes of the community being extended for a successful recovery of this building. Constructed in 1903, the building is a two-story commercial structure with 39 feet of frontage. The stone and brick facade is divided into two unequally sized bays, reflecting the building's original dual use as a bank and general store. This building is in the National Register of Historic Places. (Left, courtesy of Harold Connelly and Valley View Estates; below, author's collection.)

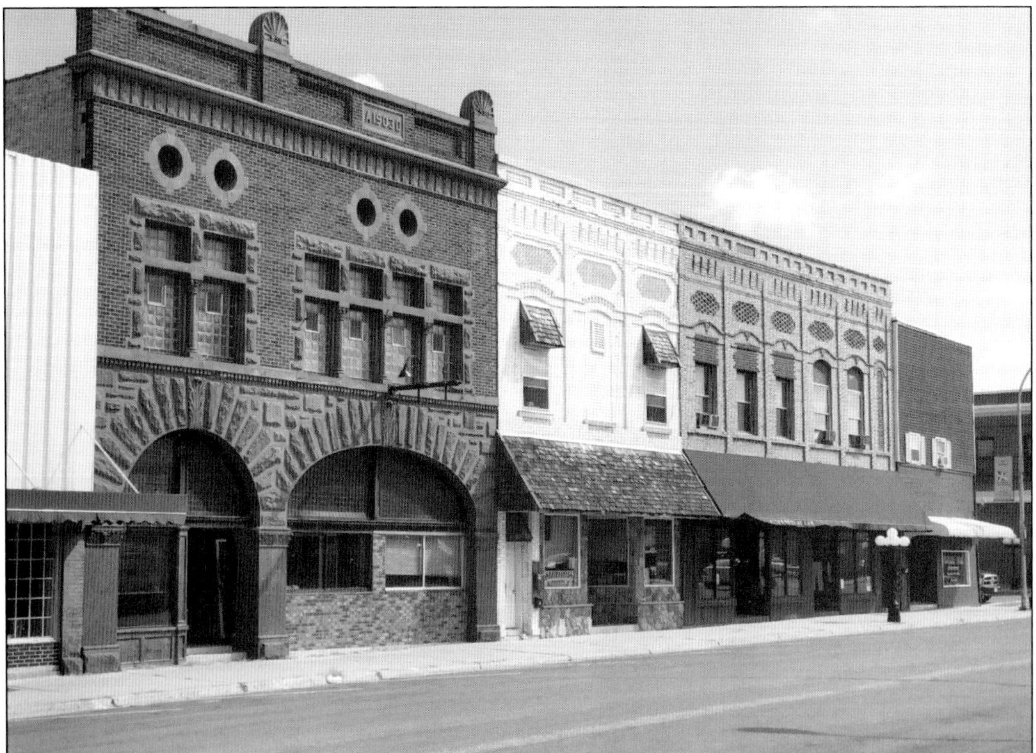

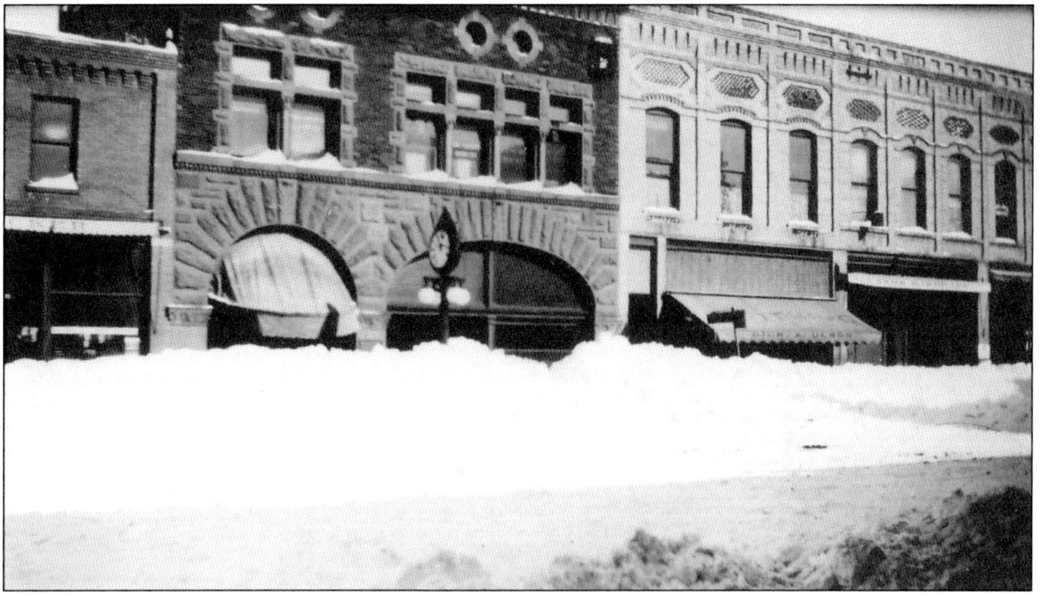

Removed in 1936, this clock, seen here in 1930 behind the snowbank and known as the Clemmensen Clock, was an illuminated timepiece that through sun and darkness, rain and snow had for about a quarter century been a landmark on "Main Street." This clock greeted many residents wandering downtown, reminding them that soon they would be needing to return home. It left no excuse to those wishing to push the boundaries of curfew. (Author's collection.)

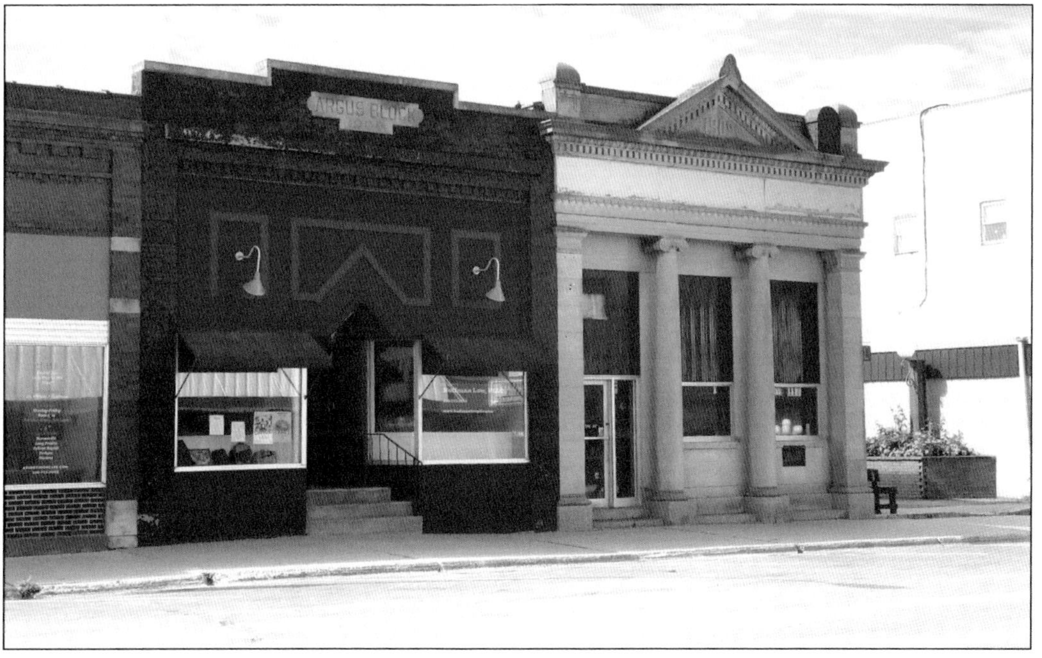

Today's Argus Building and the former First National Bank building next door are in a state of limbo. Both buildings are being remodeled in hopes of one day drawing business and visitors back downtown to enjoy what Long Prairie has to offer. The Argus Building became Chyba Tailoring and Cleaners in 1923. The bank building was donated to the city in 1964 and served as city hall. (Author's collection.)

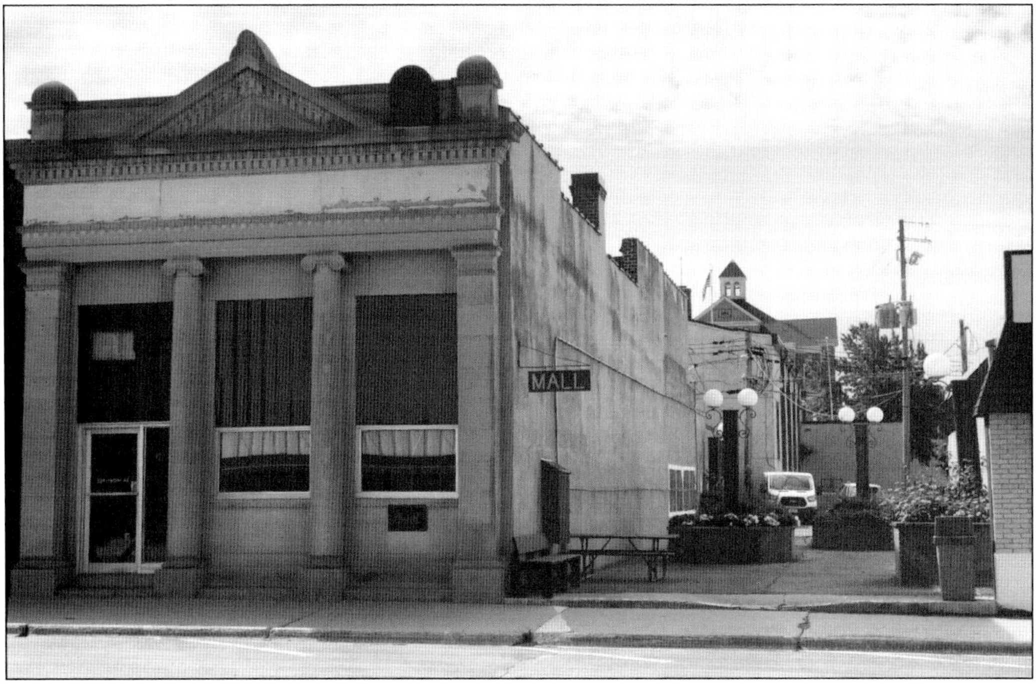

The old First National Bank building was erected in 1909 and continued in business until 1927. After a period of adjustment, the bank was taken over by the People's National Bank. People's National bought out the Bank of Long Prairie, which was also consolidated into the People's National. The bank was then known as the Bank of Long Prairie. The current mall space was the site of Huber's Meat Market. (Author's collection.)

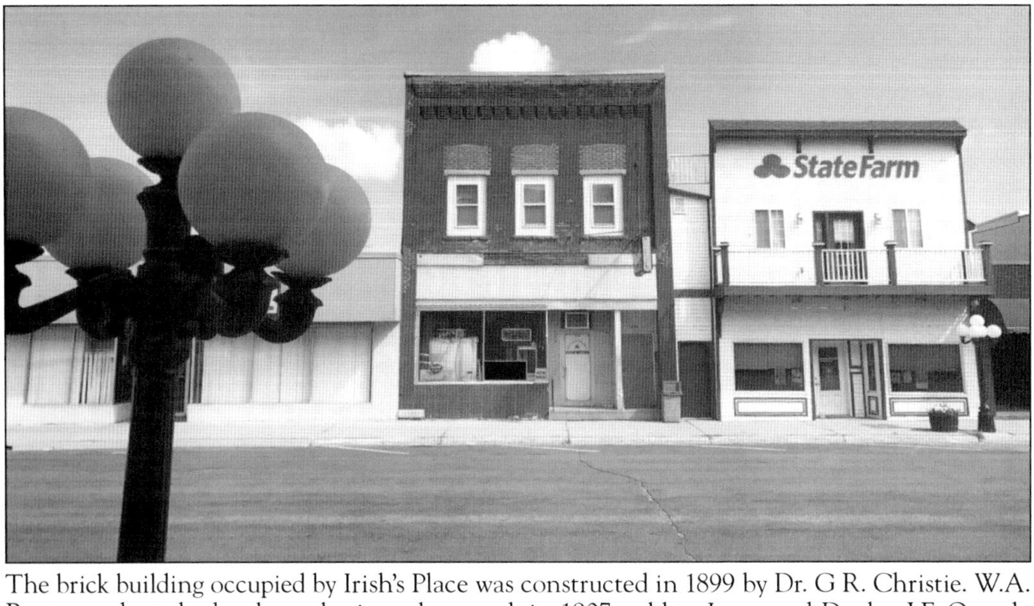

The brick building occupied by Irish's Place was constructed in 1899 by Dr. G R. Christie. W.A. Barto conducted a hardware business here and, in 1907, sold to Lano and Deuhs. J.F. Orando conducted a saloon business here until 1913. The room has been a billiard parlor, soft-drink establishment, and cardroom. A three-lane bowling alley was located on the second floor. The State Farm building was constructed in 1883. (Author's collection.)

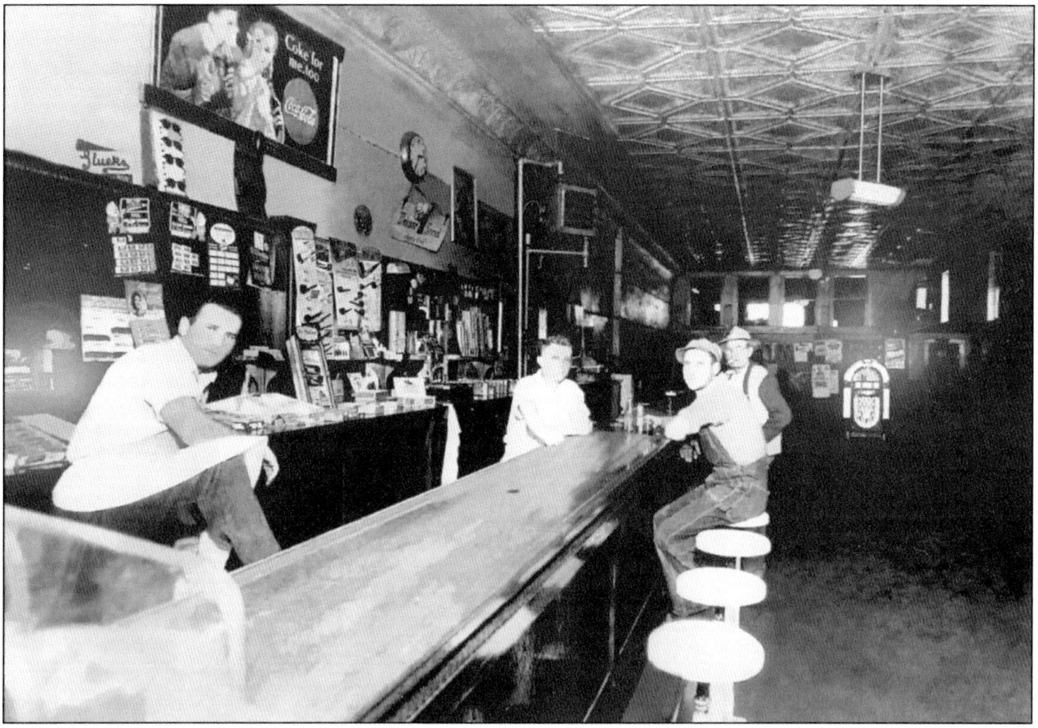

This photograph taken in the mid-1940s captures the inside of Irish's Bar located on Central Avenue. This business is still in operation, with the interior of the building remaining mostly untouched, having been kept in its original condition. This is a true throwback to the old-time mom-and-pop bar and eating establishments. The young man seen sitting at the bar is the author's grandfather, Bob Eldred. (Courtesy of Mike Dempsey.)

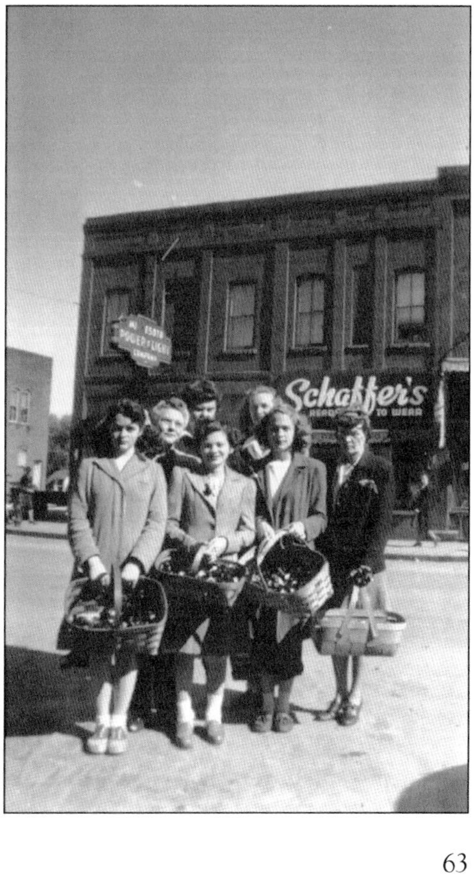

The brick building in the background of this 1946 photograph was built by J.C. Hansmeyer in about 1905. It housed various businesses: to mention a few, Dixon Bros, the Minnesota Power and Light Company, Schaffer's, and Rexall store. The second floor was the Redman Lodge around 1910. This building was destroyed by fire in 1969. These American Legion "poppy workers" are, from left to right, (first row) Nancy Lewis, Ann Rudisell, unidentified, and Mrs. C.C. Biem; (second row) Mrs. Earl Helbeck, Betty Slater, and Erma Kuehne. (Courtesy of TCHS.)

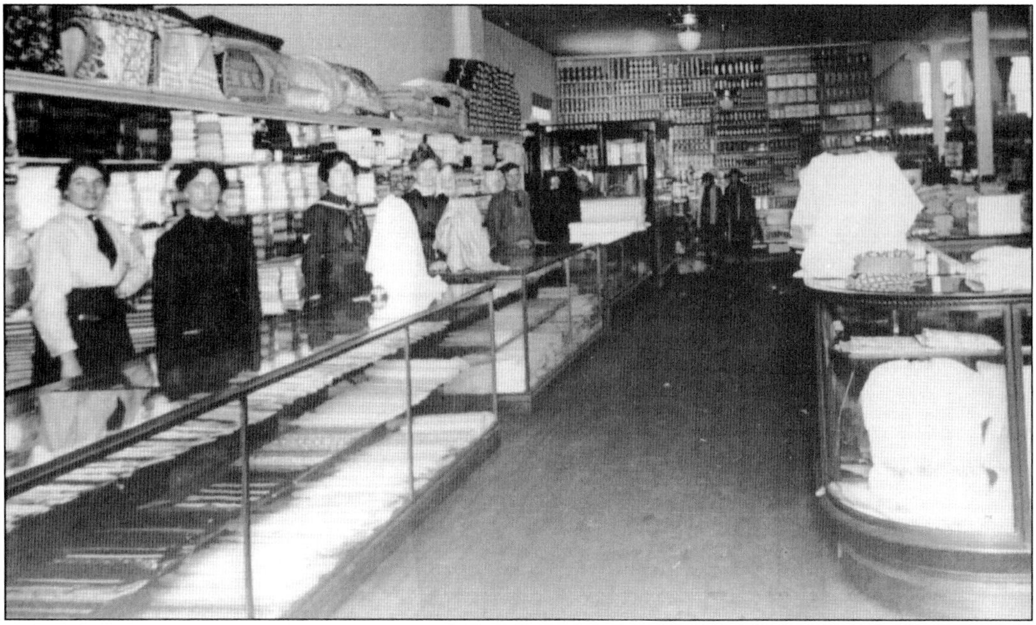

This early 1900s photograph shows the inside of the Hansmeyer Building when it was occupied by Maynard's General Store. George Maynard came to Todd County in 1866, was elected sheriff in 1886, and came to the general-store business in 1889 by purchasing the G.D. Radabaugh business interest. (Courtesy of Rich and Marge Wall.)

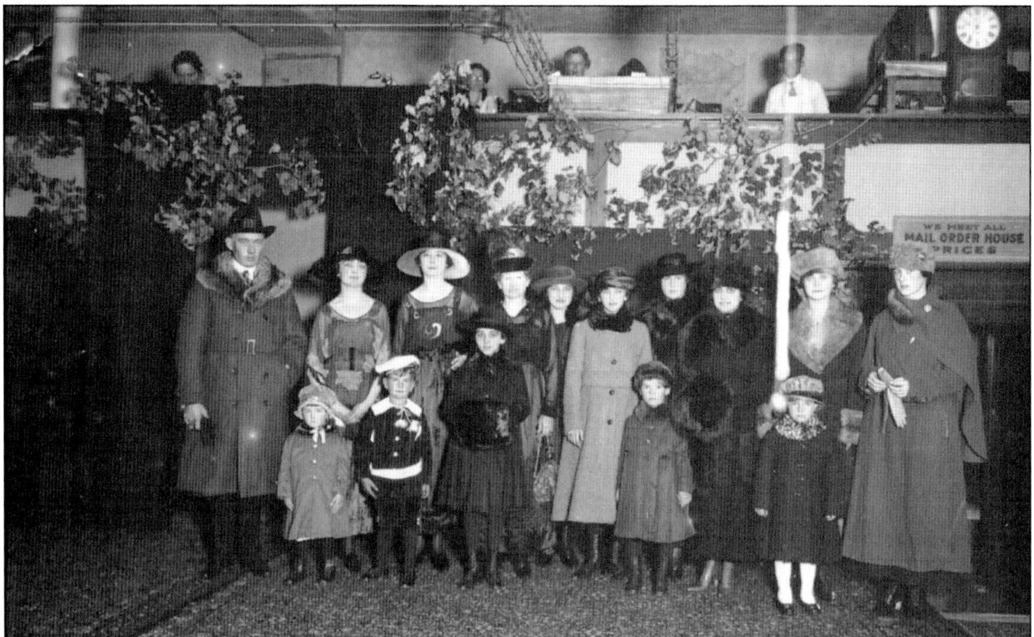

The Hart Store at 221 Central Avenue was constructed and opened in 1916. In the 1940s, it closed for a time. In October 1952, the Hart Store reopened as a major department store serving much of Todd County. The department store closed its doors for the final time in November 1986. The building had a dozen apartments located on the upper floor. This undated photograph captures the heyday of the Hart Store in Long Prairie. (Courtesy of TCHS.)

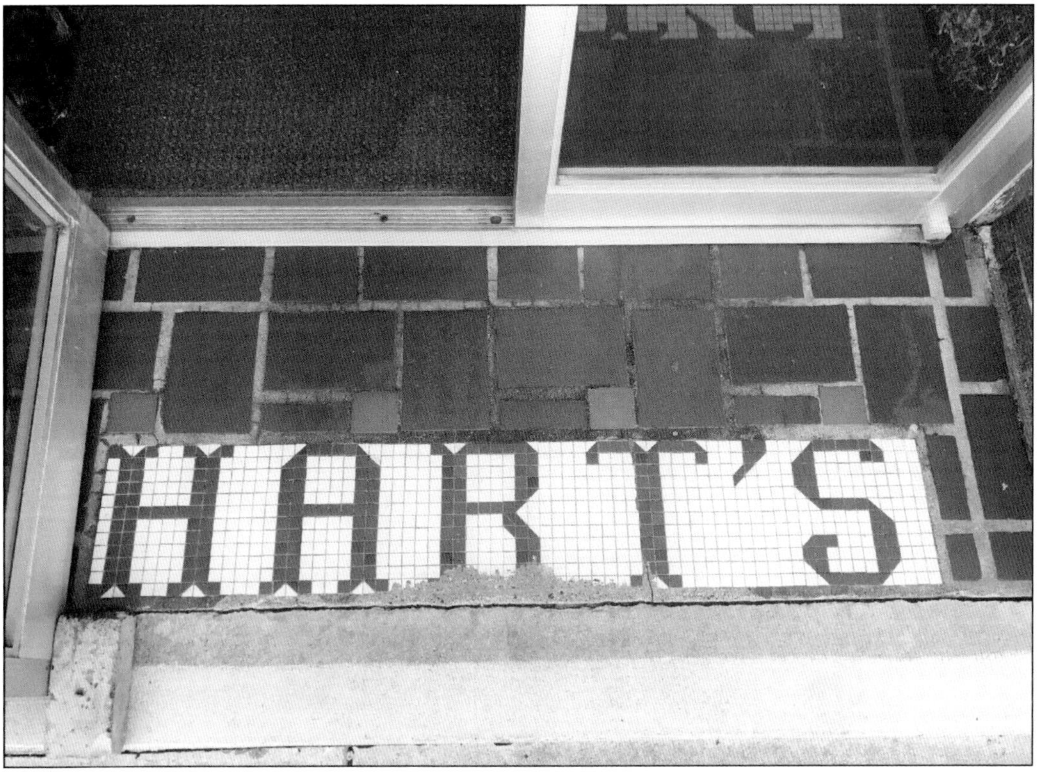

The original "Hart's" inlaid tile in the mall entrance door thresholds (above), along with the iconic "double hearts" in the arcade floor (below), have been preserved as a nod back to the original owners and the love they showed to the community. Founded by James Hart in Browerville, Minnesota, during the late 1800s, the business became known as James Hart & Sons in 1904. The store moved to Long Prairie and was set up in the Kemp Block, and in 1916, Hart erected the current Hart Mall building. The store quickly became the leading mercantile store in the county. (Both, author's collection.)

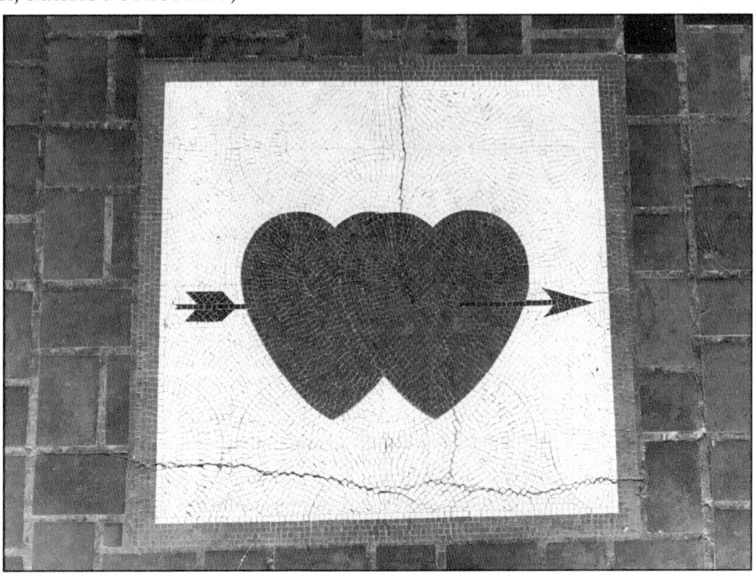

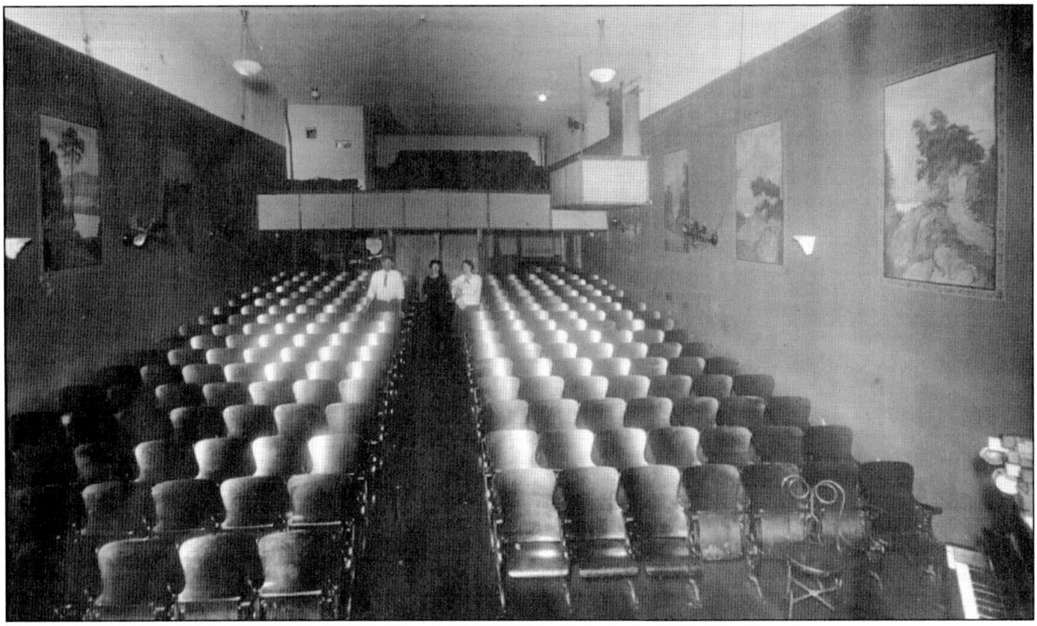

Located in the west section of the Hart Store building, owned and operated by Laurel and Wilomine Lano, the Cozy Theater was the place to be for entertainment. During the silent-film days, Mrs. Lano would sit at a piano in the front of the theater and "ad-lib" music for the crowd while watching the film. The Cozy Theater operated in this store building until 1935. (Courtesy of TCHS.)

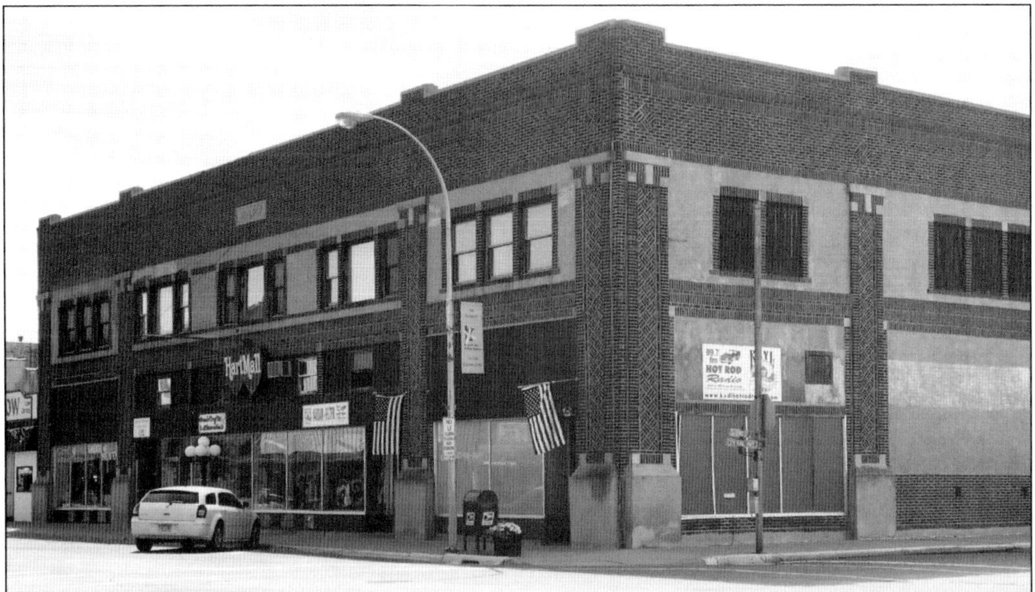

The former Hart Store building on Central Avenue had nearly been written off. Its age and condition had done their damage in the recent past, but it is now enjoying new life as the Hart Mall. The current owners, seeing potential of new life in this landmark, have begun restoration. With a full restoration of the upstairs apartments and remodeling of the main floor, new businesses have moved in and back to downtown, drawing shoppers to the historic life center of Long Prairie. (Author's collection.)

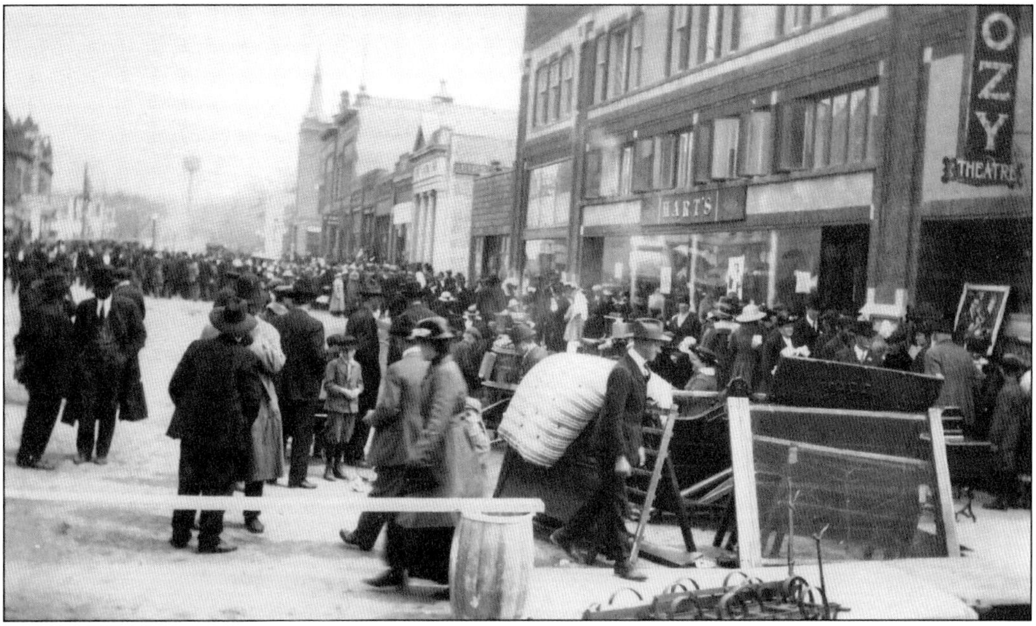

The 1918 Red Cross Auction drew citizens from far and wide to Long Prairie. This photograph captures an auction in front of the Hart Store, probably to raise funds for the organization and local support for Todd County military men. The patriotism shown by Long Prairie during World War I was well documented in the *Long Prairie Leader* newspaper and showed an immense outpouring of support for the local fighting men heading overseas. (Author's collection.)

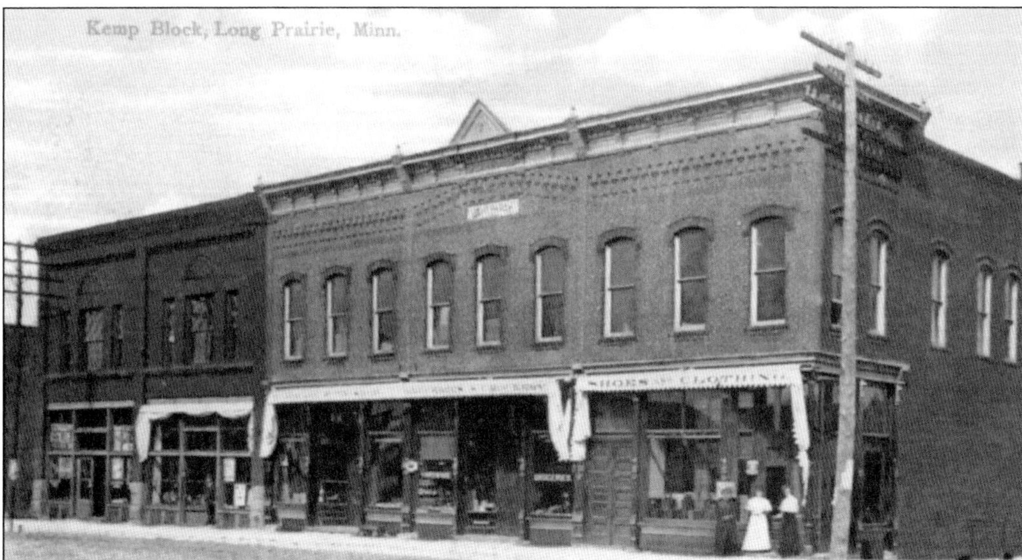

The Kemp Building was constructed in 1898 at a cost of $15,000. The upper floor was the opera house and, later, a bowling alley. The *Todd County Tribune*, a weekly newspaper, occupied the second floor for a number of years. The lower floor housed various business enterprises. James Hart & Sons Department Store occupied the building from 1907 to 1916. Eggers and Dixon Fairway Grocery store occupied the lower floor. The corner location was occupied by various drugstores over the years. (Courtesy of Barb Hamel.)

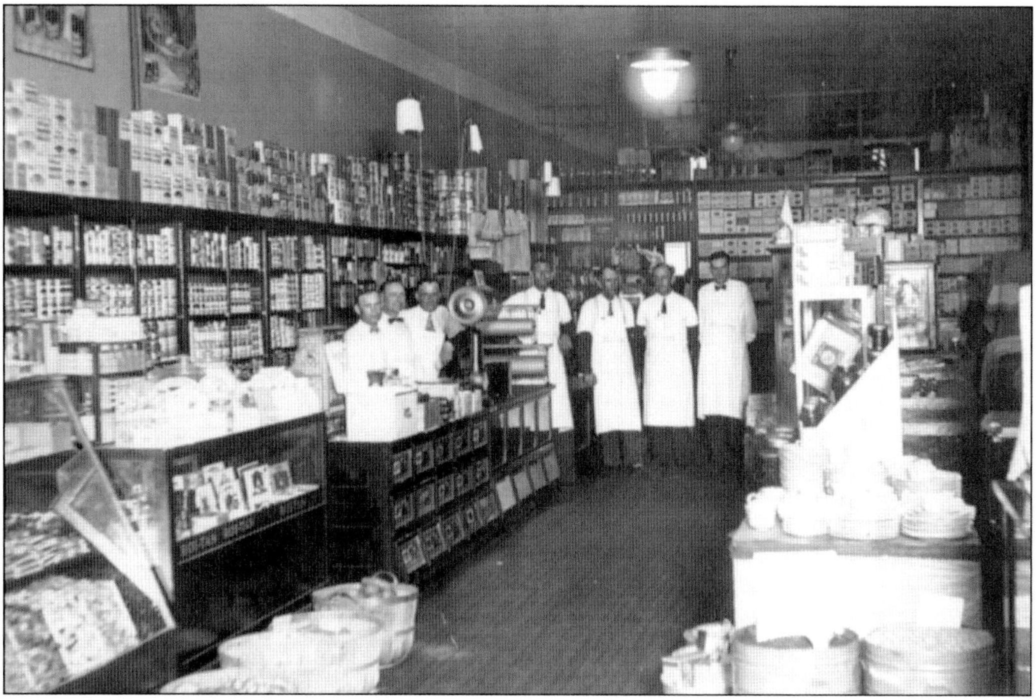

Lafayette Dixon (seen far left in this photograph of the store, located in the Kemp Building) and his brother James owned the Fairway Food Store from 1928 to 1940. After selling the store, James worked for the Great Northern Railroad in Long Prairie. He then ran a bait store behind his home at 109 Second Avenue Southwest until his death in 1961. Lafayette also worked for the railroad, as a ticket agent, after he left the food store. From 1935 to 1951, Lafayette was Todd County's 51st District nonpartisan state representative. He died in 1962. (Courtesy of Arden Truby.)

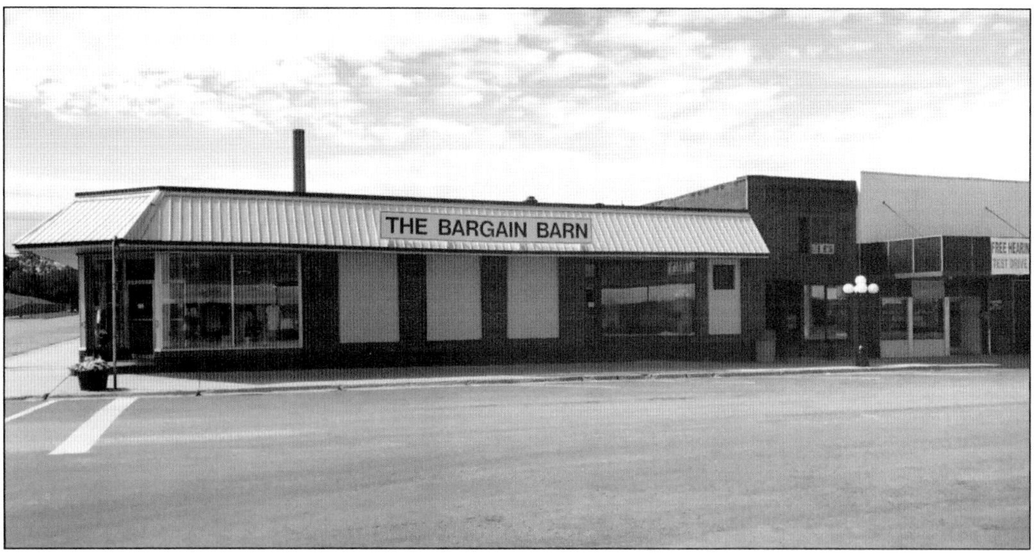

The building that currently contains the Bargain Barn on Central Avenue has a special place in the author's memory and those of many other youths of the 1970s and 1980s. This building hosted the Ben Franklin variety store, the place where kids could go to get just about anything from candy to pet fish—a venerable child's paradise. (Author's collection.)

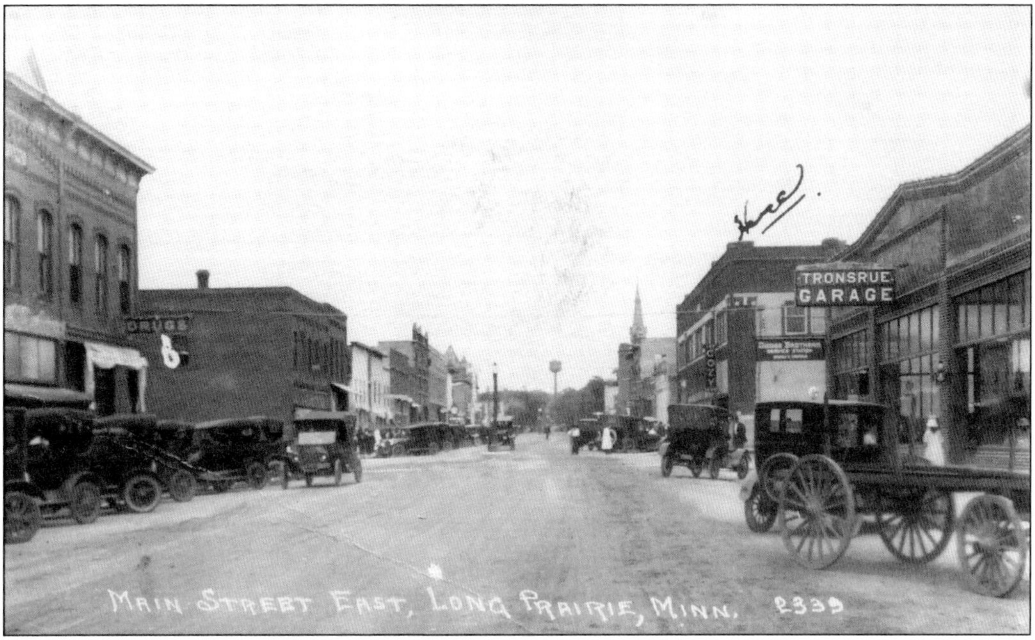

In the above 1923 photograph postcard of downtown Long Prairie, one will notice the Tronsrue Garage building, also seen below in 1937. Returning home from World War I, George Tronsrue graduated from the St. Paul School of Law and played outfield for a minor-league baseball team in St. Paul. Choosing not to practice law, he moved to Long Prairie, opening a Ford dealership in this structure, then known as the Hansmann Building. In 1921, he met and married the local home economics teacher, Ruth Cote. They lived at 24 Second Street North the rest of their days. Tronsrue was appointed postmaster for a time around 1937. He was elected probate judge in 1950, but died of a heart attack months after. Ruth died during surgery in 1975. Touted as "fireproof" when built in 1914, this garage building was destroyed in a spectacular fire in March 1951. (Both, author's collection.)

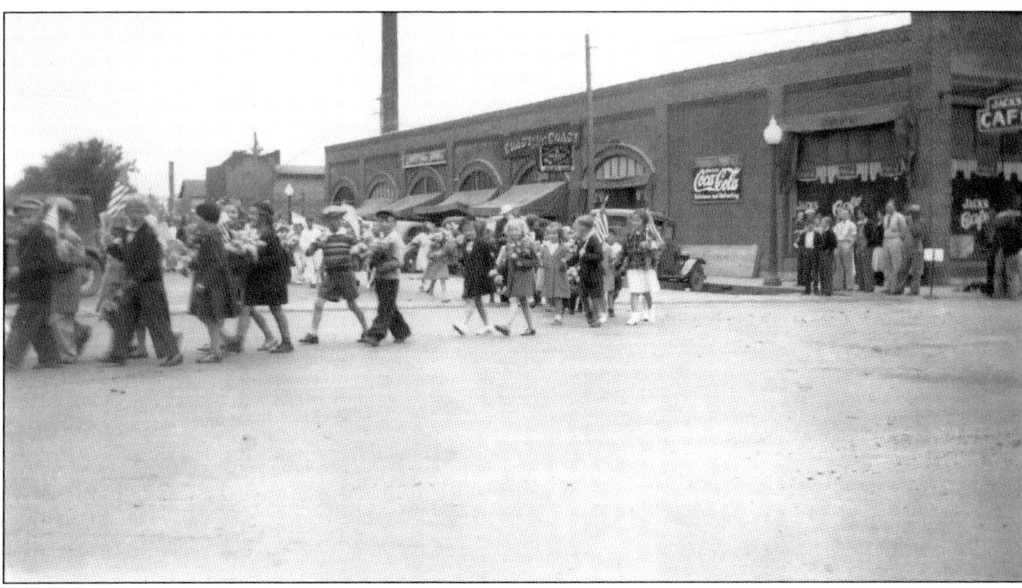

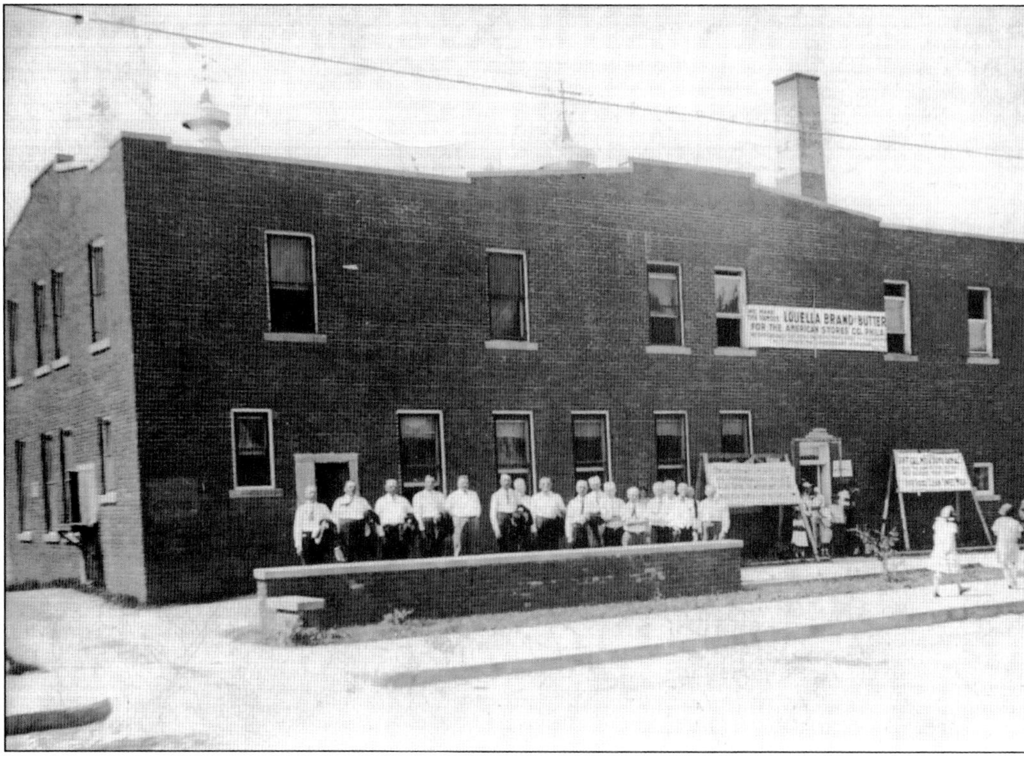

Above, this former Long Prairie Creamery building was erected in 1916. Before that time, the Long Prairie Creamery was located along the river on the north side of town near the present city disposal plant. The last milk can rolled into this creamery in 1987. Below, the building is currently owned by the Bjerga Feed Stores and is used as a storage location for company items. The aged structure and patina of the building are often used as vintage backdrops for photographs by local photographers. The future of this hub of Long Prairie rural history is uncertain. (Above, courtesy of Linda Armstrong; below, author's collection.)

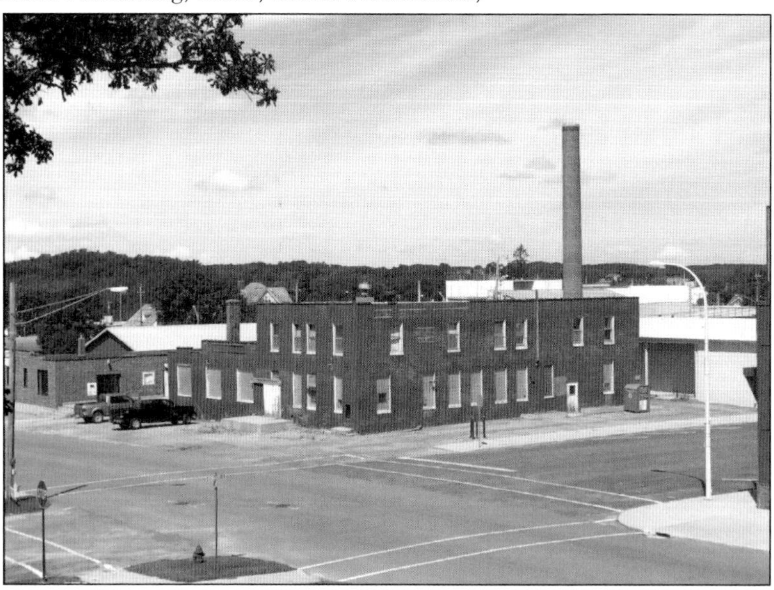

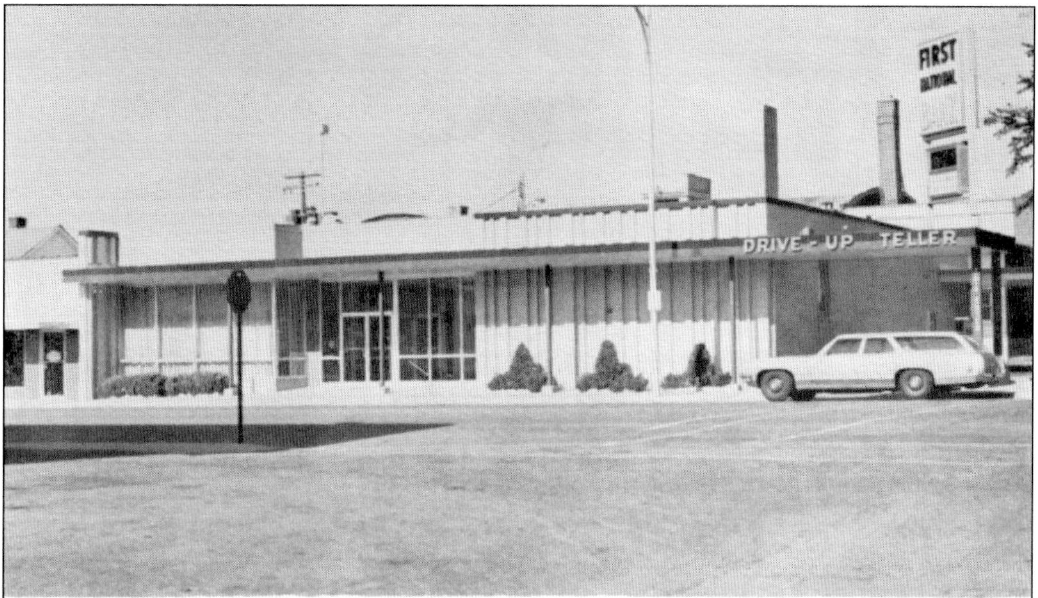

First National Bank—Long Prairie, Minn.

H.W. Schroeder began his banking career in Long Prairie in 1906 as a teller in the People's National Bank of Long Prairie. In 1927, the People's National bought out the Bank of Long Prairie, which was consolidated into the People's National, and after the purchase, the bank was then known as the Bank of Long Prairie. In 1963, the present bank building, seen here in the 1970s, was erected; the bank was then moved to these new quarters, and the name was again changed, to the First National Bank. (Author's collection.)

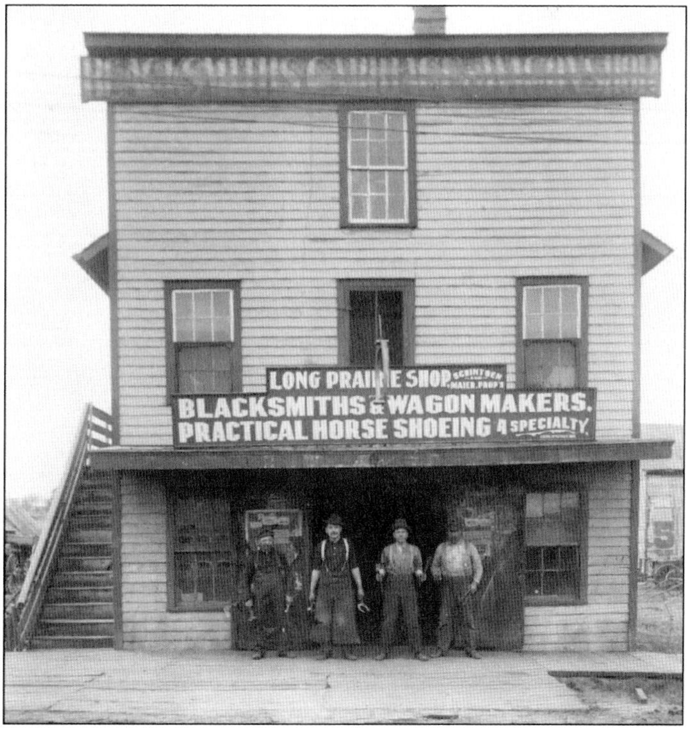

Located on the present site of the former Cozy Theater/KEYL/Food Shelf building and old Delight Shop/D&J Stylist building sat the leading blacksmith shop of its day: the Schintgen and Meier Blacksmith Shop. This shop also manufactured wagons and sleds, and did much of the horseshoeing for the community. A Mr. Meier was instrumental in getting day current from the local light plant for the residents of Long Prairie. (Courtesy of TCHS.)

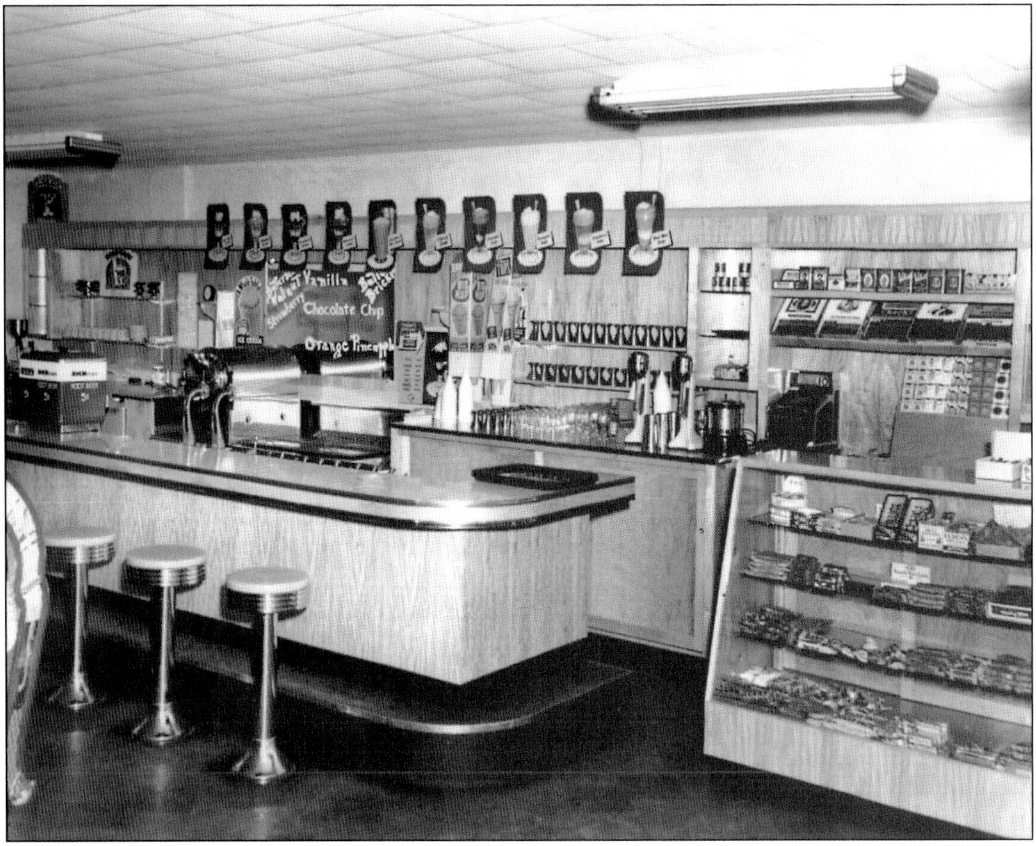

The Delight Shop opened for business on August 8, 1947. This building still stands today at 125 Central Avenue. Owned and operated by Reiny Schinske and with a jukebox and pinball machines, it was the place to be for high school teens of the day. It is said many teenage relationships started and ended in these booths. Popcorn was 5¢. Moviegoers would stop in and buy their candy and popcorn here before stepping next door to the Cozy Theater to watch movies. The Delight Shop closed in 1967. Many items from the Delight Shop have been donated by the Schinske family to the Todd County Museum for display. (Both, courtesy of Tony and Janet Schinske.)

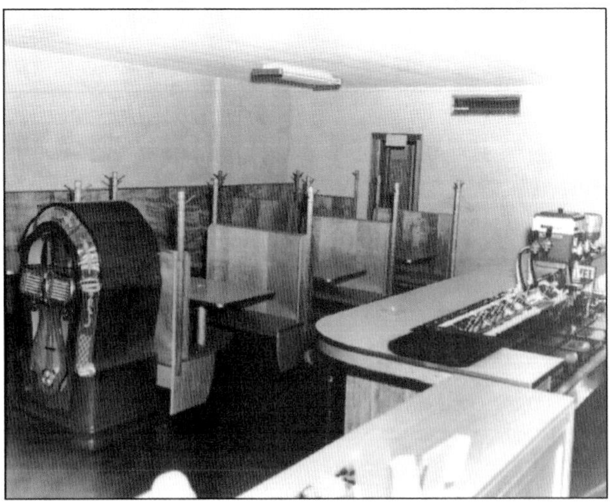

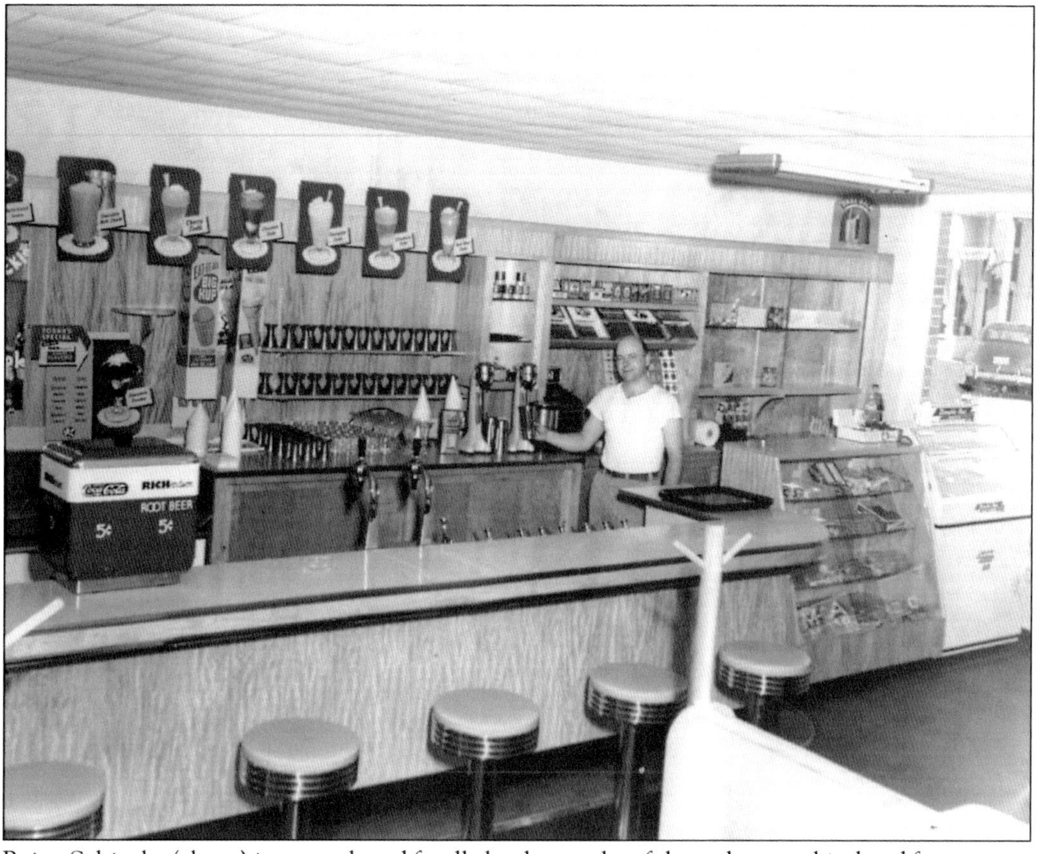

Reiny Schinske (above) is remembered fondly by the youths of those days as a kind and funny man. Schinske would always brighten one's day. Dorothy Smith bought the Delight Shop building in 1967 and converted it into a hair salon. Her shop had been located in the former Miller Building across Central Avenue from the Reichert Hotel building prior to moving into the former Delight Shop location. Sheryl Lunsford bought the hair salon business from Smith in about 1970 or 1971. The building was then sold out to Bob Johnson, who had a gift shop and hair salon there. (Both, courtesy of Tony and Janet Schinske.)

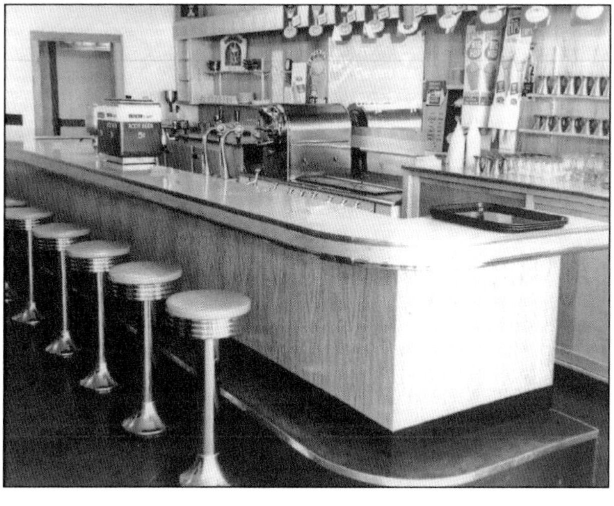

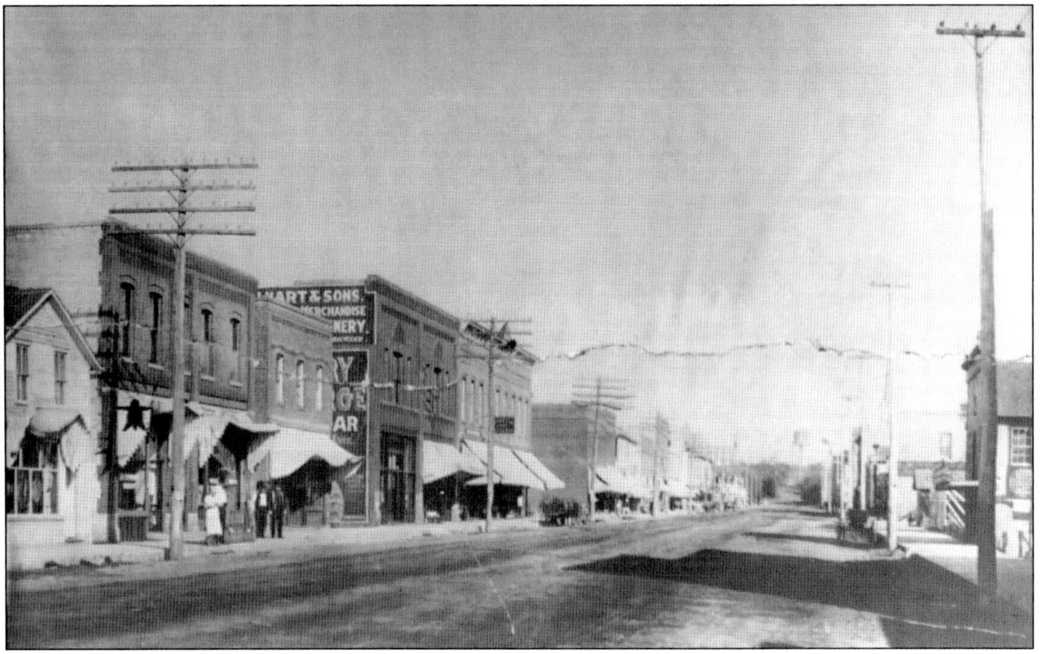

The view in this photograph of downtown looks east up Osakis Street (now Central Avenue). In this c. 1910 image, note the advertisement for James Hart & Sons painted on the side of the building. This painted advertisement is still visible today, though faded. This building was the original location of the Hart Store in Long Prairie before the current Hart Mall building was constructed in 1916. The Schintgen and Meier Blacksmith Shop is also visible on the right in this photograph. (Courtesy of Ron Wienhold.)

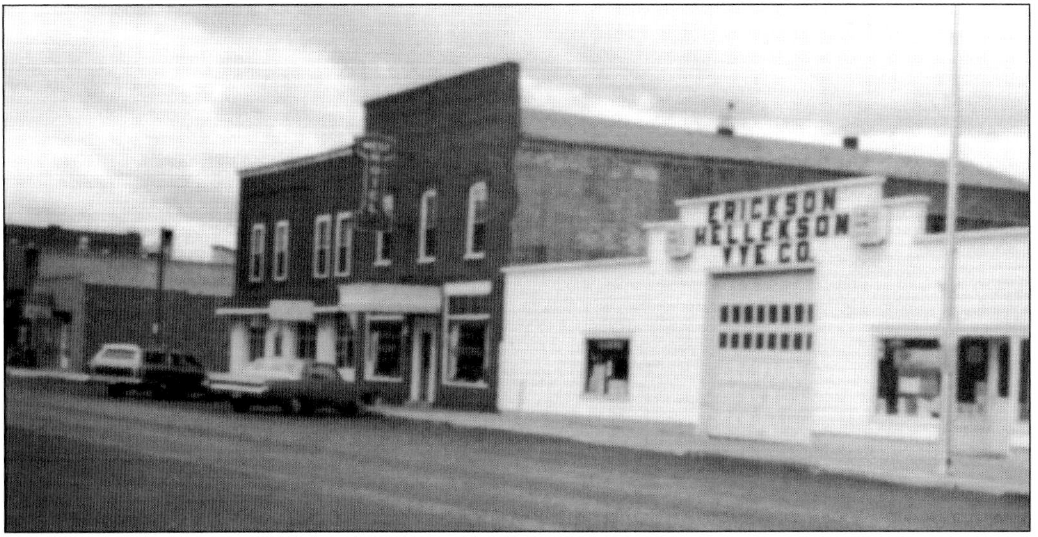

The West Hotel, seen here in 1971, was owned and operated by a Mr. Menard for many years and, for a time, was known as "the Farmer's Home." Other owners were Perry Knapp, Leo Clavin, Cleve and Alida Eldred, and Chuck Eldred. Lumber businesses occupied the corner next to the West Hotel for many years. Some of these lumberyards were the North Star Lumber Company, the Hennifen Lumber Company, Herman Albright, H.C. Wolfarth and Sons, and, seen here, the Erickson-Helleckson-Vye Co. (Courtesy of Harold Connelly and Valley View Estates.)

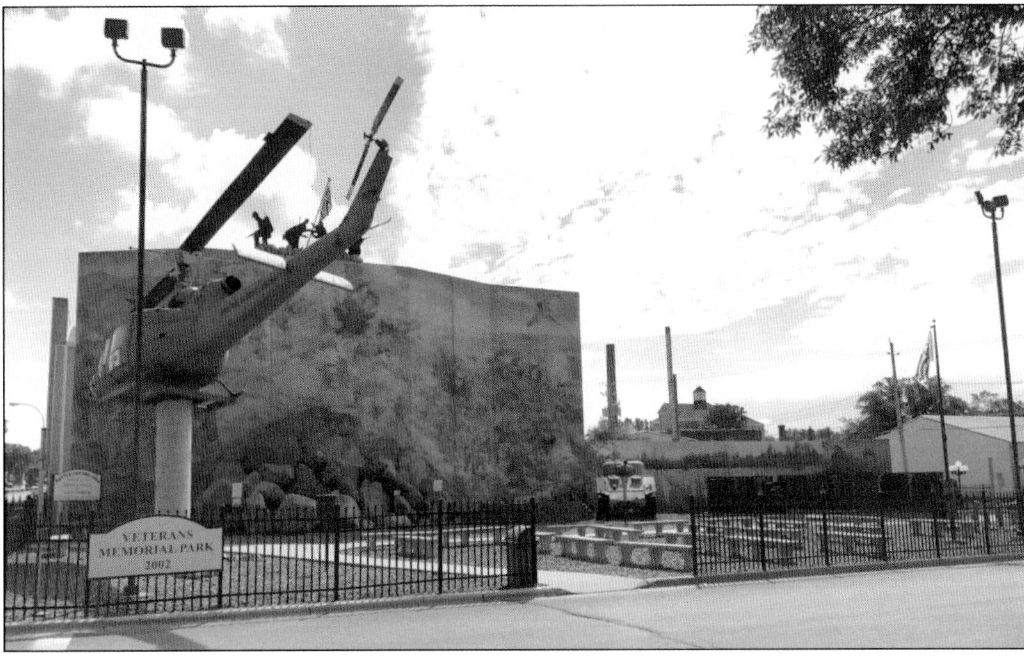

Dedicated August 10, 2002, Veterans Memorial Park is located at the corner of Central Avenue and First Street South. It was built by banker Roger Johnston, who commissioned Army reservist Kimberly Lawler to skillfully depict several scenes that tower to a height of five stories. At the top is a one-and-a-half-story steel depiction of the first flag raising at Mount Suribachi. The author hauled up the first US Coast Guard flag to fly over this park during the dedication, which was also attended by Charles W. Lindberg, who was, at the time, the last surviving member of the group to first raise the flag on Iwo Jima. (Author's collection.)

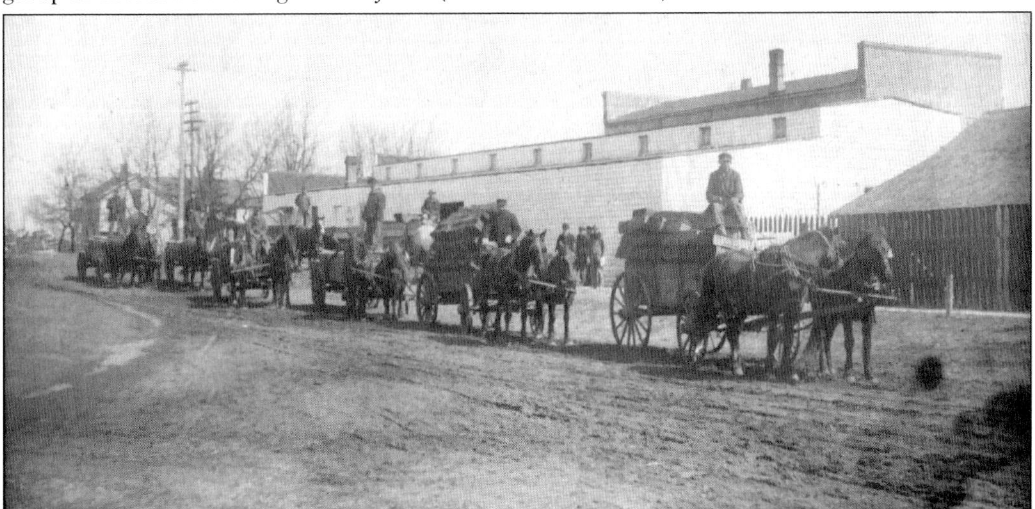

This 1915 photograph captures a shingle-hauling train for the new Nick Drikes barn in Round Prairie Township, from the Albright Lumber Company. Long Prairie had many lumber companies throughout its history, all supplying lumber for the growing village. The lumber building in this photograph was torn down in the 1980s, and this is the current site of the World War II memorial. (Courtesy of TCHS.)

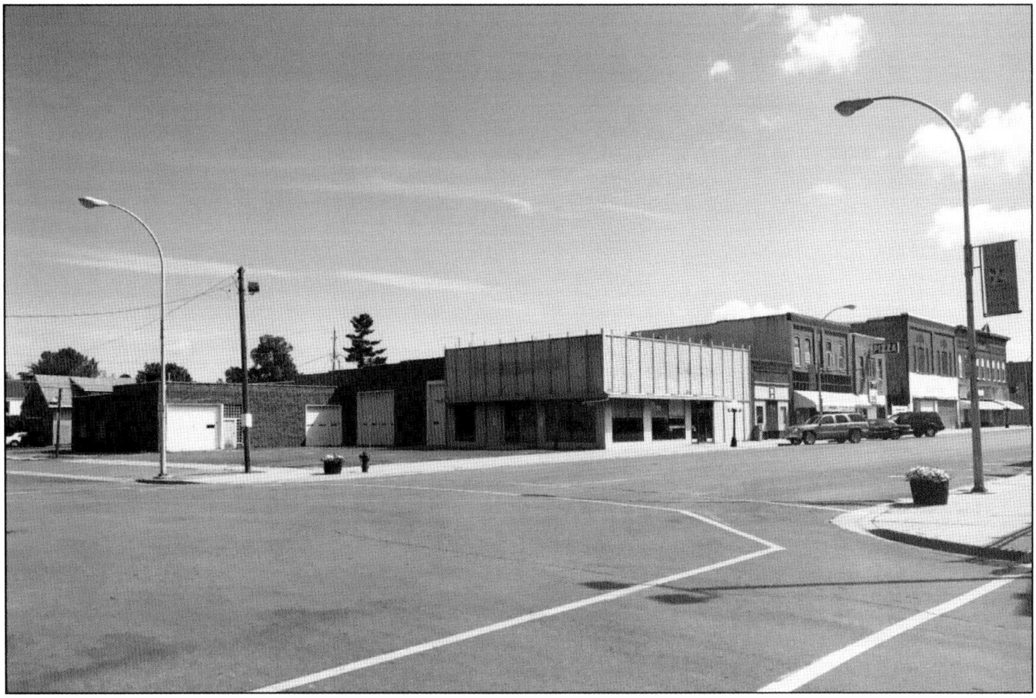

The section of the former Blais Ford agency salesroom, seen above, was built by Ray Ostrander, and a confectionery business was conducted in this section for many years. A while ago, the Stephen Bottling Works was located in the rear of this lot. The present corner car lot contained two residences at one time; one of them housed the Andrie Abstract Company, and the second was the home of Ray Ostrander, and prior to that, was the Swan Thornquist home, as mentioned on page 29. A fire practically destroyed the Andrie Abstract Company, and both properties were cleared. The first modern gasoline service station in Long Prairie was built on this corner by Standard Oil Company, as seen below in 1941 at the far left of the photograph. (Both, author's collection.)

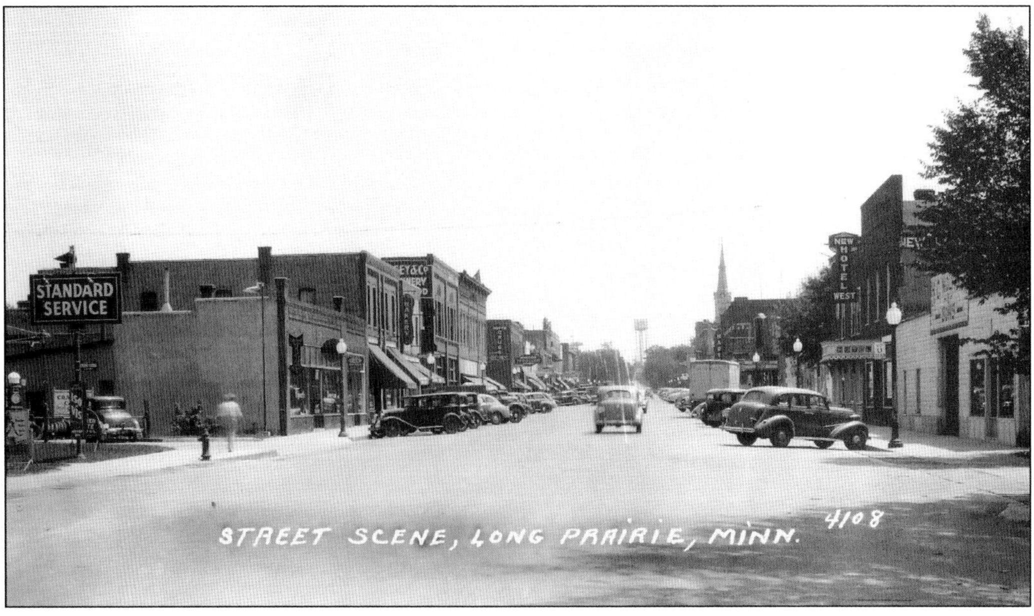

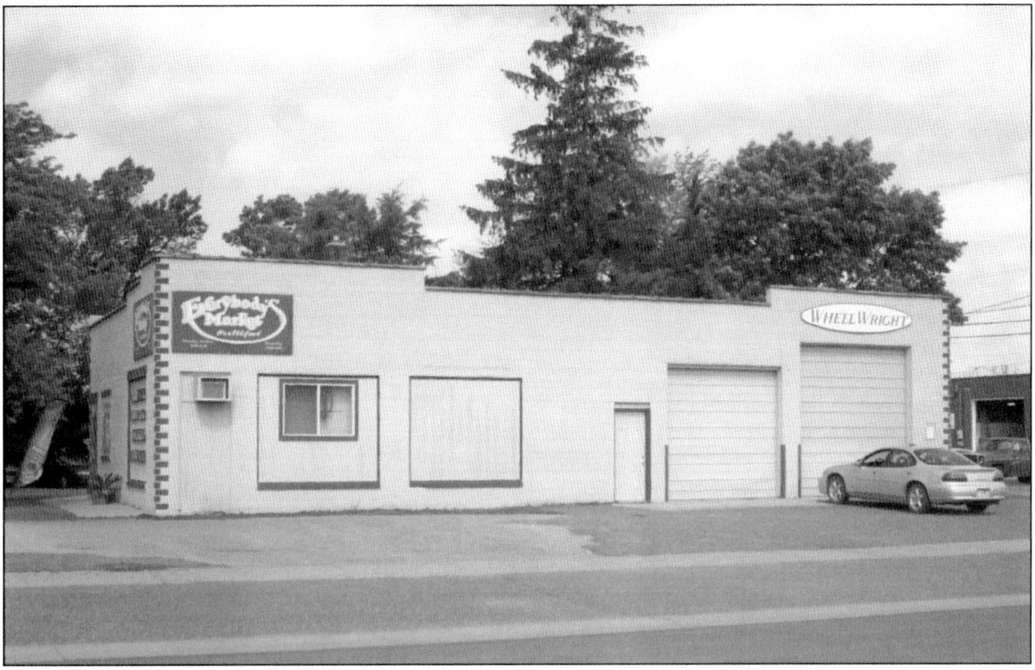

Of the many service stations that served Long Prairie since the arrival of the automobile, this building is one of the only remaining early service stations. Standing on the corner of Central Avenue and First Street North, it was built in the late 1940s as the Central Cooperative Oil Association. It sold gasoline, oil, batteries, and tires and also carried appliances. Since the mid-1980s, the building has been the home of Everybody's Market health-food store. Wheel Wright bicycle shop is also in this building. (Author's collection.)

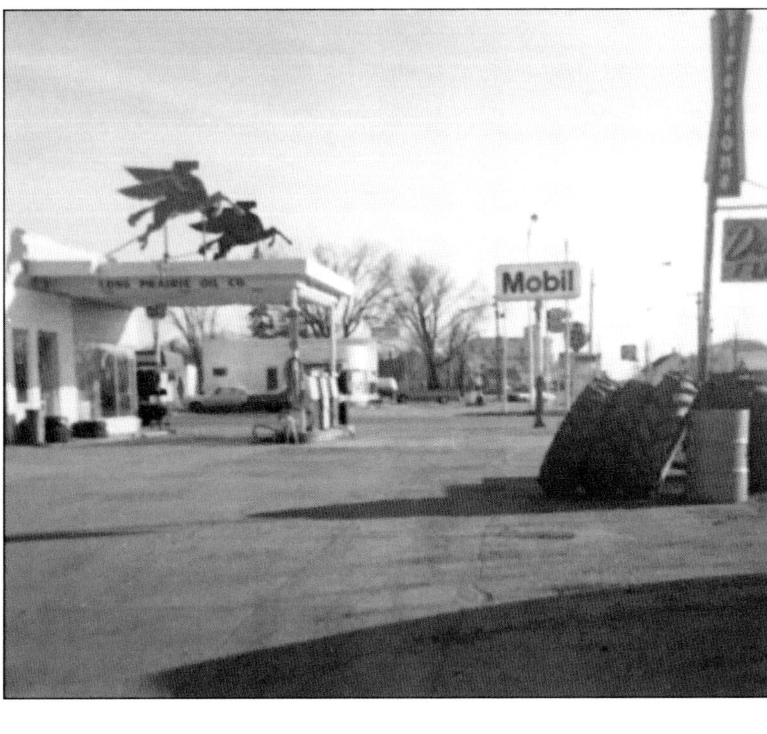

This 1971 photograph captures the many gas stations that occupied Lake Street near the intersection with Central Avenue. In a two-block area, there were five service stations. They included a Sinclair station, which stood behind the photographer's view here; a Mobil station; a 76 station; a Shell station; and just beyond that, a Super America station. (Courtesy of Harold Connelly and Valley View Estates.)

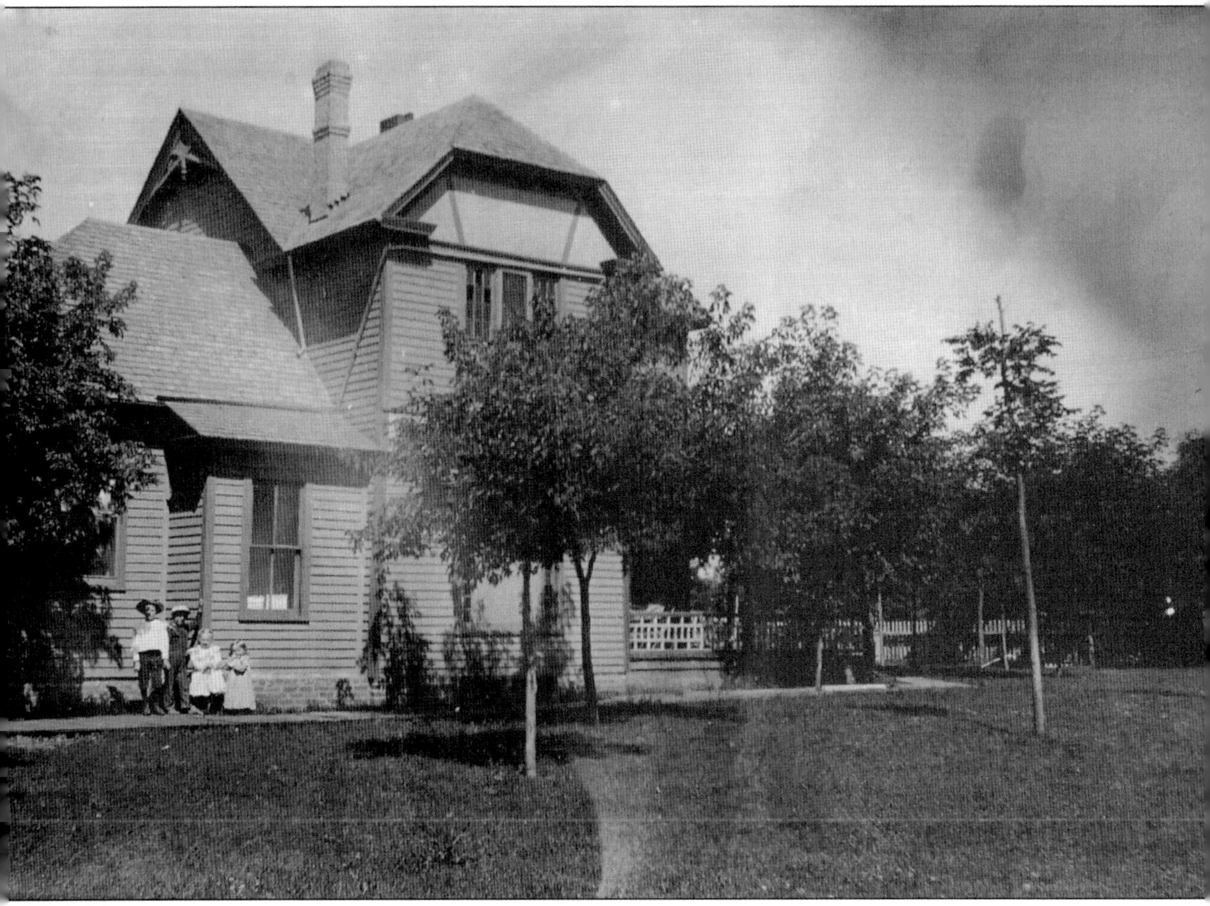

In 1887, Dr. Christie married Susan West (1859–1910), a schoolteacher, in Milwaukee, Wisconsin. In the 1890s, George and Susan lived in the "old house" seen here. This home was occupied by the Christie family prior to the construction of the current house in 1903. The old house sat right about where the Countryside Restaurant building is now and was removed in 1973 to make room for the Geno's parking lot. Dr. George and Susan had four children: George West Christie (1890–1956), Robert Laing Christie (1892–1976), Edith Lisle Christie (1894–1902), and Donald Rittenhouse Christie (1896–1985). Edith died at the age of eight from peritonitis and septicemia. Susan helped establish the Long Prairie Literary Society in 1893. In the literary society report celebrating one century, Susan is remembered for her piano accompaniment in Chautauqua performances held at the local opera house. (Courtesy of the Christie Home Museum.)

Three

Off Main Street

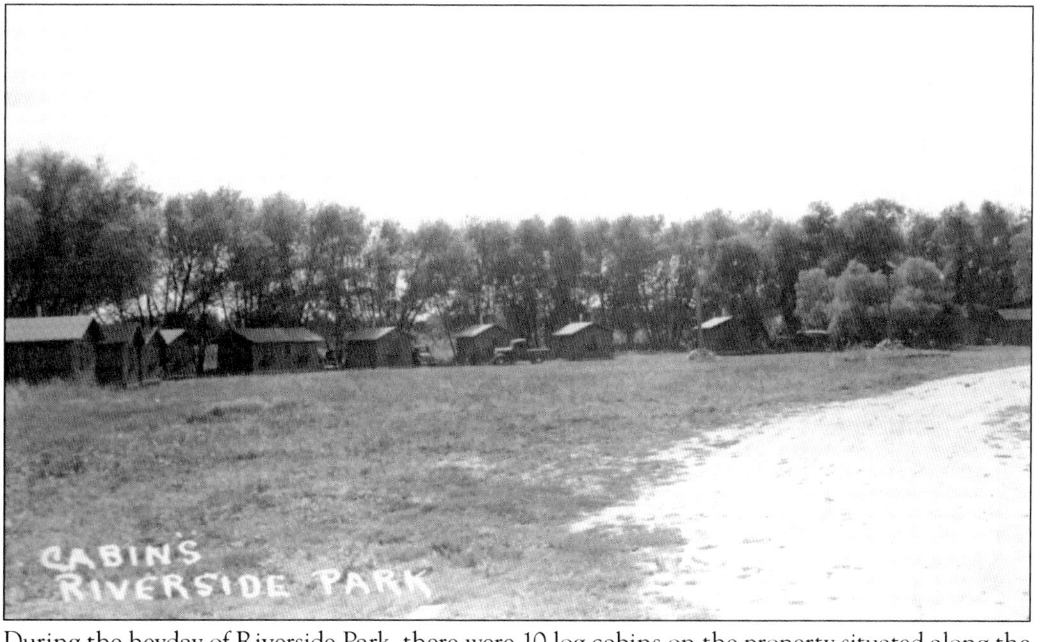

During the heyday of Riverside Park, there were 10 log cabins on the property situated along the riverbank, as seen here. These cabins were utilized by various groups as a retreat location, with some even being rented as temporary residences. When the park was auctioned off in 1943, the cabins were removed. One of the cabins was purchased and moved to a private residence on the east shore of Lake Charlotte; it still stands today. (Author's collection.)

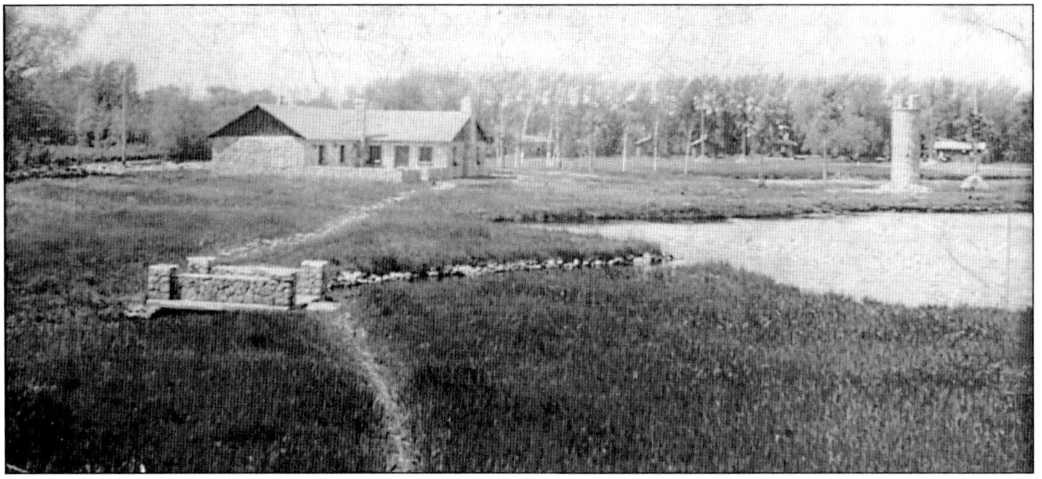

Riverside Park was conceived of, developed, and built by the Works Progress Administration (WPA) during the drought years of the mid-1930s and completed in 1936. The project called for the development of two and a half acres of pastureland along the bank of the Long Prairie River, near the intersection of Highways 71 and 27. The Sportsman's Club building, seen above, was used as a gathering place. Boy Scouts would hold retreats and banquets here. During the "wet years" of the early to mid-1940s, the park flooded often, and with most of the men gone to fight in World War II, fell into disrepair. The city abandoned the park in 1943 and sold it at auction. It was purchased by a private party who renamed the park Fairview Park for a time, but it was abandoned again. The park took on an unofficial name, "Mosquito Park." (Both, author's collection.)

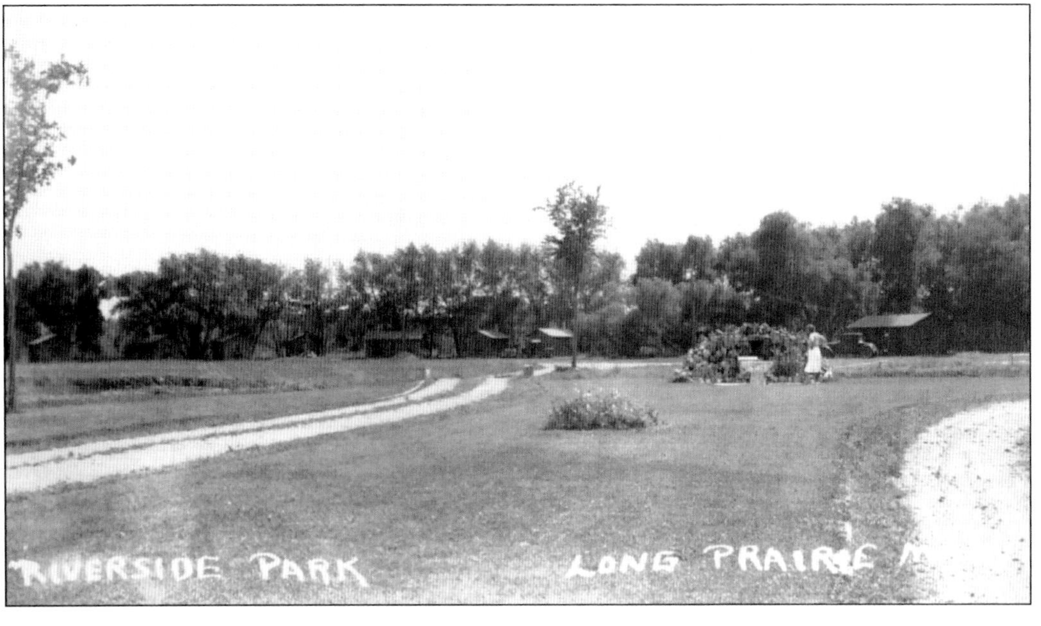

The Huber Packing Plant constructed in 1937 was the precursor to Prairie Packing, seen here in 1971. It was and still is one of the leading businesses in Long Prairie. Adolph Huber, a local butcher, constructed and used the building for slaughtering and storage of meats. The original building was 38 by 98 feet in size and included a basement. In the basement were the hide room, a tank room, and the necessary boilers for heating and scalding purposes. (Courtesy of Harold Connelly and Valley View Estates.)

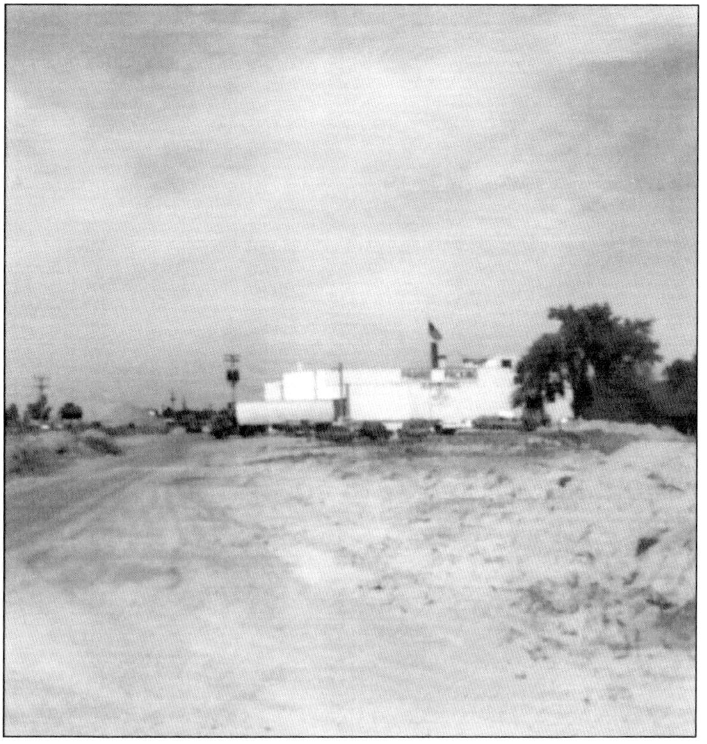

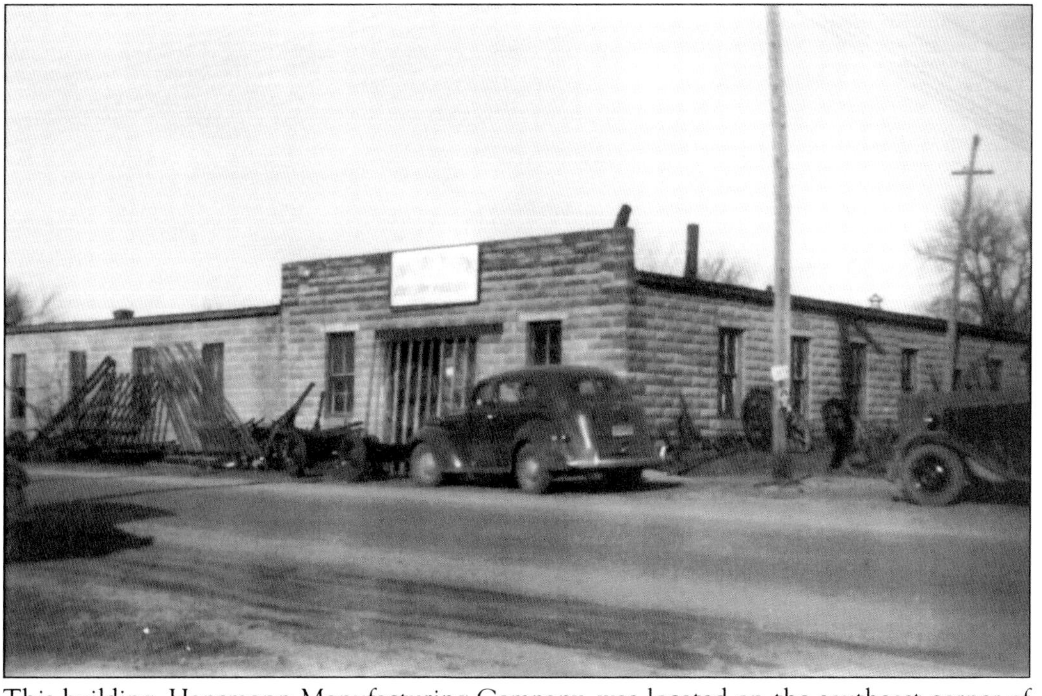

This building, Hansmann Manufacturing Company, was located on the southeast corner of Highways 71 and 27, where South Side Auto building now stands. It was constructed by Paul Hansmann, who produced a line of tractor hitches to include a drill hitch, binder hitch, and plow engine guide. (Courtesy of Doris Visser.)

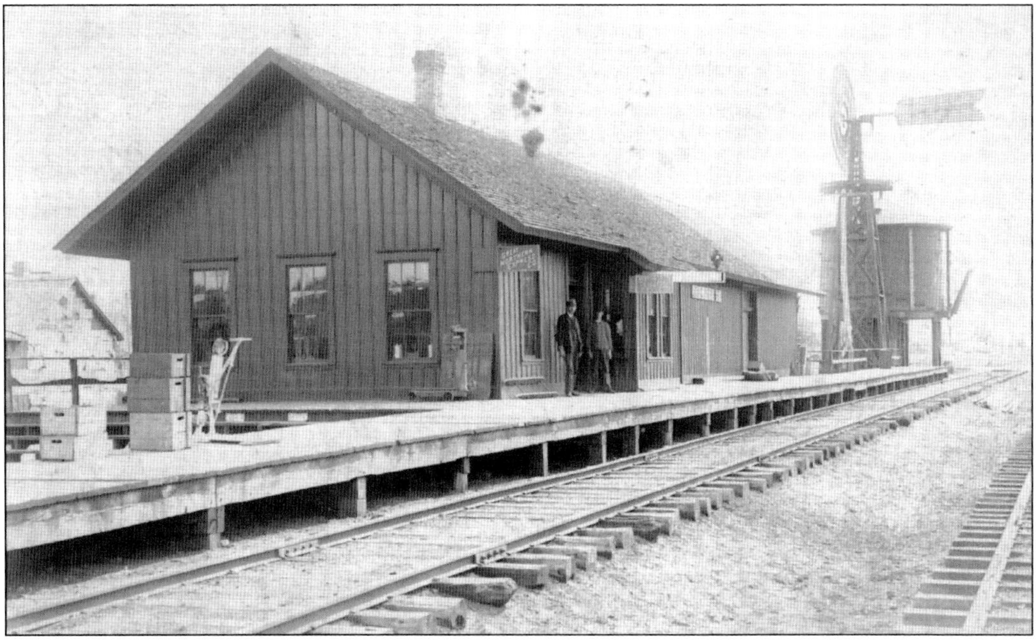

These photographs of the Long Prairie depot, taken in 1900 (above) and 1960 (below), provide an idea of how little the depot building changed over the years. The winter of 1950–1951 saw the last passenger run of the Great Northern Railroad K-Line, which served Long Prairie for over 70 years. Some of the travelers that rode the train that day included a group consisting of Cherall, Jerry, and Stevie Markuson; Betty Wilds; Sherly and Betty Miller; Geraldine and Betty Blair; and Mary Jo, John, and Jo Wickum. The passengers boarded the train in Long Prairie and rode it south to Sauk Centre, Minnesota, where Ray Wickum picked them up and drove them home in a car. The depot sat on the rail line straight west from the current Long Prairie Plumbing and Heating or just northwest of the current Subway restaurant. (Both, courtesy of TCHS.)

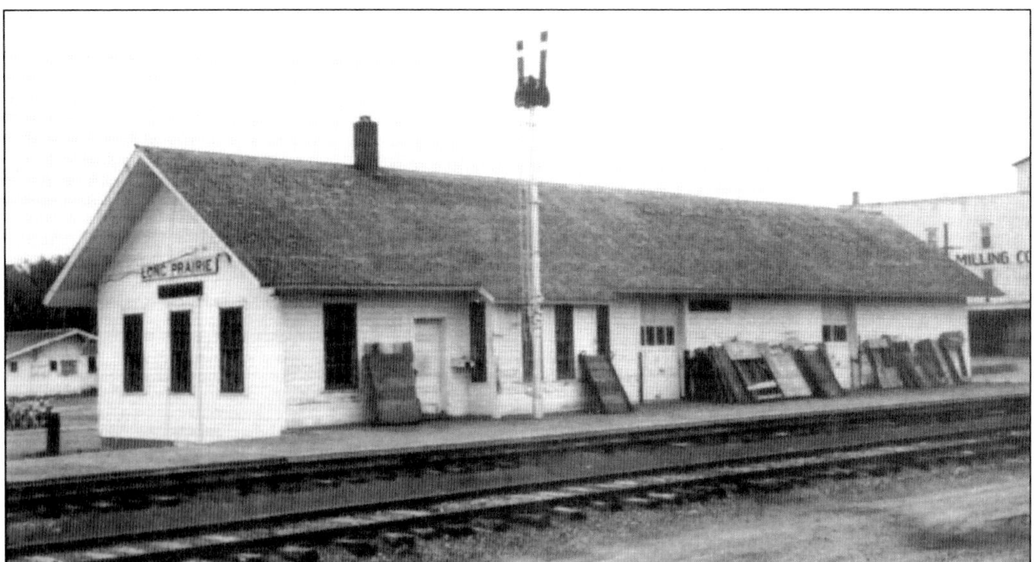

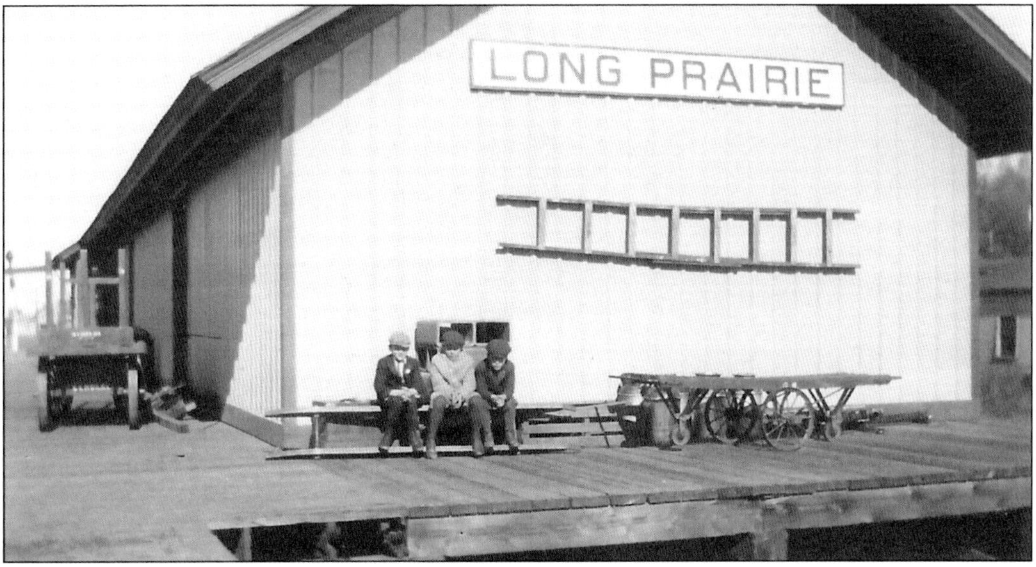

The Long Prairie depot was the stepping-off point for those visiting Long Prairie for nearly a century. The rail line made it to Long Prairie about 1880. The original depot building was moved when the railroad ceased operations in 1983. The old depot still stands, located on the north side of town in front of the wastewater treatment plant. (Author's collection.)

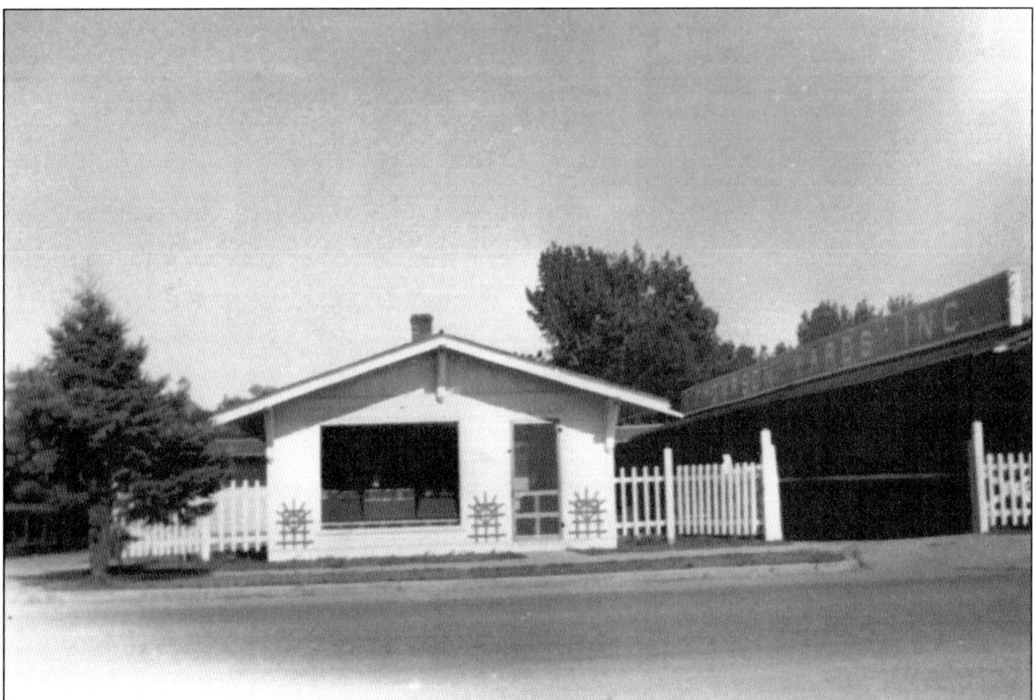

Located on what is now the site of Long Prairie Plumbing and Heating and the law offices of Brown & Krueger, the Thompson Lumber Yard was one of the leading lumberyards of its day. This lumberyard began operation in 1937 when it was purchased from George Steiner, who had been engaged in the lumber business at this location for eight years prior. (Author's collection.)

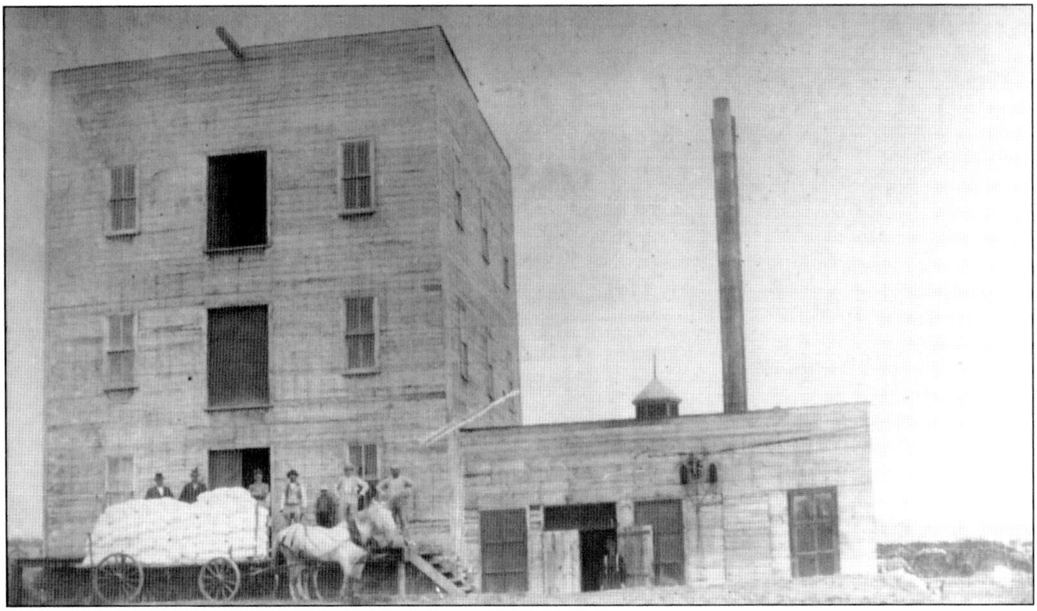

The Long Prairie Milling building was originally constructed as part of the first municipal lighting plant in Long Prairie. It sat in the area across the street from the old hospital on Second Avenue South (above). The plant building was then moved using horsepower and greased timbers (below) west down Second Avenue to what is now the location of Burger King. This was so that the milling company would be next to the railroad, thus becoming Long Prairie Milling Company in 1894. It was the largest milling organization in Todd County at the time, grinding 200 barrels daily. This building was taken down in 1988. (Both, TCHS.)

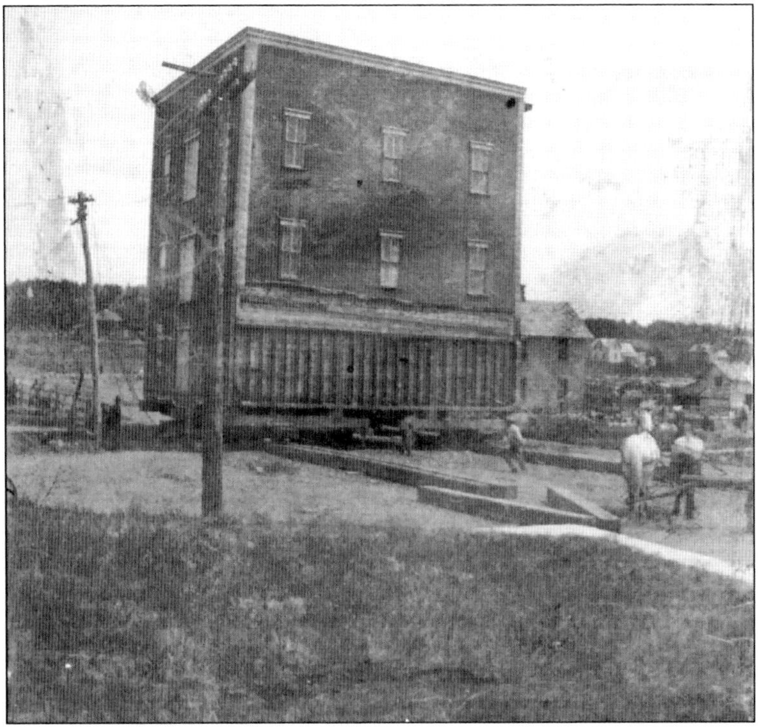

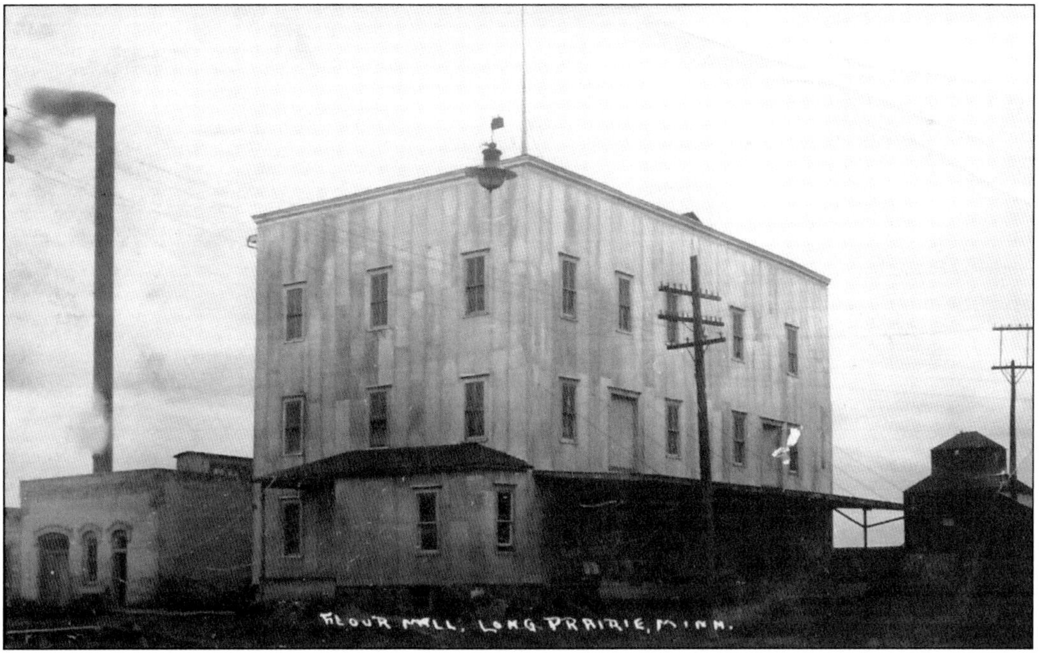

Once established on the site along the railroad, the Long Prairie Milling Company became known as the home of the famous X-Ray and Leaf Patent flours. The largest milling operation at the time in Long Prairie and Todd County, this mill held great prominence throughout the state in its time, rivaling the mills of Minneapolis and St. Paul. The former mill building was P&R Ag Services at the time it was torn down. (Courtesy of Barb Hamel.)

In 1870, the first school district and high school were organized in Long Prairie. In 1882, more accommodations became necessary, and a new site was advised. This first high school was built at the current site of Soldier Field athletic grounds on the north side of Long Prairie. This block has been in the possession of Long Prairie school system ever since this first school was built. (Author's collection.)

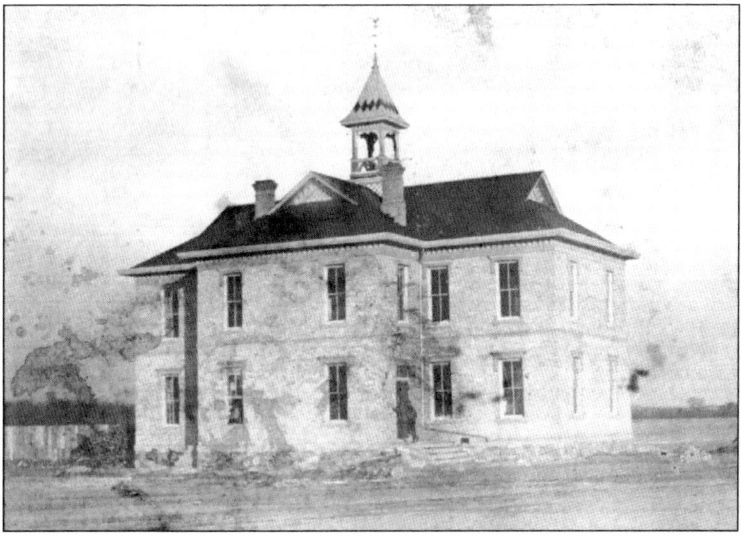

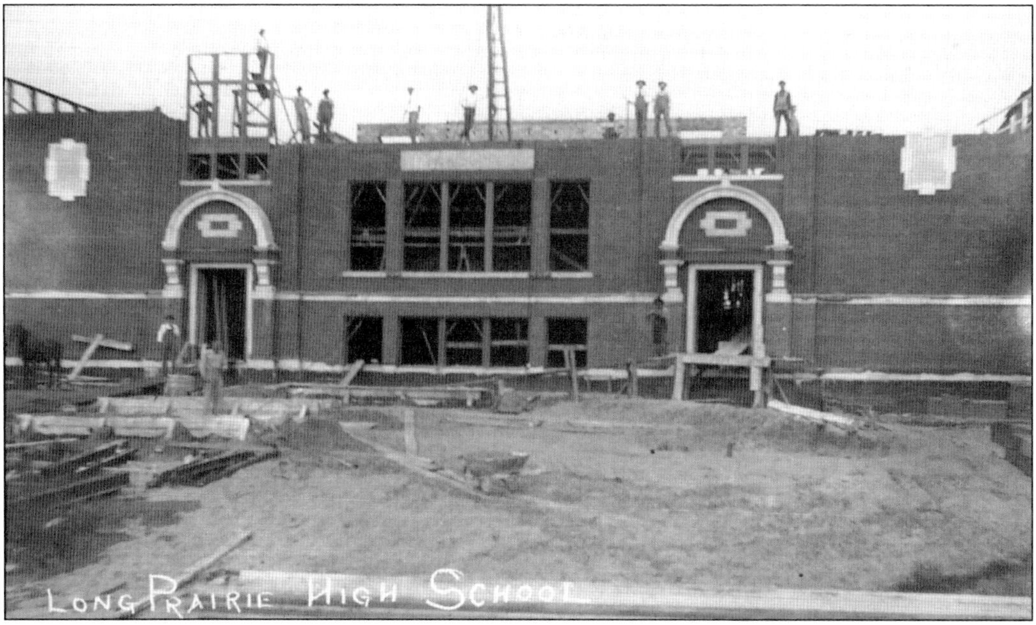

The 1908 high school building was constructed at a cost of $40,000. In 1921, the "new" high school building was completed, and the 1908 property became an elementary school. The school building had three floors. The bottom, or basement, floor included a gym that doubled as the cafeteria. The space also had a stage where children performed different programs. In addition to some storerooms, this level also held a kindergarten classroom. The author attended kindergarten here. The middle floor held a music room and first- through fourth-grade classrooms. The top floor held the fifth- and sixth-grade classrooms, along with a science lab and the high school math, English, and social studies classrooms. The elementary school offices were also located on this floor. With the city school expansion project taking place in the early 1980s, the old 1908 building met its end during the summer of 1981. (Both, author's collection.)

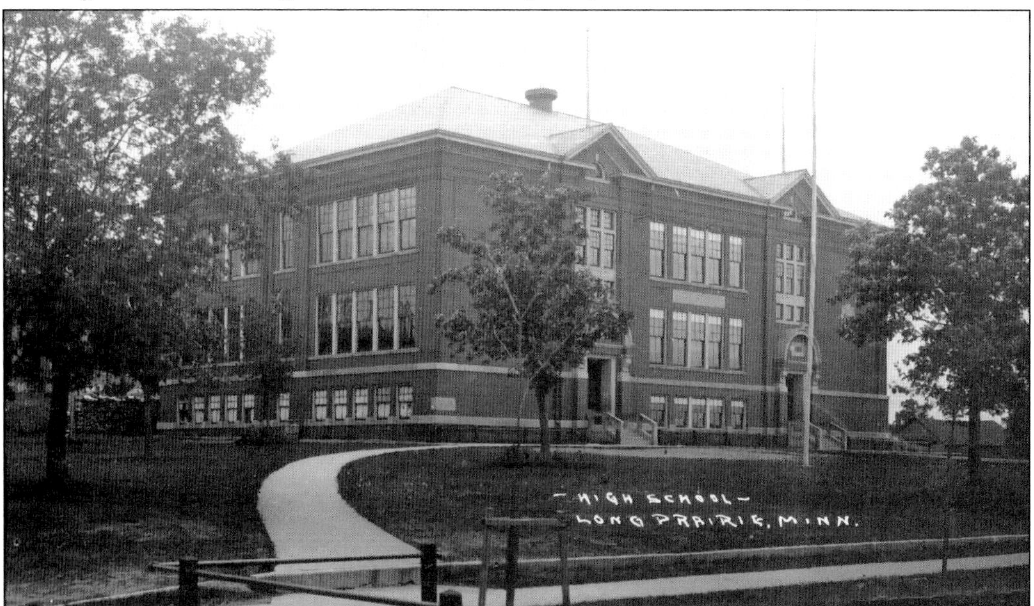

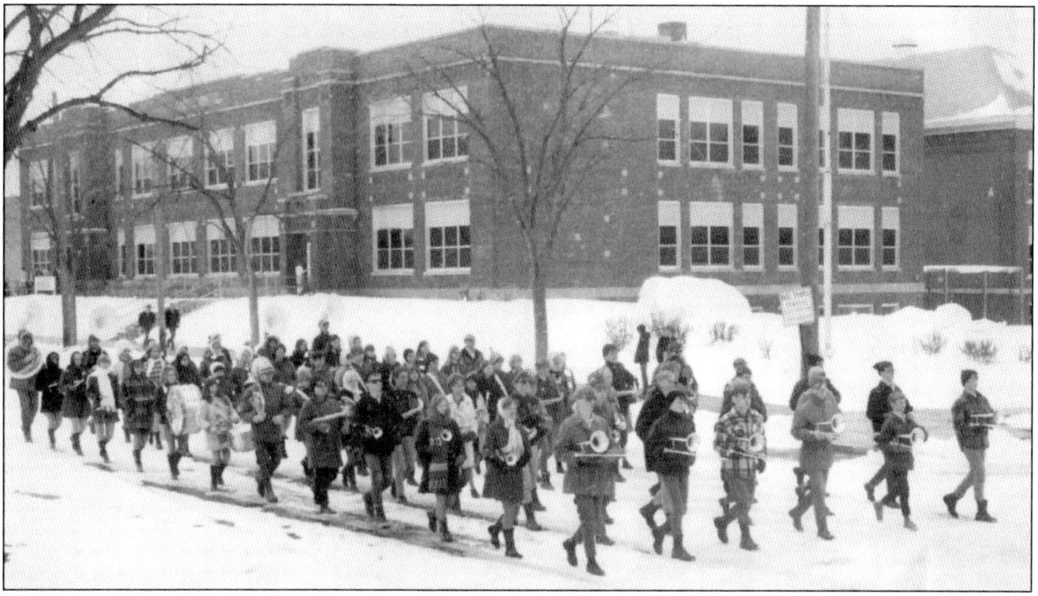

Built in 1921, this new high school was one of two major improvements in Long Prairie that year. In 1958, a major addition was made to the south end of this school building to include school offices, kitchen and cafeteria, a gymnasium with locker rooms, and a band room. After 76 years of service educating the youth of Long Prairie and combining with the Grey Eagle school system in 1993, a larger high school building was needed. The 1921 section was demolished in 1997. The location remains under the ownership of the Long Prairie school district. The site has been redeveloped to host various school district offices and classrooms. These before and after photographs were taken from the same location; the above was taken in 1970, and one can see the 1921 building, with the 1908 building sitting behind it to the west. (Both, author's collection.)

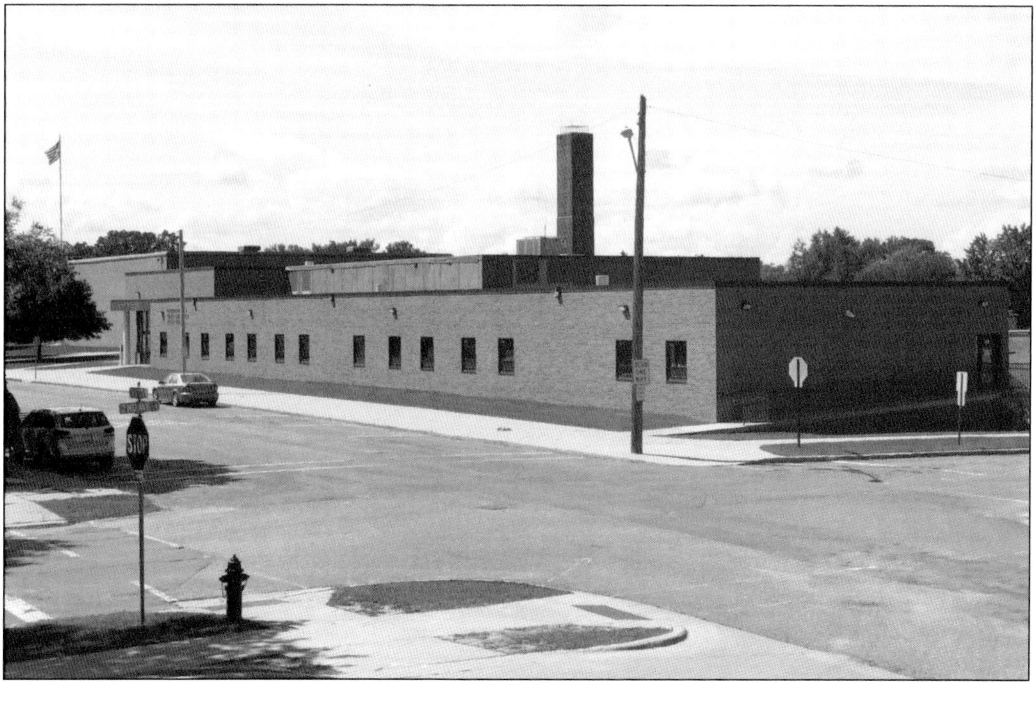

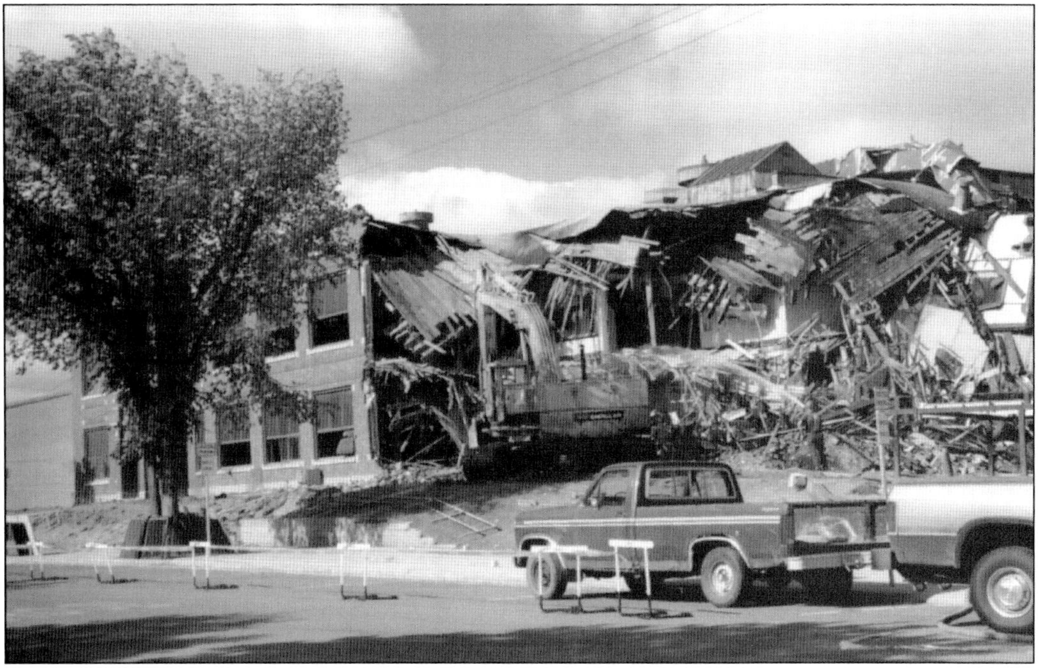

The 1921 building fell to the wrecking ball the summer of 1997. Those attending this old Long Prairie High School probably had heard the rumor of a swimming pool in the 1921 school building, though hardly a soul knew where it may have been. The rumor went so far to say that a student drowned in the pool, causing its permanent closure. During the demolition of this school, the mystery seemed to have been solved when the pool was exposed, having been under the former school kitchen, as seen below. According to an article in the *Long Prairie Leader* during the 1921 school construction, "The swimming pool is not to be finished for some time, the building containing only the construction necessary to put the swimming pool in at such time as the board deems best." (Both, courtesy of Darlene Eldred.)

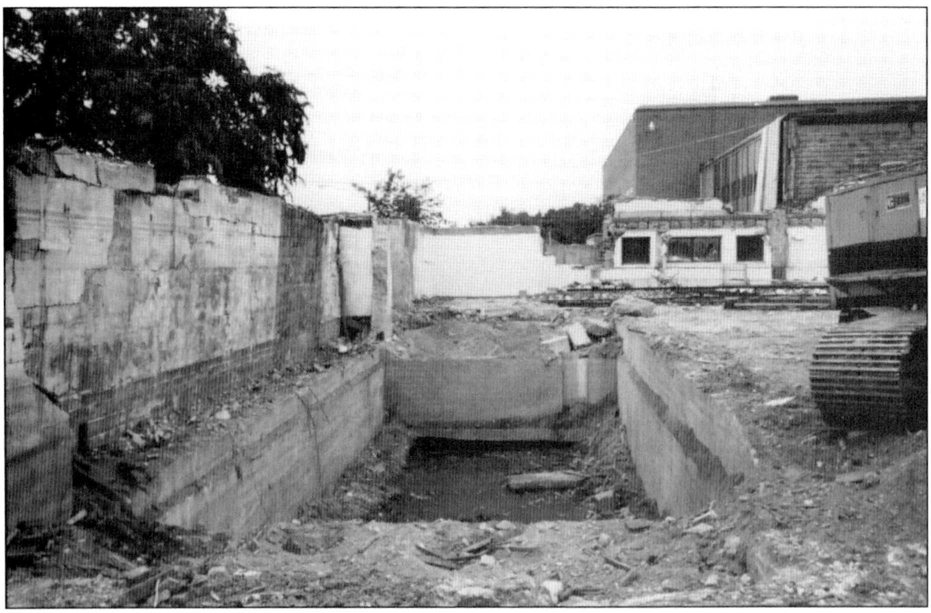

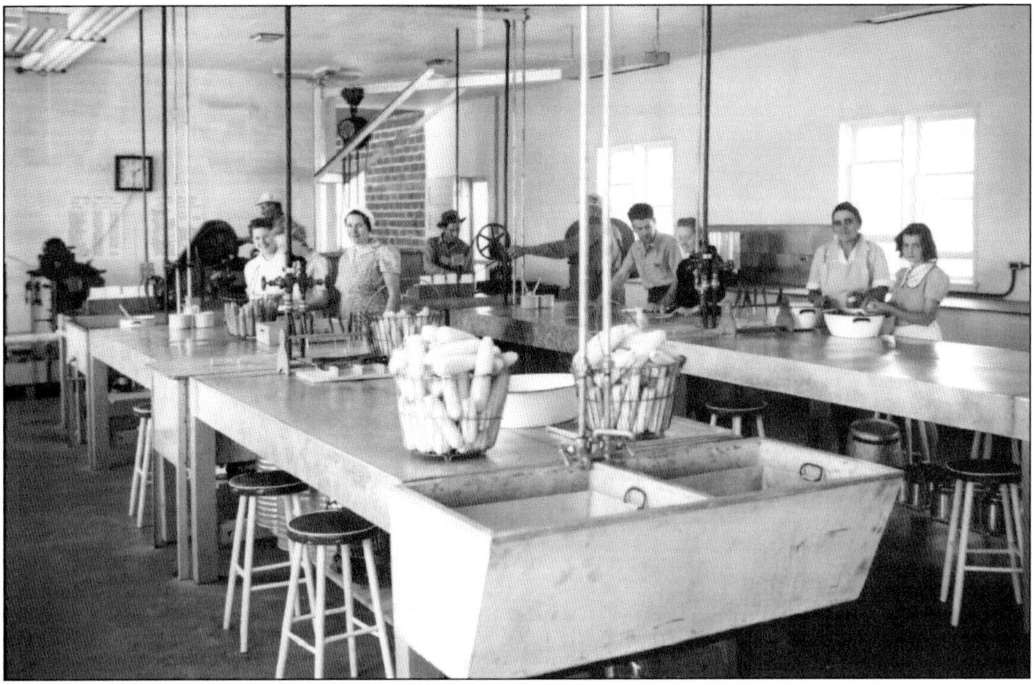

As seen in the photograph above, the town cannery was a place where families could go to preserve and can their goods. Built around 1941, it was quite active during the World War II years. It was a humped-roof Quonset-hut-type building. It was located just east of the T-intersection of First Street South and Third Avenue South on the former high school lot, as seen below on the far left of this mid-1950s photograph, made just prior to the 1957 high school add-on. The WPA-constructed stone wall and bleachers are all that remain in this photograph. In the late 1940s or early 1950s, the cannery was converted into school classrooms. Throughout its time, wood shop, metal shop, and drafting classes took place in the building. Later, choir and art classes used the building. It was torn down in the mid-1980s to make room for the school expansion. (Above, courtesy of TCHS; below, courtesy of Barb Hamel.)

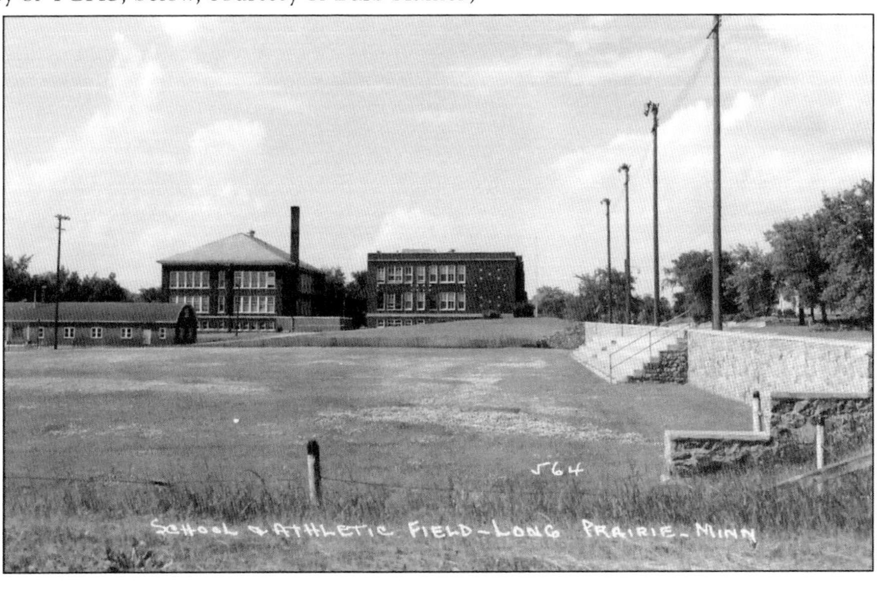

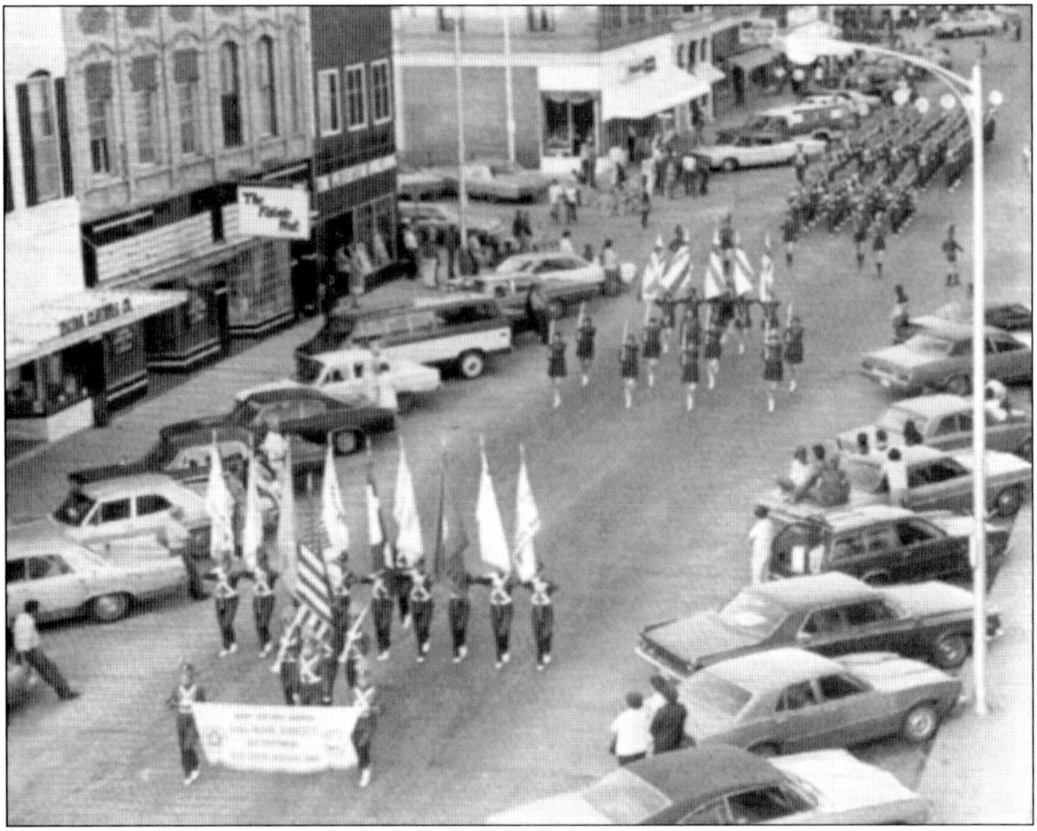

Minnesota's Marching M'Bassadors of Long Prairie High School hold a special place in the history of Long Prairie. Directed by Ray Gove dating back to 1963 through his retirement in 1999, this marching band has a competition recorded rivaled by none. The pride this band brought to this small west central Minnesota town of 3,000 people was electrifying. Residents that lived in the community during these years cannot forget the summer, and sometimes, winter days when this band marched up and down the town streets perfecting its craft under Gove's tutelage. Traffic would gladly stop to allow the band to pass as it prepared for the next competition. Small children would follow the band, marching alongside in step, dreaming of the day they would be old enough and privileged enough to join the ranks of the "toy soldiers." (Both, TCHS.)

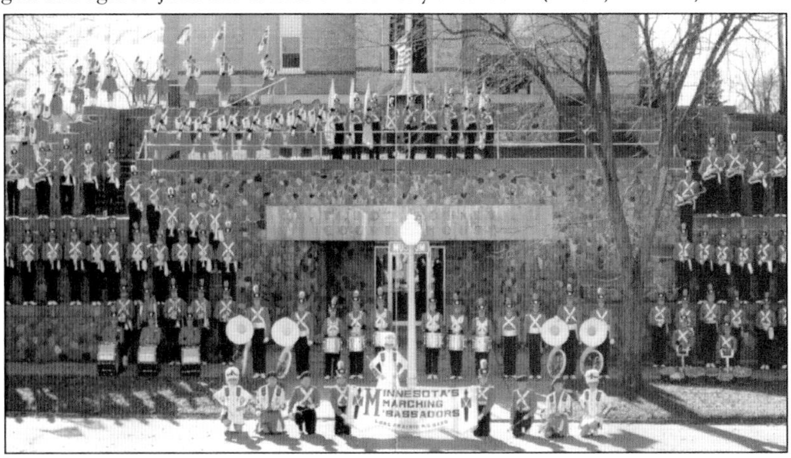

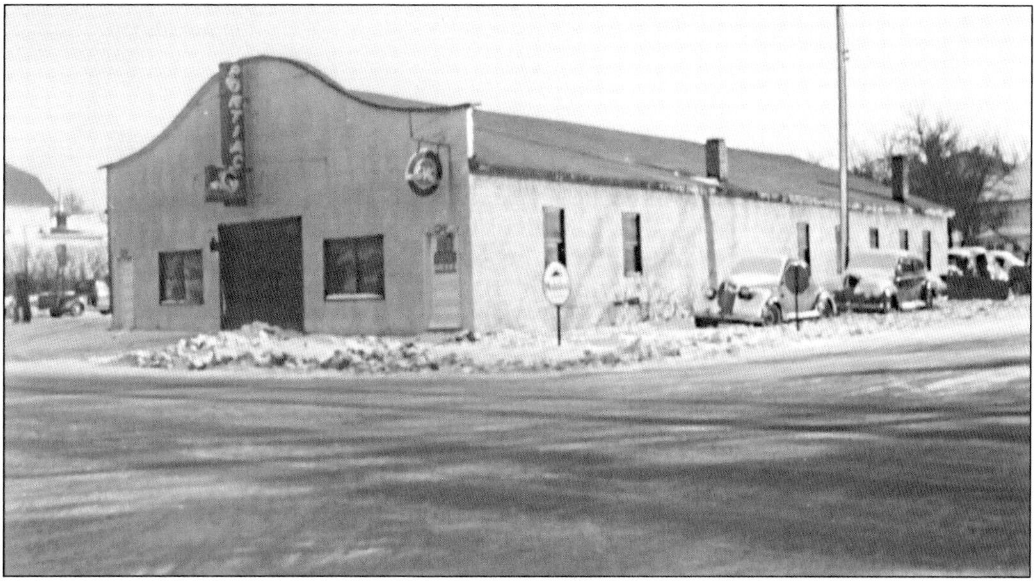

Arnold Griep, after working for several other repair businesses in Long Prairie, decided to go into business for himself. Around 1935, he leased the Hansmann Garage on the corner of First Street South and First Avenue South (seen above) and began an automotive repair shop. In the spring of 1952, the Grieps broke ground on a new building at this same location. The work was begun the fall of 1952 and completed in the spring of 1953 (seen below). Angie and Arnold retired from the automotive business in 1961. After the dealership closed, the Grieps rented the building, which was converted into a SuperValu grocery with Don Frost as proprietor. This building became Lux Hardware and Lumber from 1977 until 1982, and then became Dueber's Department Store from 1991 to 1996. The building still stands, operating as the Veterans of Foreign Wars Club from 1996 to 2017. (Both, courtesy of Jim Notch.)

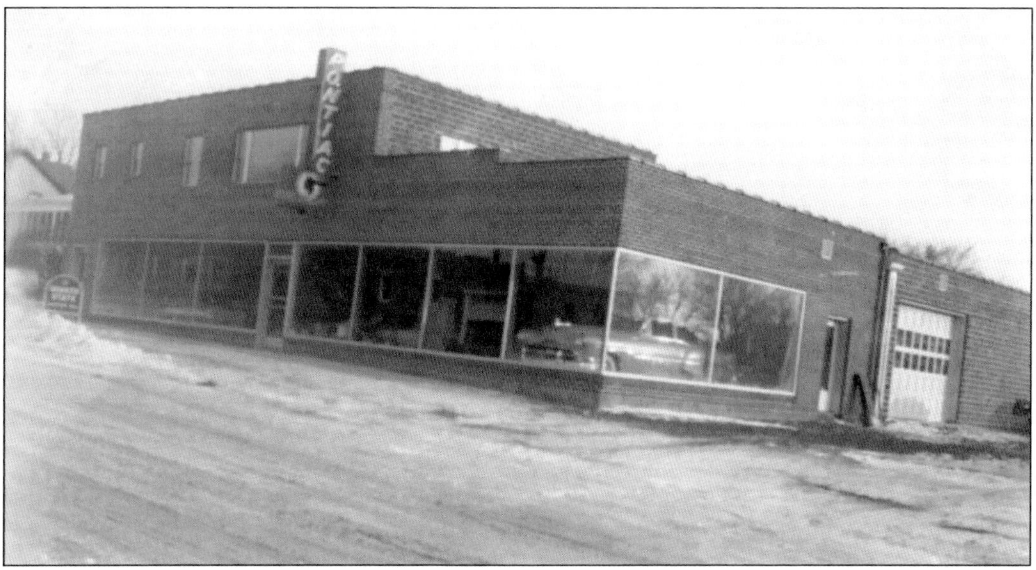

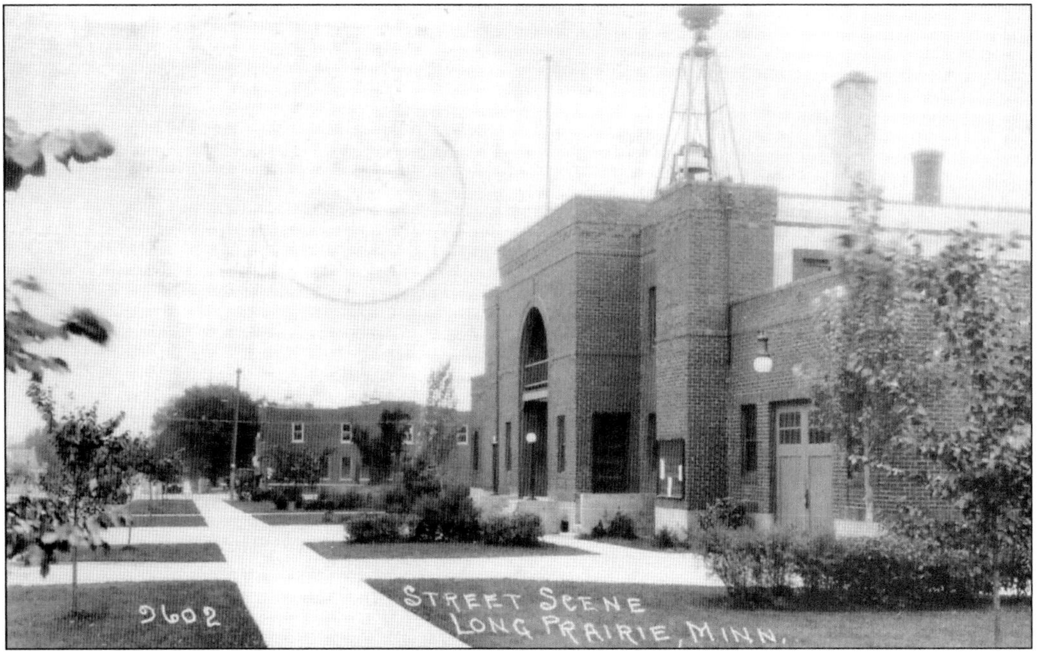

The Long Prairie Armory was built in 1921. Upon its completion, the fire department and city council chambers were moved into portions of this building. The Long Prairie Fire Department was organized in 1889 and used the east garage for fire truck and equipment storage. The armory was also used for many city celebration events and was the central mobilization site for Todd County soldiers for many years. (Courtesy of Barb Hamel.)

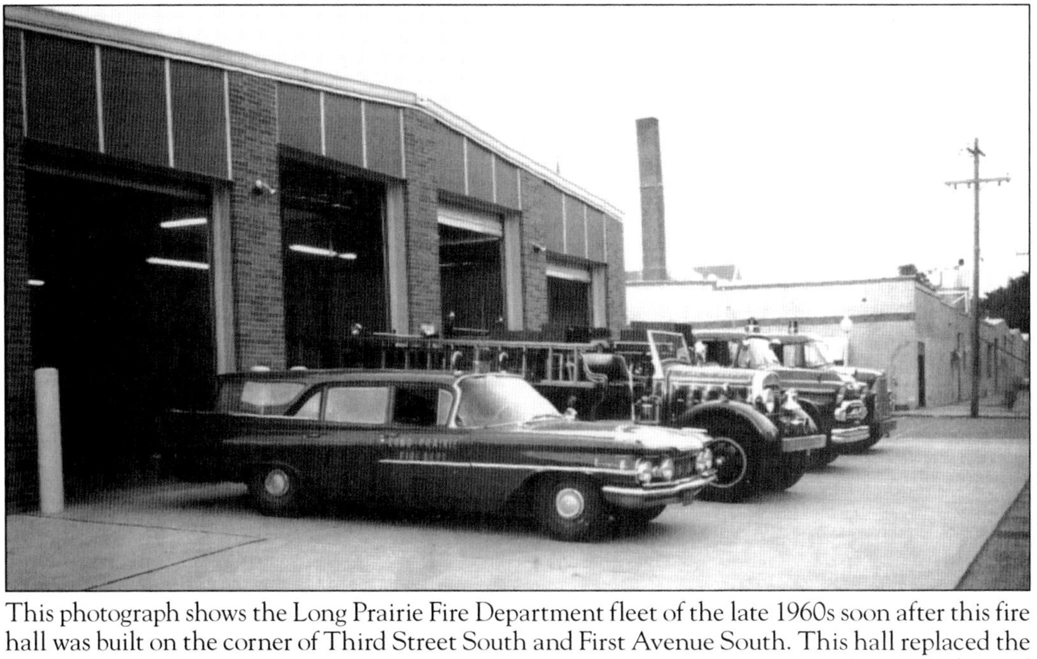

This photograph shows the Long Prairie Fire Department fleet of the late 1960s soon after this fire hall was built on the corner of Third Street South and First Avenue South. This hall replaced the fire hall that, at the time, was located next door in the Long Prairie Armory, which was deemed too small for the fire equipment needed for a modern city fire department. This building is now utilized by the CentraCare Health System for its ambulance fleet. (Courtesy of TCHS.)

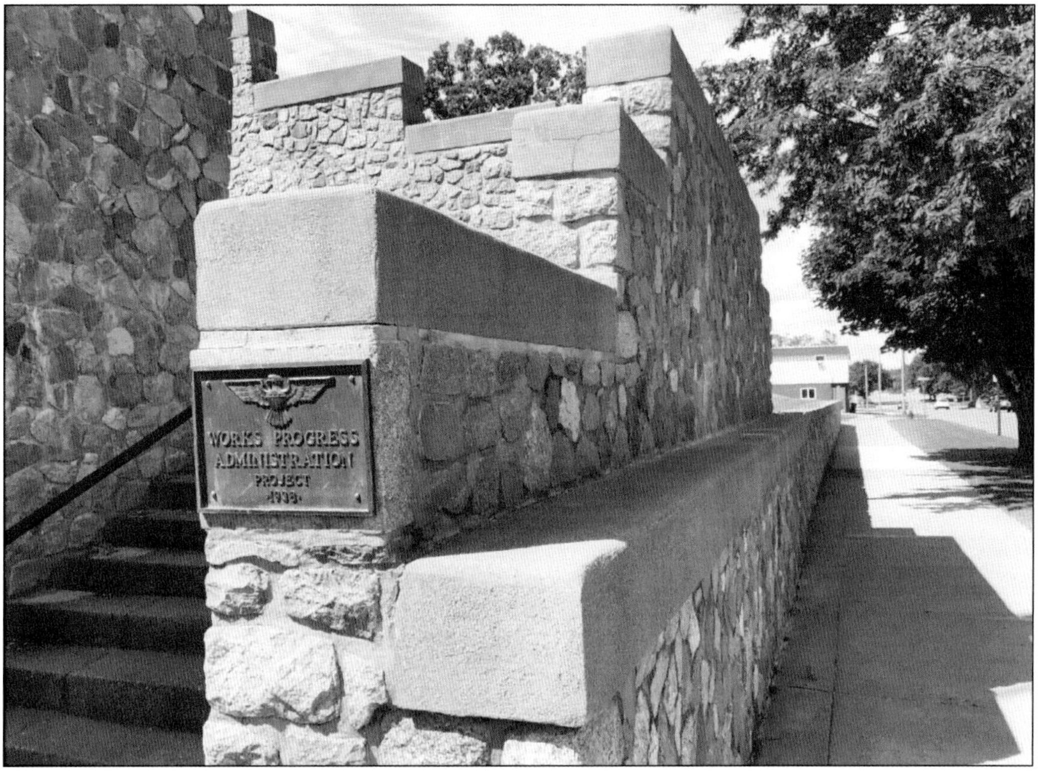

The courthouse square retaining wall was originally ordered by the county board in 1897. Constructed of large fieldstones, the wall completely encircled the courthouse hill for many years. Many a child walked the wall to and from school, and some will remember the cannonball that was cemented into the southeast corner of the old wall. Many alterations over the years have changed its look. In 1938, the Works Progress Administration made the most significant change to the wall when an underground entrance and double-stone staircase were added to the north side of the wall. For a time, there was a large steel door in the wall on the west side of the block, which housed a civil defense shelter in the Cold War era. (Both, author's collection.)

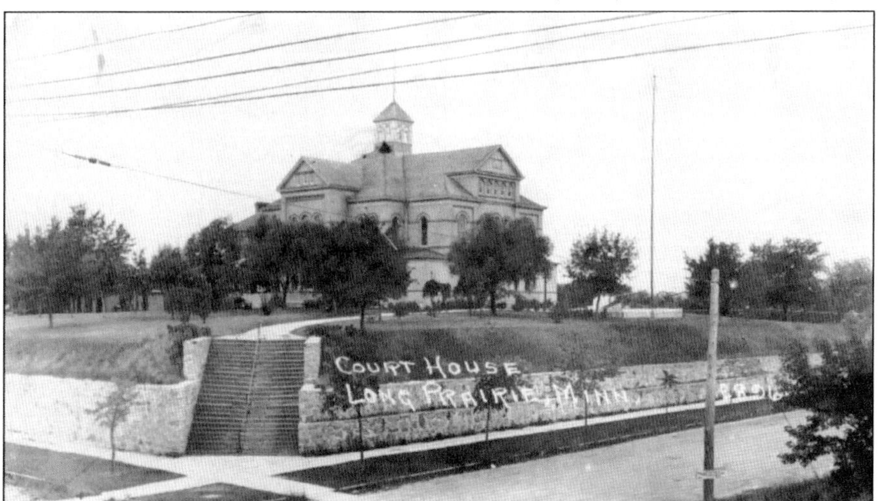

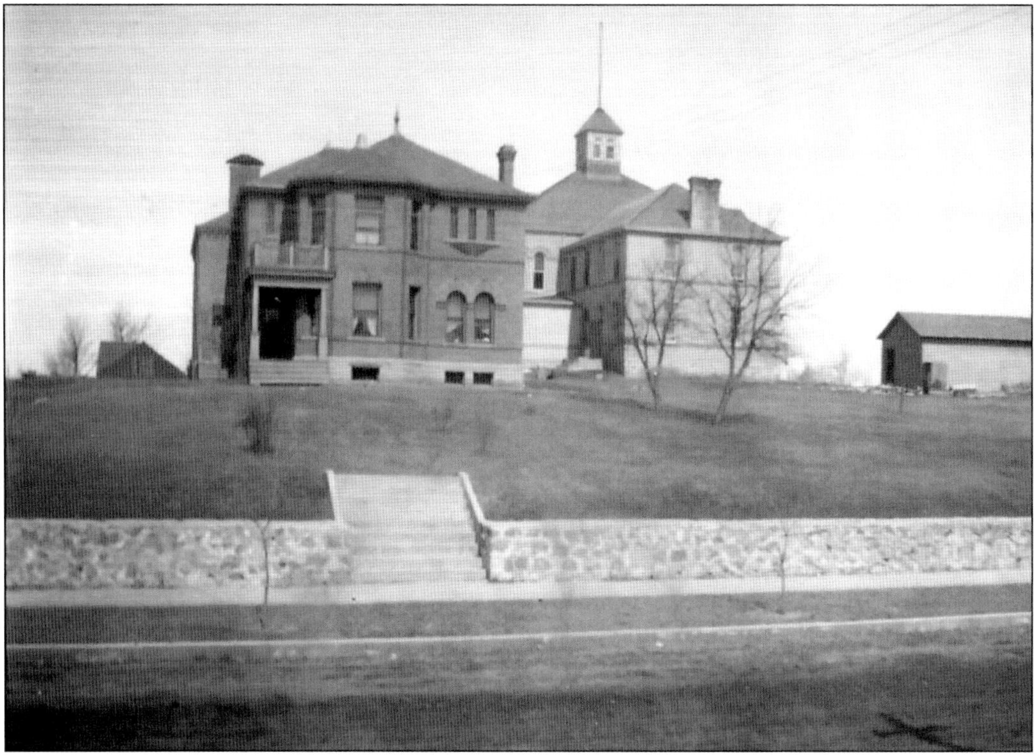

This undated photograph shows the Todd County jail building, erected in 1900 and used until 1985, when it was demolished. There were nine cells, with four on the first floor, five upstairs, and one for women. All the cells had bunk-style beds, except the women's cell, which had a single bed. The jail could house a total of 17 prisoners. The sheriff's quarters were attached. The only evidence remaining of the jail consists of the concrete steps and rail that are still visible in the stone retaining wall south of the old courthouse. (Courtesy of TCHS.)

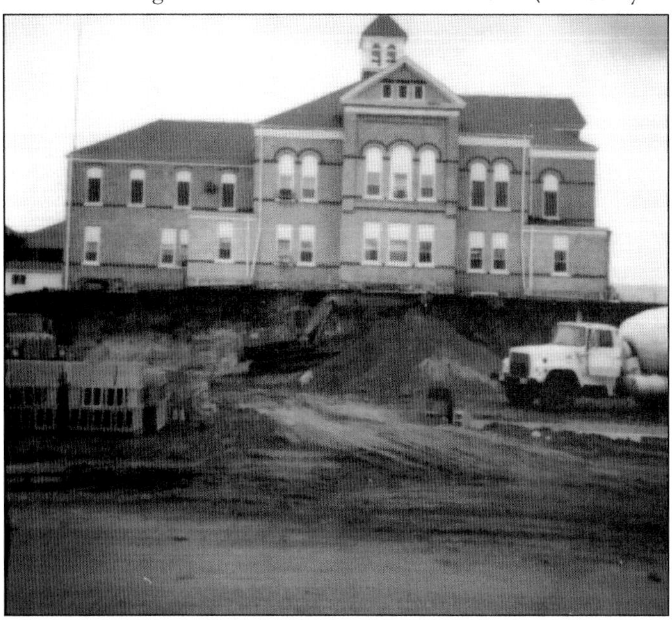

Construction for a new jail facility was started in July 1984, as seen here, in anticipation of the old Todd County jail meeting its fate in 1985. In June 1995, ground was broken for a new court facility, which was added to the north side of this new jail. The facility is now known as the Todd County Government Center and Law Enforcement/Detention Center. (Courtesy of TCHS.)

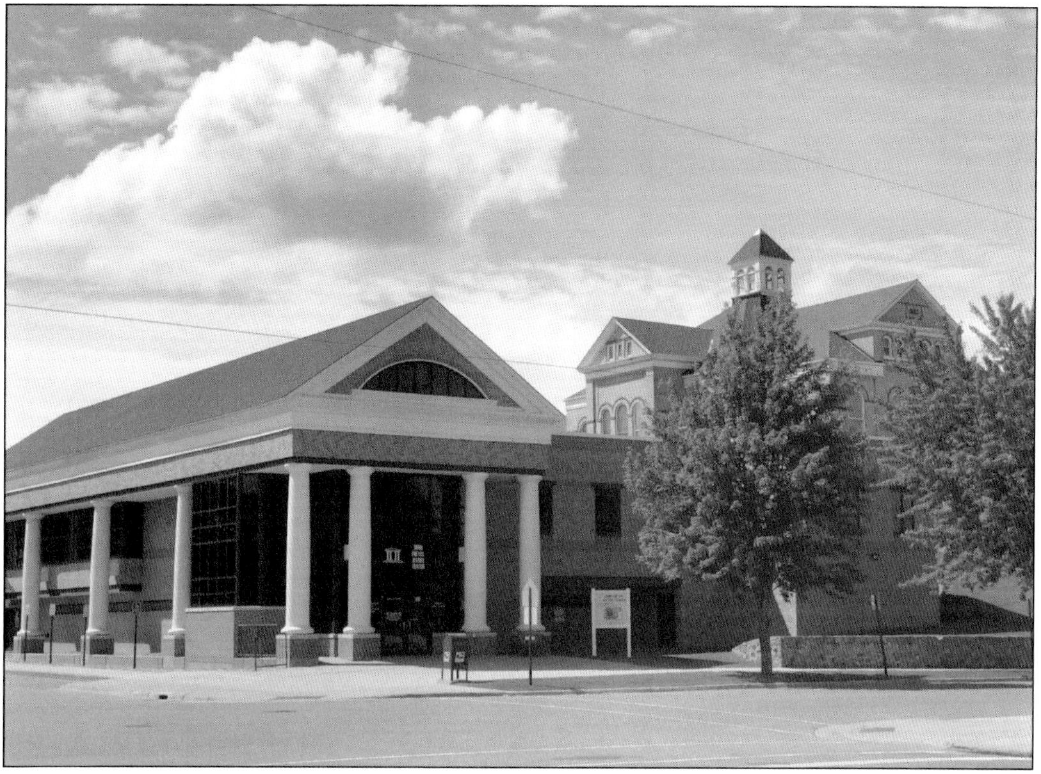

Sitting proudly atop the hill, the Todd County Courthouse was built in 1883. The first jail was built in 1900 and was used until 1985. New jail facility construction began in July 1984. Additionally, a new court facility was constructed in June 1995. These buildings remain on the original specified townsite, initially platted as Lincoln Square. (Author's collection.)

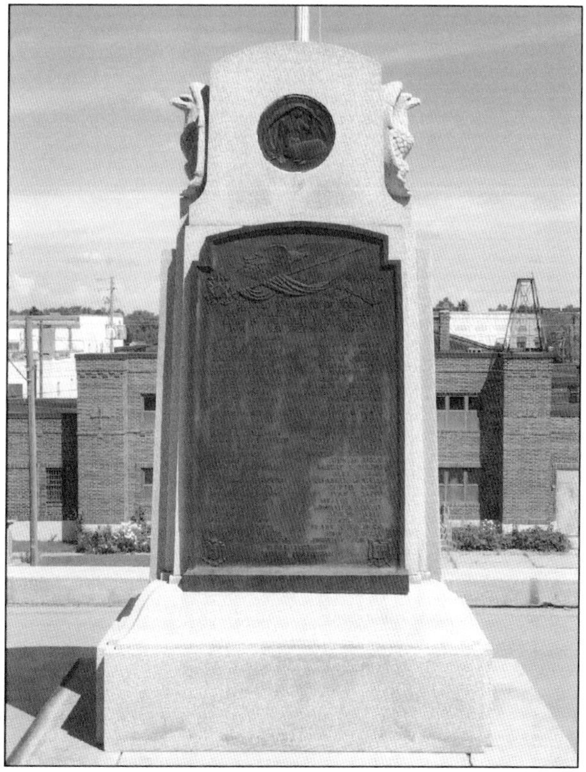

In December 1918, William E. Lee tendered to the county a monument to be erected in the honor of Todd County soldiers who gave their lives in World War I. The monument was placed on the Courthouse Square, and the names of the soldiers were inscribed on tablets. John Karl Daniels, a St. Paul sculptor, was chosen to do the sculpture work. The monument was dedicated on June 3, 1920. (Author's collection.)

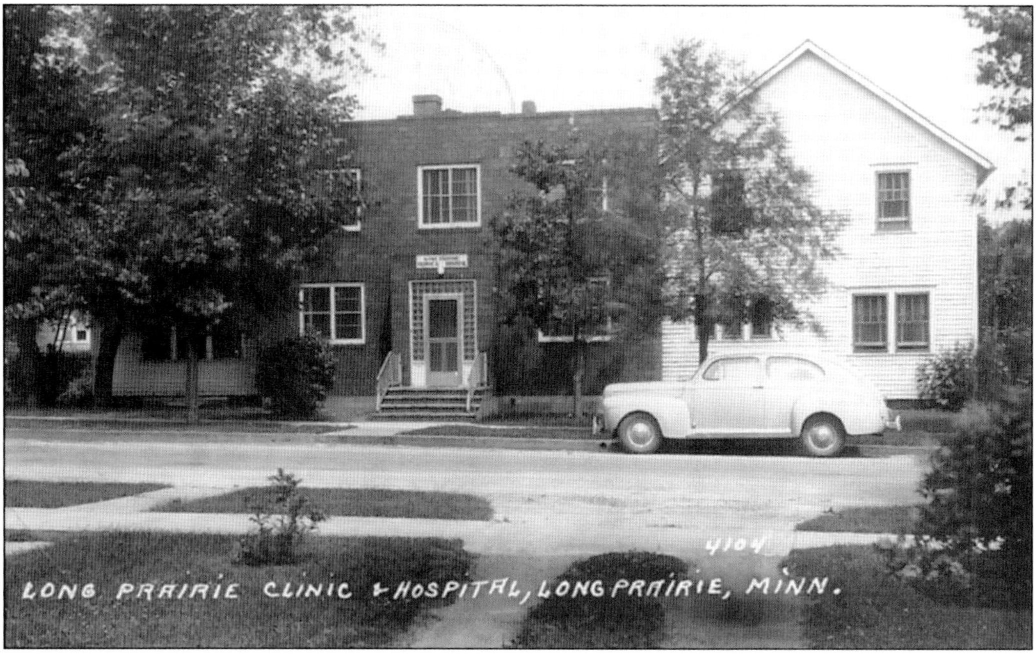

The first true hospital in Long Prairie at 310 Second Avenue South was built by Dr. B.F. Van Valkenburg, who converted an old residence and a barn into a hospital, a part of which was converted into the present St. Mary's Nursing Home. The old-time medical doctors were Dr. G.R. and Robert Christie, Dr. Fisher, and Dr. Van Valkenburg. Dr. Maurice Mosby took over the "Van Hospital," and in 1954, the fire marshal required an elevator and sprinkler system be installed. Dr. Mosby requested a new hospital building from the city. This was met with resistance, so Dr. Mosby ran for and won the mayoral race. A new hospital and clinic were built in 1956. The old Van Hospital was offered to St. Mary's for $1 and turned into a nursing home. This former hospital building is now apartments. (Both, author's collection.)

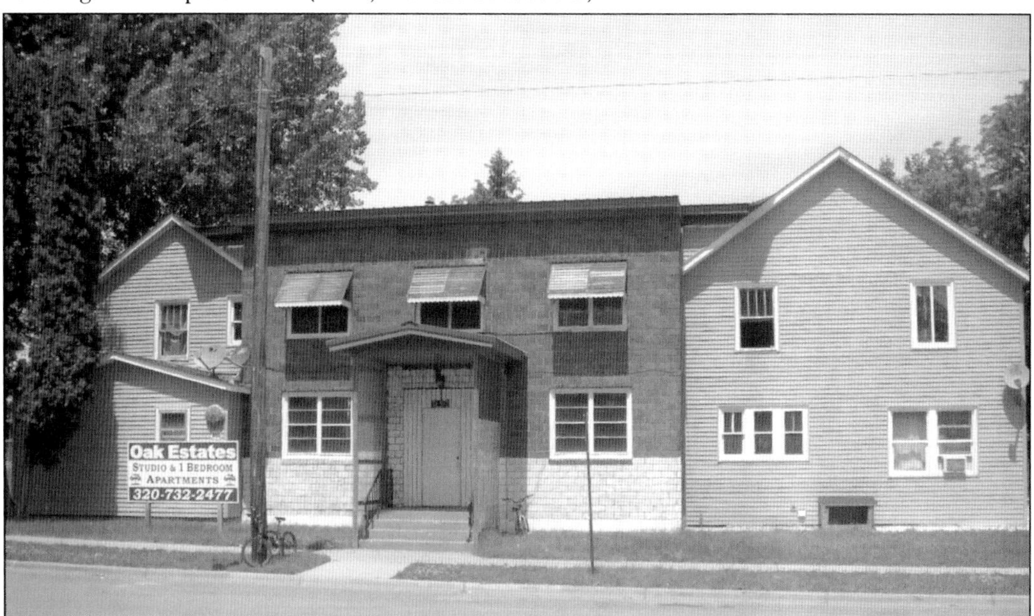

Trinity Lutheran Church in Long Prairie can trace its lineage as far back as 1870, when Pastor Victor Both became the first pastor in Todd County. Prior to construction and dedication of this church in 1882, services were held in locations such as the courthouse and the Long Prairie public school. This church was torn down in 1968 and buried in place on the corner of Sixth Street Southeast and First Avenue Southeast, where the concrete basketball court is located. The image at right captures the church in 1929. The photograph below was taken in 1941 and shows the addition of a classroom on the southeast corner of the church. (Both, author's collection.)

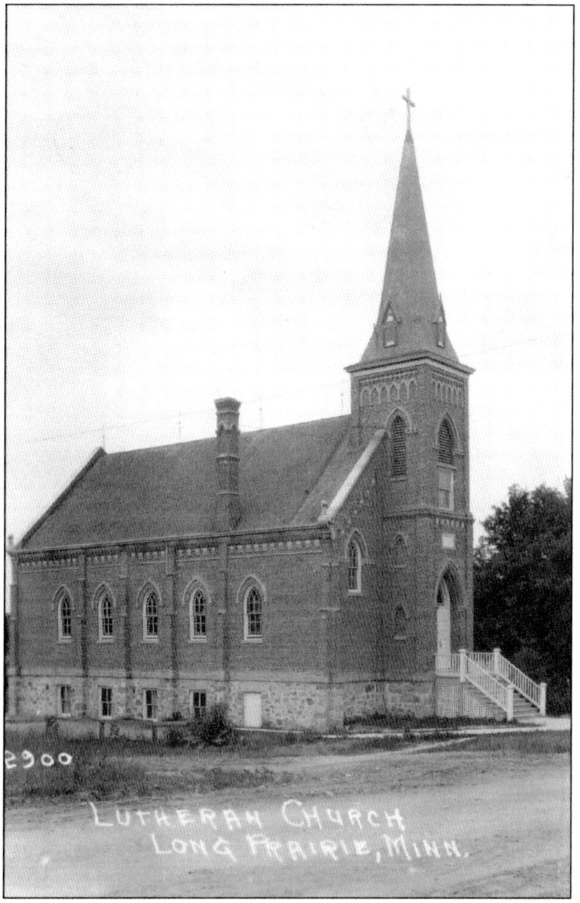

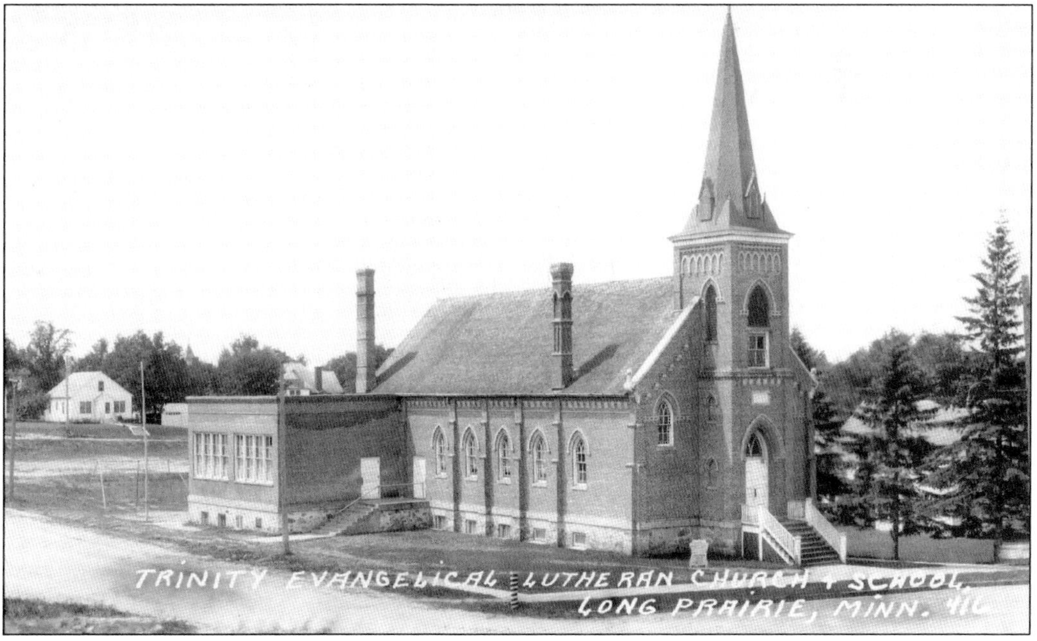

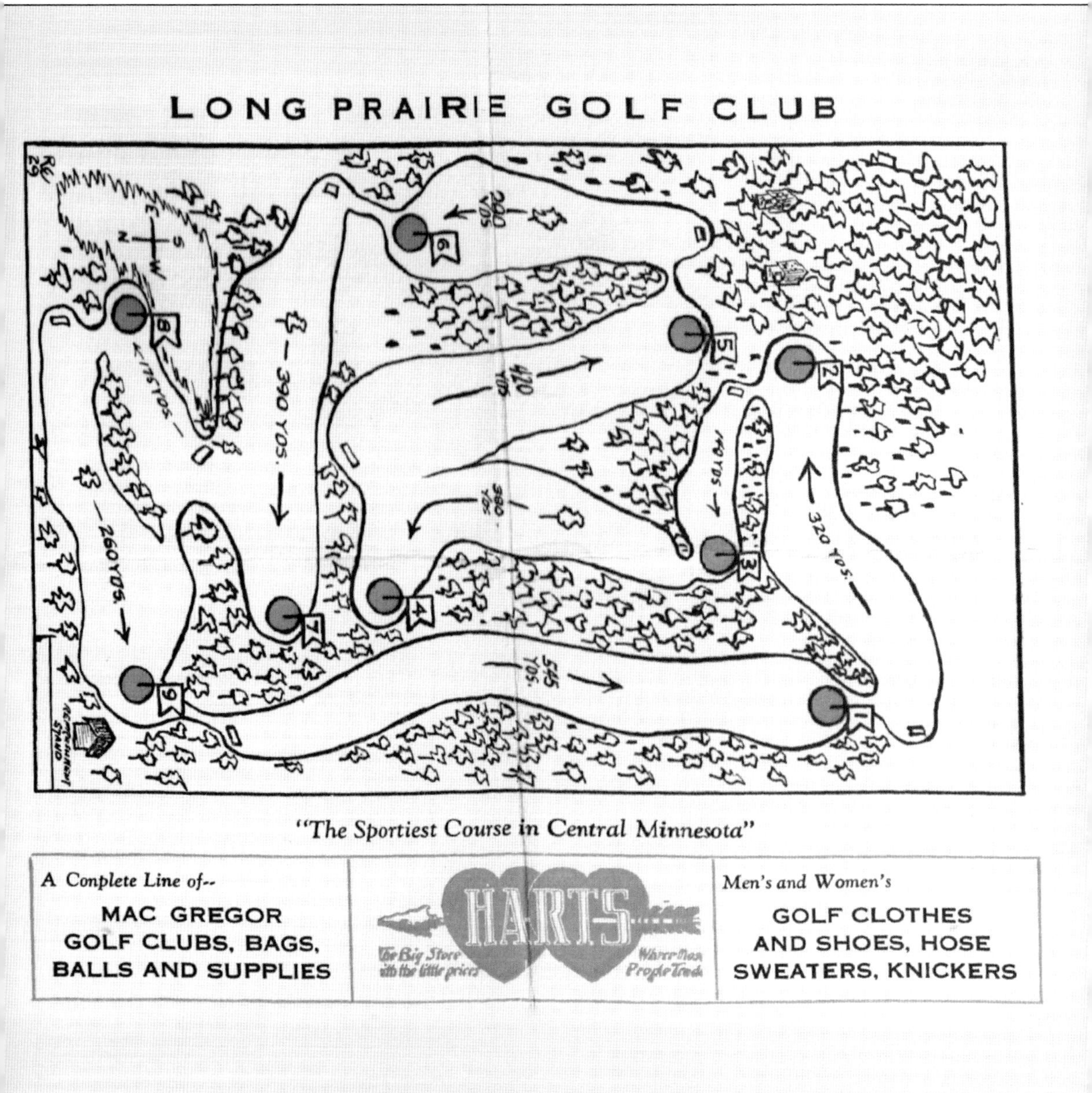

The Long Prairie Country Club was organized in 1926 with 22 original stakeholders. Tom Vardon, brother of Harry Vardon, assisted in laying out the nine-hole course and the original sand greens, as seen here on an early scorecard. A column written in a 1926 *Leader* states, "A Long Prairie golf club has been organized and it has leased ground for the construction of a course. Workman are already busy preparing the course and it is expected to be available for use by the middle of summer." The column goes on to say, "The club will have the use of 60 acres and the lease carries the option for purchase within five years. . . . Those who play golf say that the Long Prairie course will be a very good one, having many natural advantages." The property known then as the Davis farm had been used as a cow pasture for anyone in the village who owned cows at that time. (Author's collection.)

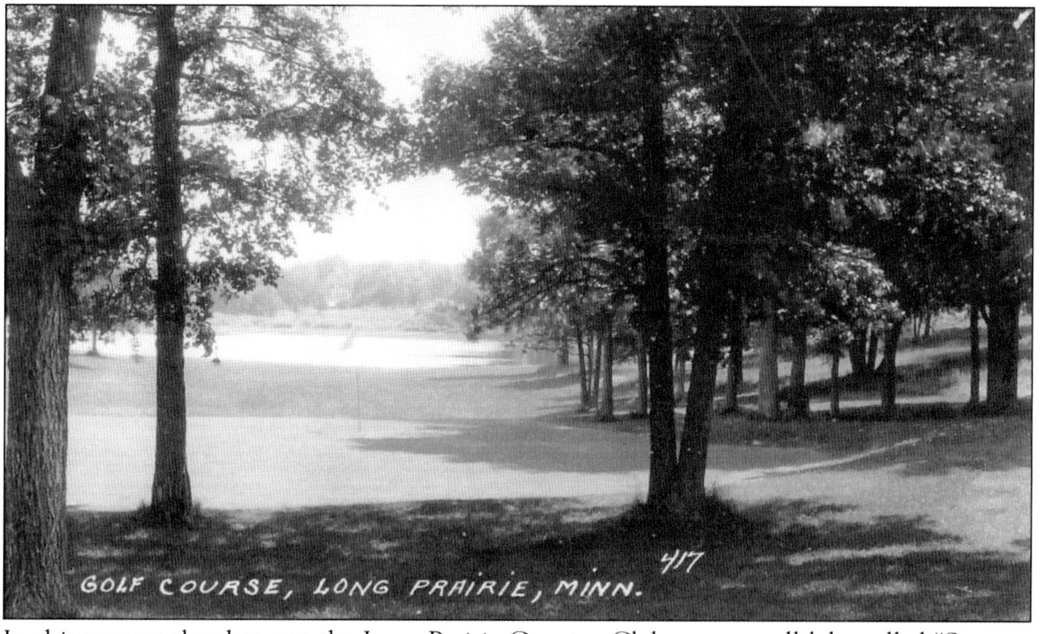

In this pasture that became the Long Prairie Country Club was a small lake called "Senners Slough." The course has been redesigned over the years, with Senners Slough being utilized for irrigation water. The water level had been lowered over the years, lessening the footprint of the slough. As seen above in 1941 and below in 1941, during very heavy rain events, the slough floods and Senners Slough returns, seemingly to remind the golfers that it once existed. A 1939 Farmall A tractor, purchased in 1941, is still in use today on the grounds, towing sprayers and mowers and occasionally used for getting equipment out of the mud of Senners Slough. (Above, author's collection; below, courtesy of Kathy Gugat Harris.)

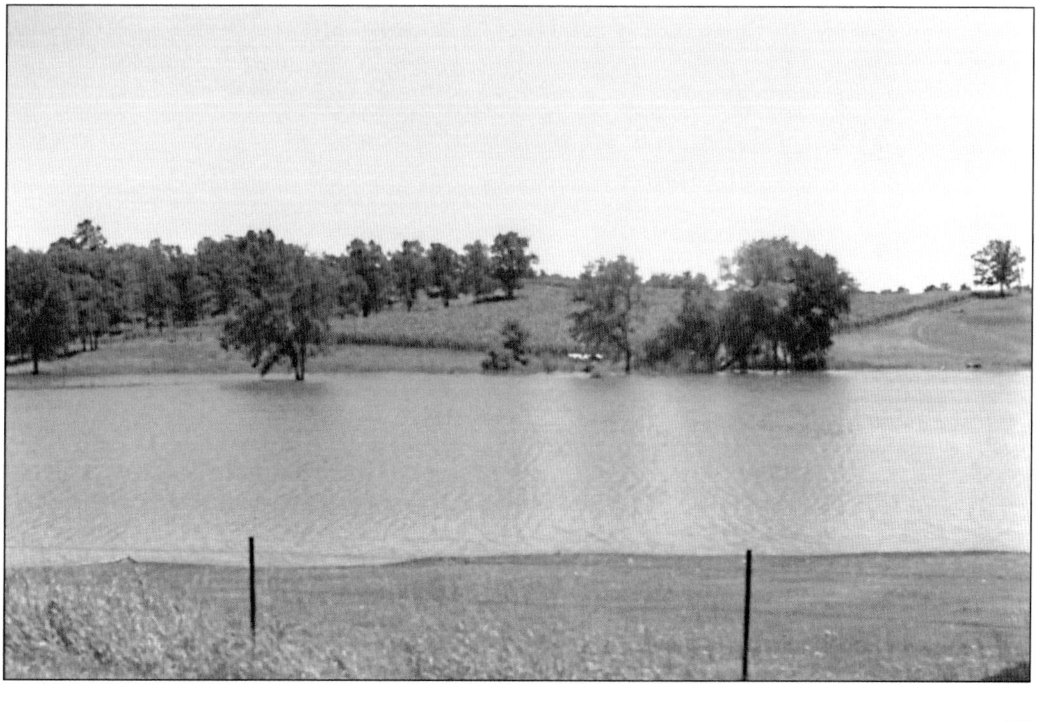

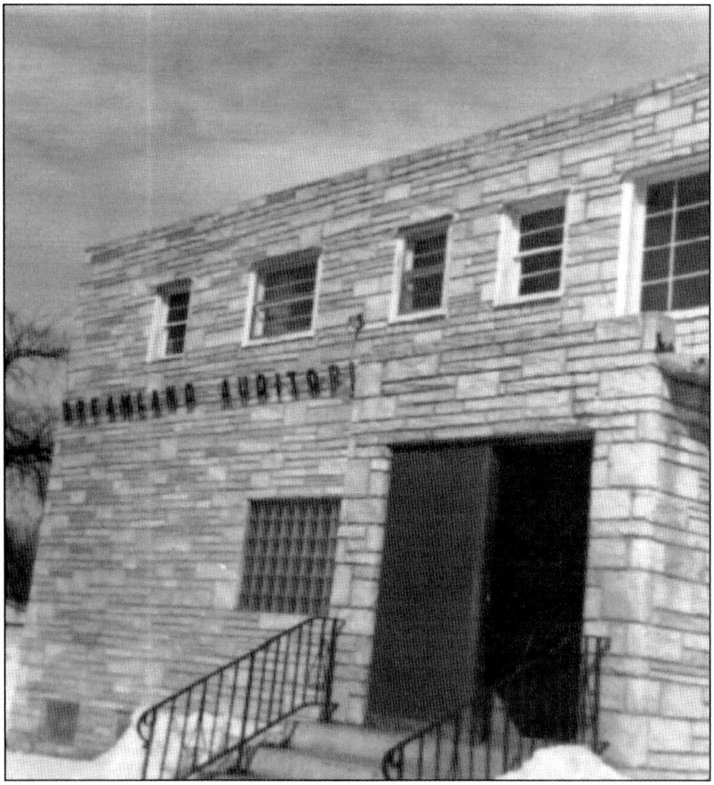

Dreamland roller-skating rink was built by Blanche and Henry Buelow in 1948. There was a time when the high school used Dreamland for its basketball games. Dreamland no longer stands; it was demolished in 2007 to make room for the construction of a bank. "Ma and Pa" Buelow, as they were called, are remembered as wonderful people by those who knew them. They would teach square dancing on roller skates for all who were brave enough. Dreamland was the place to be on Fridays, Saturdays, and Sundays for kids of all ages. (Both, courtesy of Harold Connelly and Valley View Estates.)

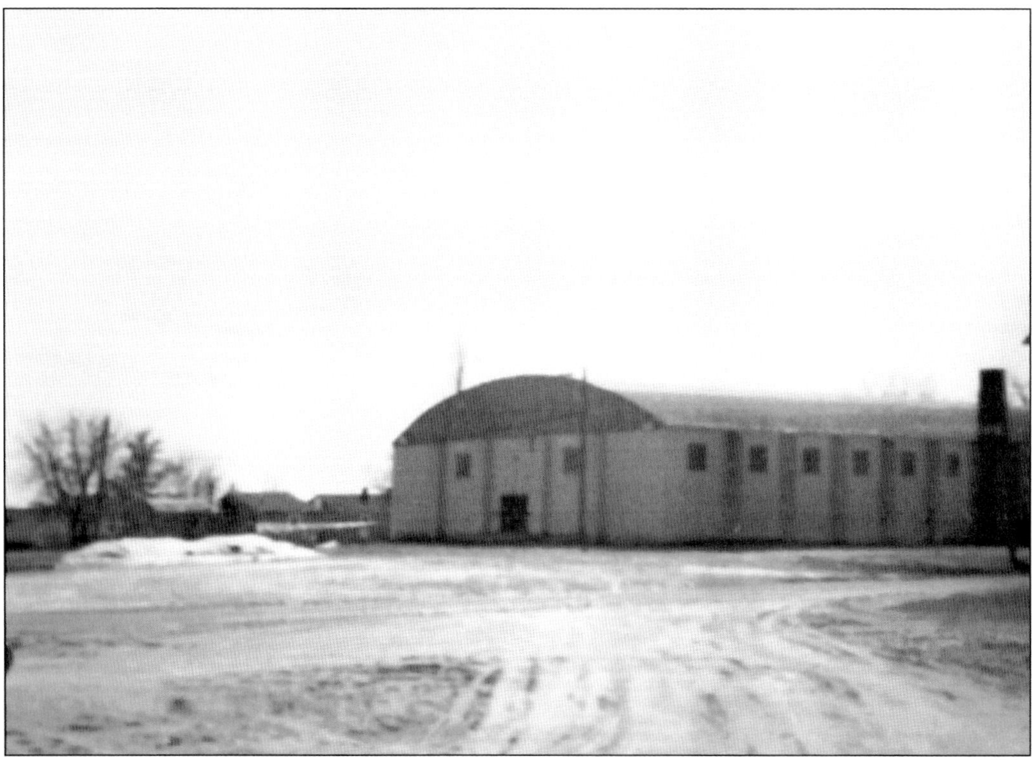

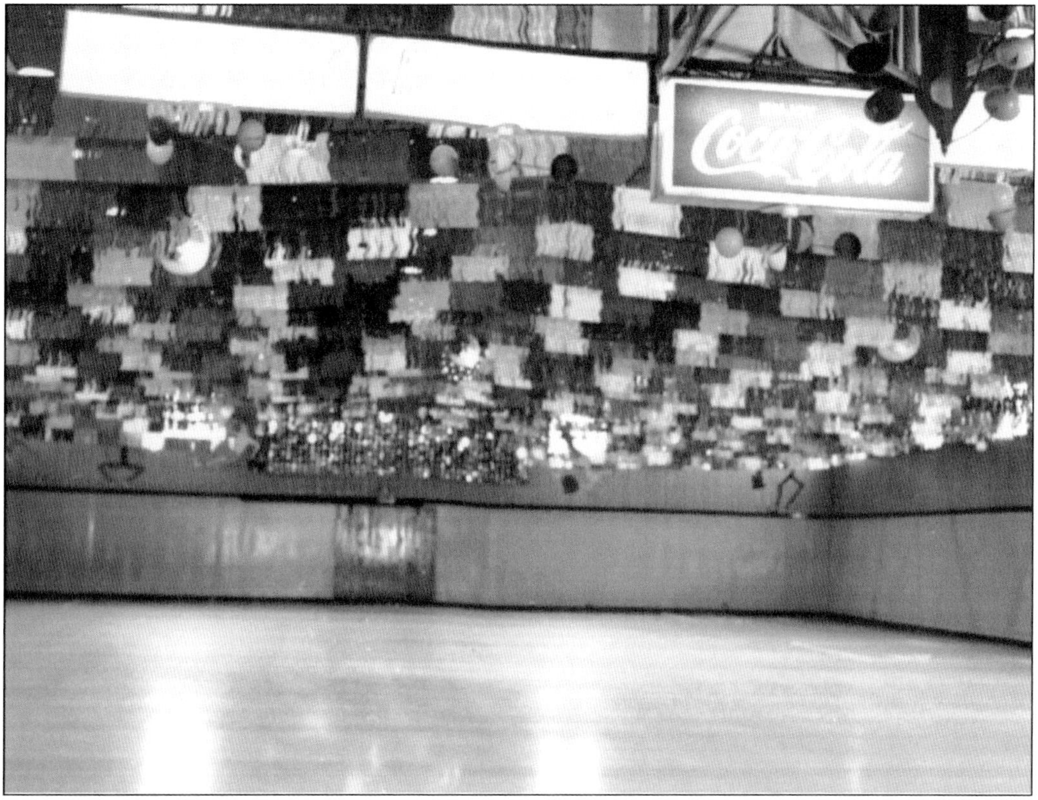

The inside of the Dreamland Auditorium consisted of the large roller-skating floor constructed of polished hardwood, as seen above. There was also a lounge area, seen below, a snack shop, and an arcade area. As the music played, the "person behind the curtain" would call out different skate "events." These events included the "All Skate," "Two Step," "Special," and the one event that caused the most anxiety to rush through the room—the "Couples Only" skate. Many young couples met their future spouse during these "Couples Only" skates. Bob and Jan Adams owned and operated Dreamland from 1972 to 1975. They would bring in bands and have concerts in the auditorium, converting the skate floor to a dance floor. (Both, courtesy of Elisha Adams.)

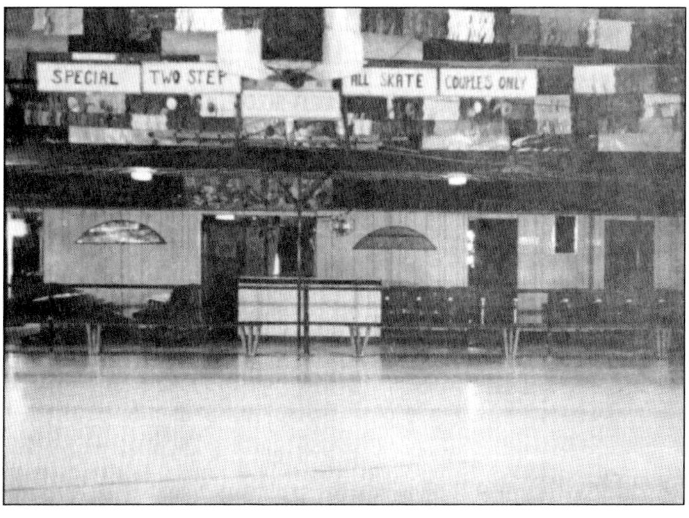

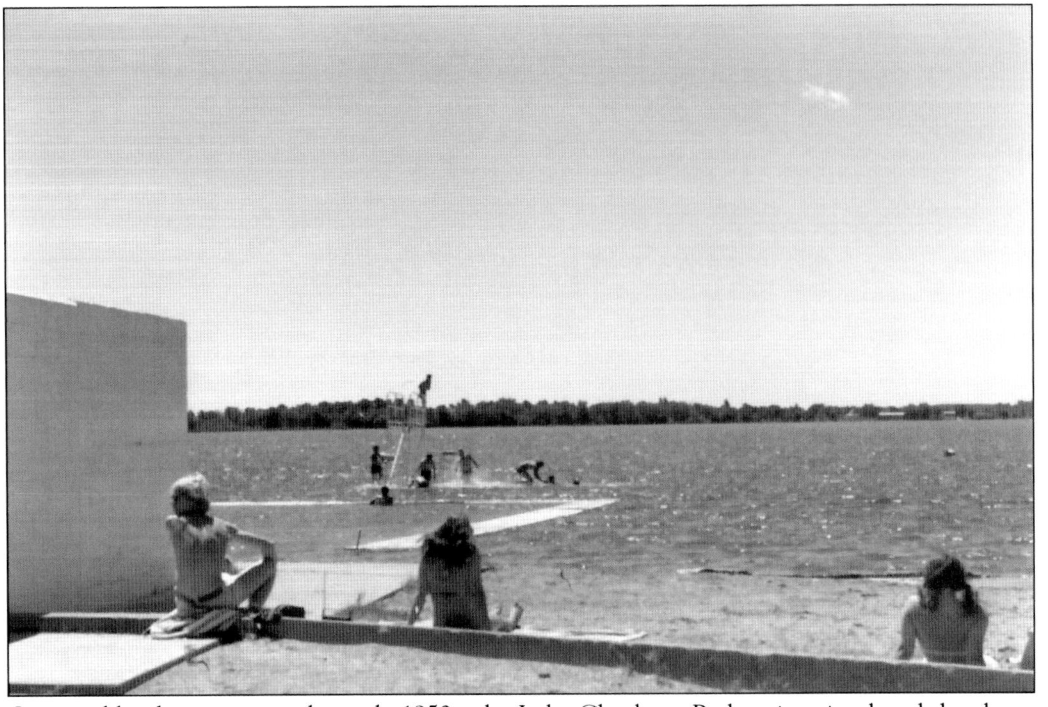

Operated by the city since the early 1950s, the Lake Charlotte Park swimming beach has been the "cooling-off" place for the residents of Long Prairie. Since that time, a summer has not gone by without the screaming and splashing of the town youths enjoying the cool, clear waters of Lake Charlotte. The layout of the buildings and the swimming docks has changed over the years. The former diving-board platform has been replaced with a floating swim platform. These 1972 photographs show the rise in the water level after an extremely heavy rain event that caused heavy flooding in Long Prairie. (Both, courtesy of Kathy Gugat Harris.)

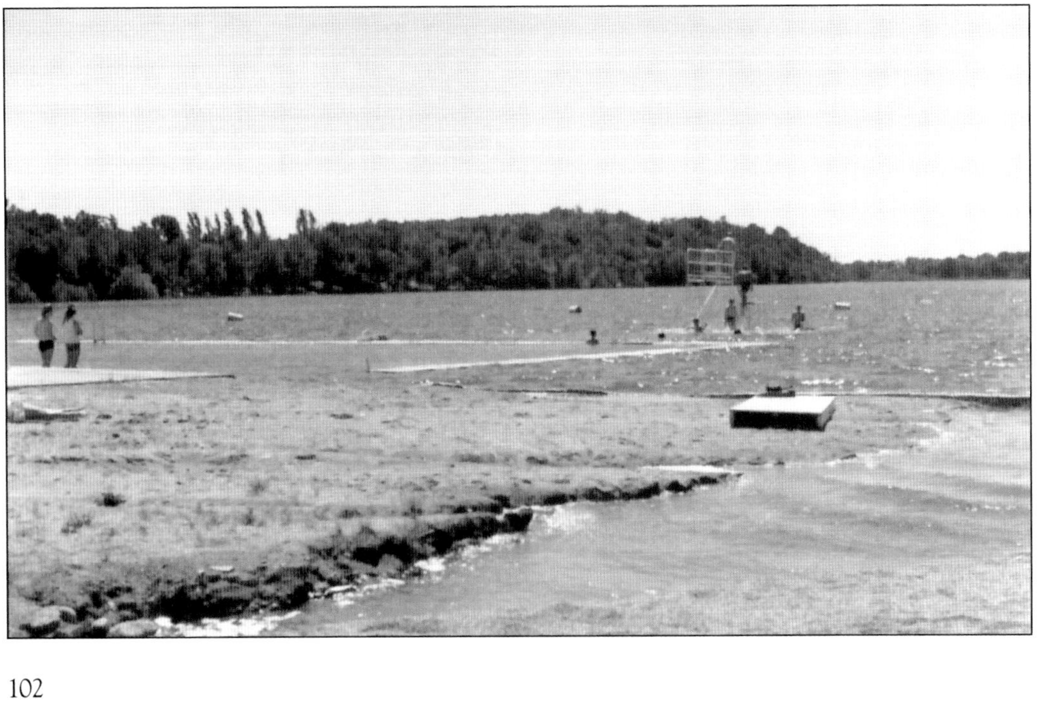

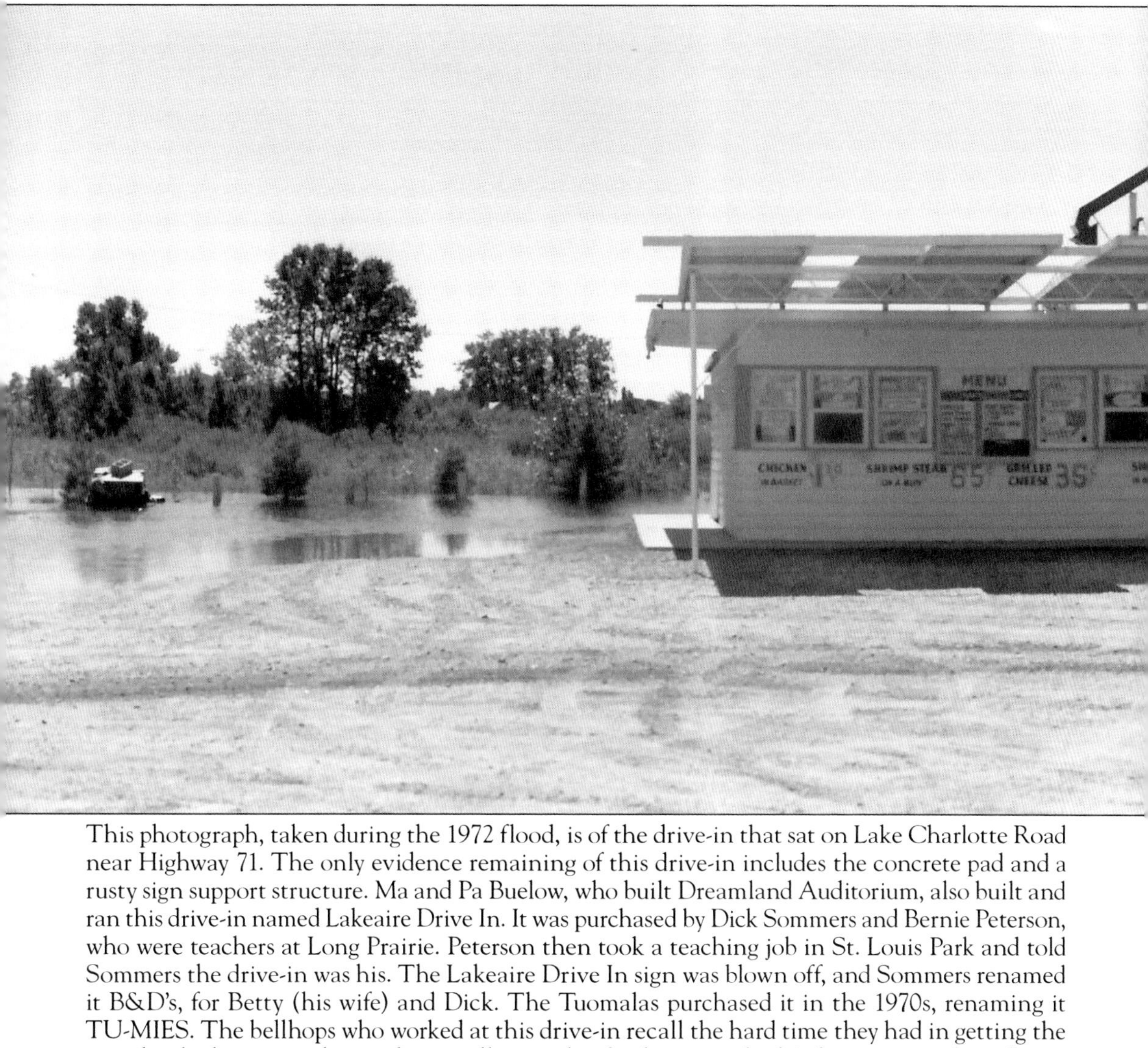

This photograph, taken during the 1972 flood, is of the drive-in that sat on Lake Charlotte Road near Highway 71. The only evidence remaining of this drive-in includes the concrete pad and a rusty sign support structure. Ma and Pa Buelow, who built Dreamland Auditorium, also built and ran this drive-in named Lakeaire Drive In. It was purchased by Dick Sommers and Bernie Peterson, who were teachers at Long Prairie. Peterson then took a teaching job in St. Louis Park and told Sommers the drive-in was his. The Lakeaire Drive In sign was blown off, and Sommers renamed it B&D's, for Betty (his wife) and Dick. The Tuomalas purchased it in the 1970s, renaming it TU-MIES. The bellhops who worked at this drive-in recall the hard time they had in getting the trays hooked on a window without spilling malts, food, or everybody's favorite, root beer floats, on the driver. Unfortunately, that very thing did happen from time to time. (Courtesy of Kathy Gugat Harris.)

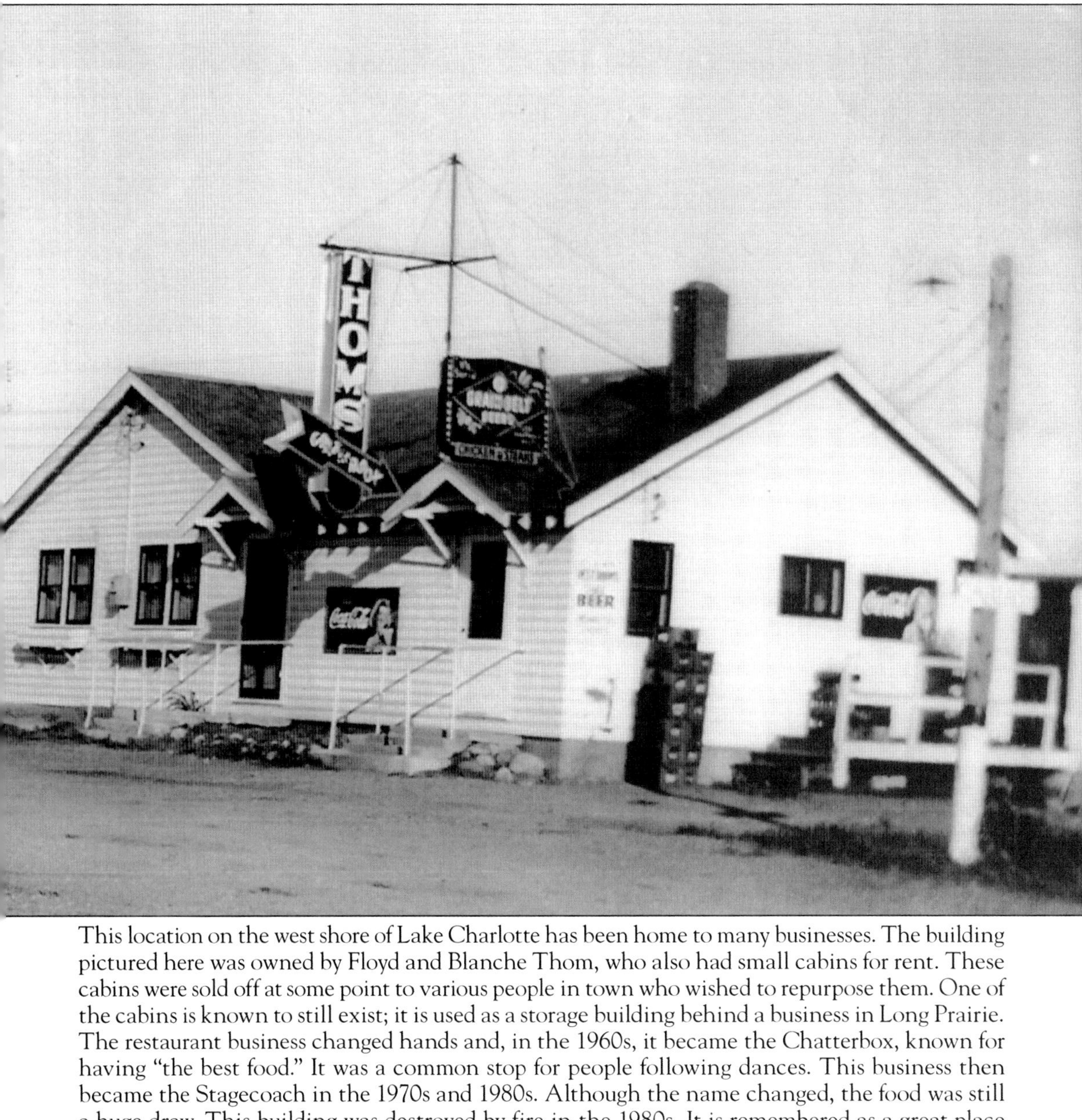

This location on the west shore of Lake Charlotte has been home to many businesses. The building pictured here was owned by Floyd and Blanche Thom, who also had small cabins for rent. These cabins were sold off at some point to various people in town who wished to repurpose them. One of the cabins is known to still exist; it is used as a storage building behind a business in Long Prairie. The restaurant business changed hands and, in the 1960s, it became the Chatterbox, known for having "the best food." It was a common stop for people following dances. This business then became the Stagecoach in the 1970s and 1980s. Although the name changed, the food was still a huge draw. This building was destroyed by fire in the 1980s. It is remembered as a great place for that midnight burger. (Courtesy of TCHS.)

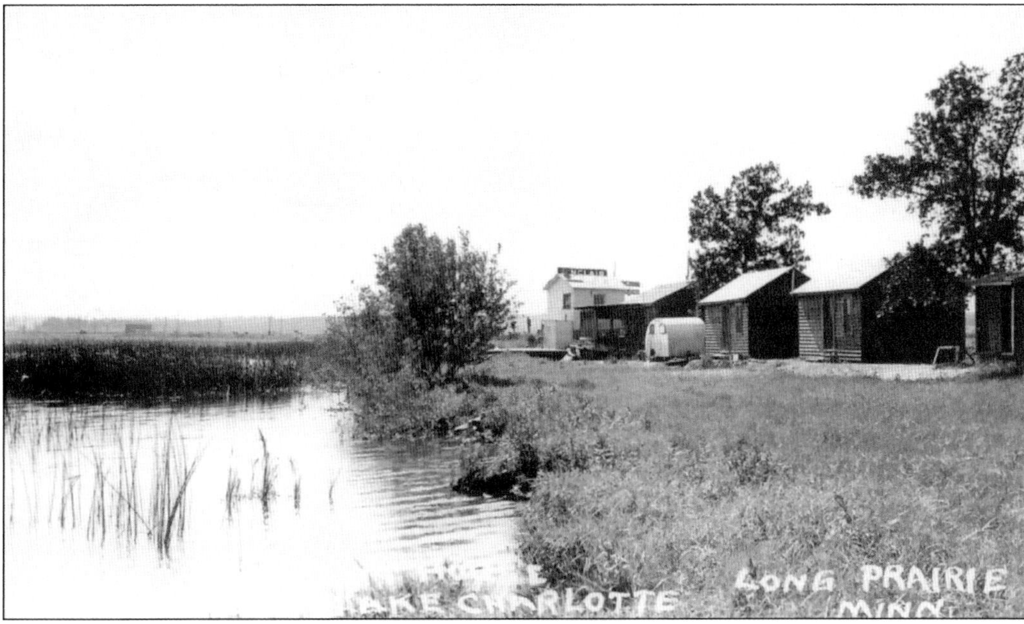

This 1940s photograph postcard captures the small cabins that sat on the lakeshore right behind Thom's Restaurant—as discussed on the previous page. The owners, Blanch and Floyd Thom, lived in a cabin just to the northeast along the shoreline. (Author's collection.)

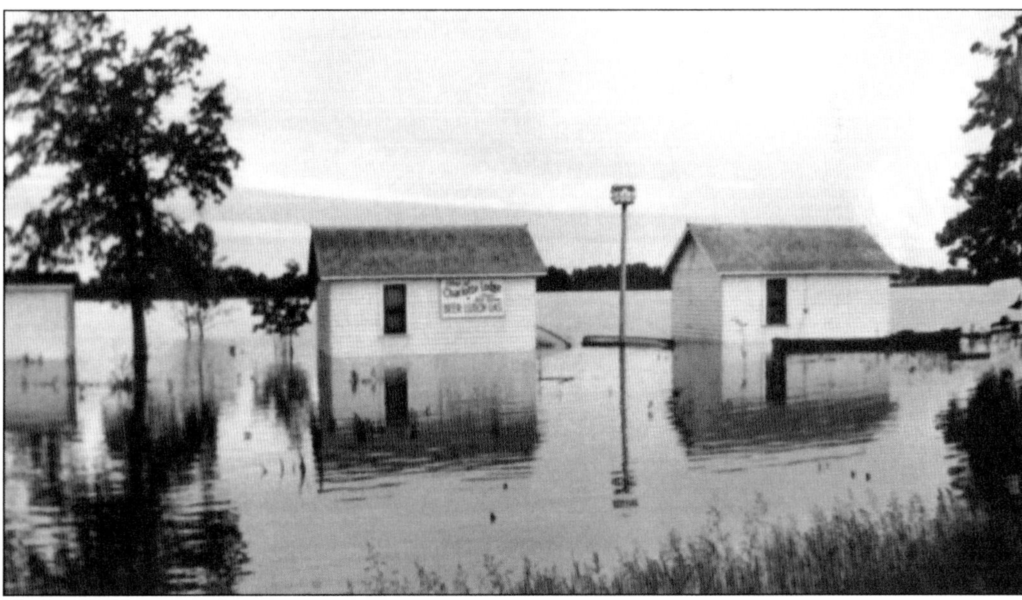

This undated photograph captures Lake Charlotte flooding out some cabins belonging to the Lake Charlotte Lodge. This lodge stood on the south end of the lake at 22406 US Highway 71, a location currently owned by the Dempsey family. (Courtesy of the Christie Home Museum.)

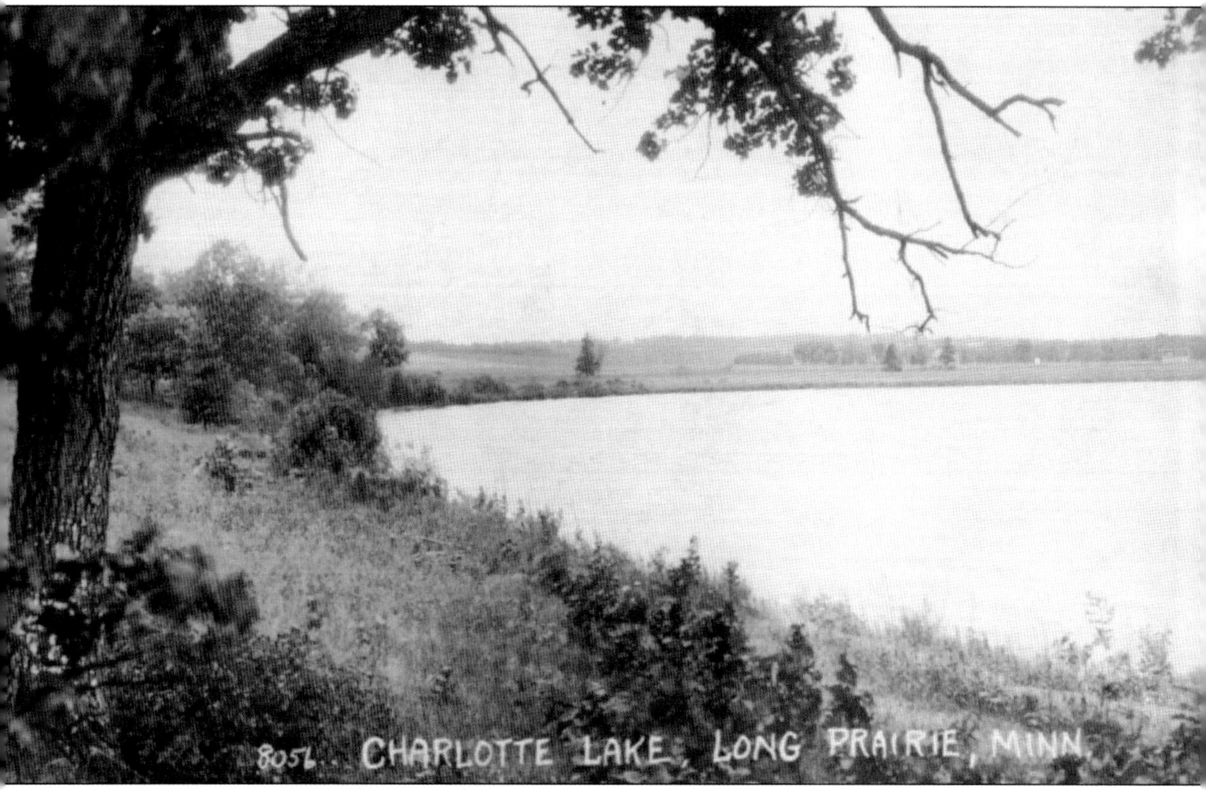

This undated image with a view looking west captures the undeveloped south end of Lake Charlotte. One can barely pick out the homestead that sat to the west of today's Sportsman's Club. The south end of the lake holds an interesting story, as told by O.B. DeLaurier: "On July 3, 1873, he [Thomas Cooper] came to Long Prairie to make appropriate arrangements for the celebration of the birthday of his adopted country. He probably made arrangements, for on his way home, he drowned in the little stream that empties into Lake Charlotte at the southwest corner of the lake. He does not appear to have had any relatives and he was buried on the south side of the little creek where the body was taken from the water. Our mother told us that later the line of the road was shifted a little and when so changed, the track passed over the foot of the grave, but Thomas has not objected." So, when passing over that little bridge, a tip of the hat to Thomas Cooper may be appropriate. (Author's collection.)

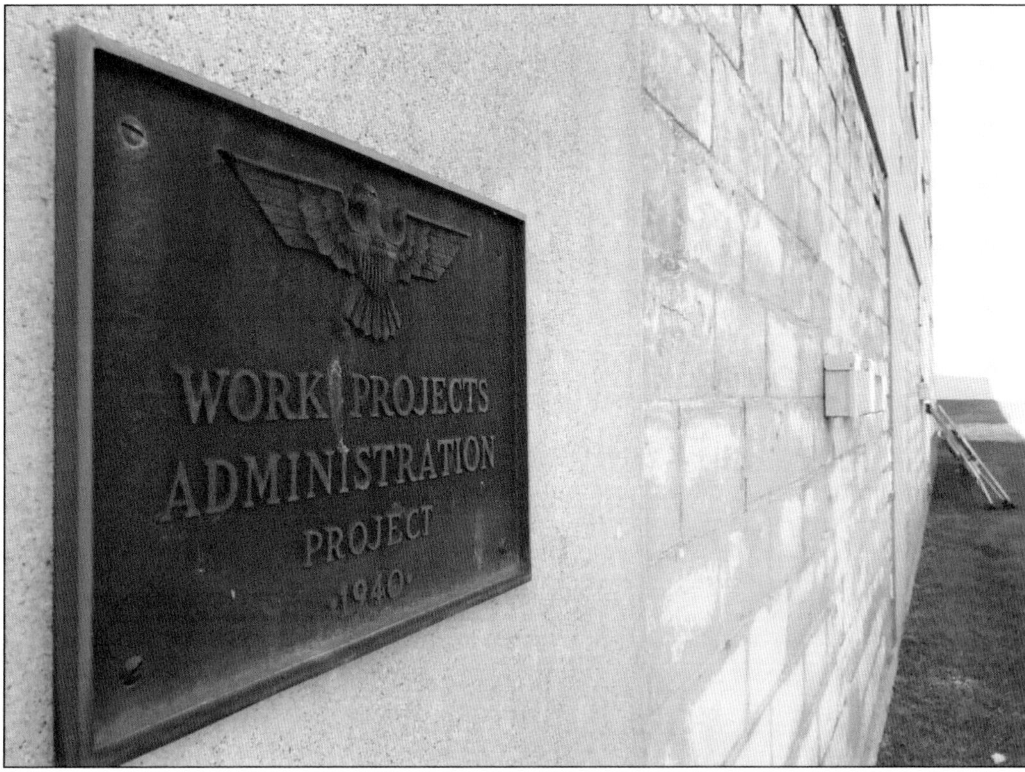

The fairgrounds are located in the northeastern part of Long Prairie. The Todd County Fair Grandstand was constructed in 1940. It was the largest WPA (Work Projects Administration) project in the county. The workers began pouring concrete in the spring. The grandstand was a labor-intensive effort. The size of the work crew was doubled in May 1940 to ensure a portion of the grandstand would be done in time for the August fair. The workers spent hours and hours in hard hand labor. The workers poured cement for six steps at a time, working from dawn to late evening. The interior of the grandstand was designed for use as a dormitory and display room. During the spring of 1940, another grant was received to add a second section to the grandstand, which doubled the capacity. (Both, author's collection.)

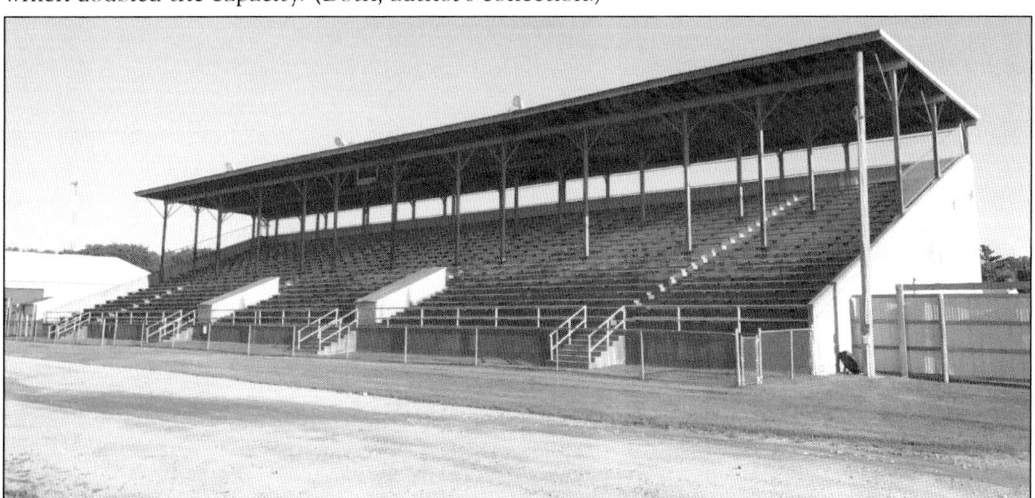

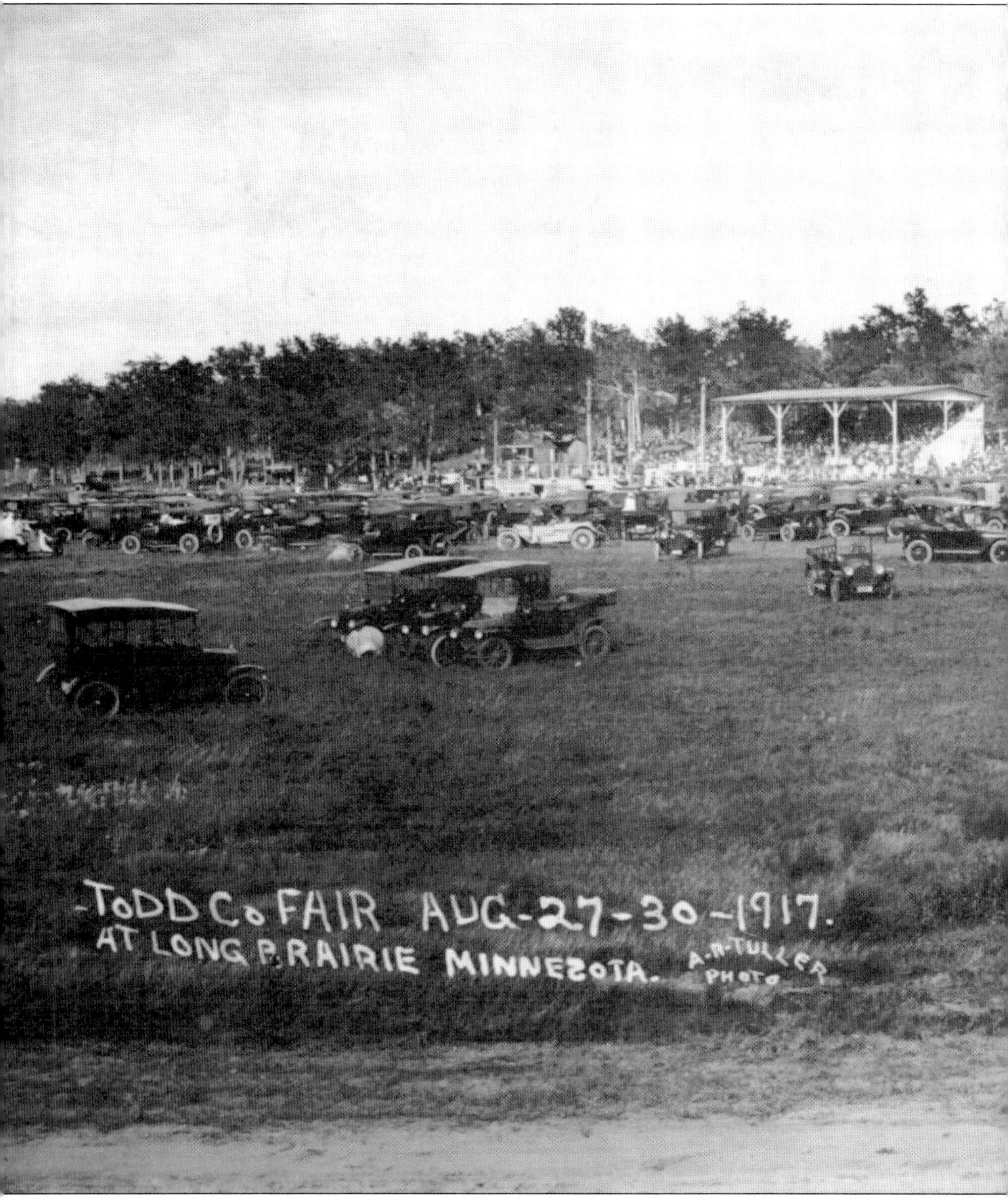

This 1917 real-photo postcard offers a glimpse of the Todd County Fair's popularity through this time in the last century. This photograph was taken about from where the current grandstand is located and the view looks northwest toward the current site of Long Prairie Grey Eagle High School. As previously stated, the grandstand in the distance stood about where the sandstone

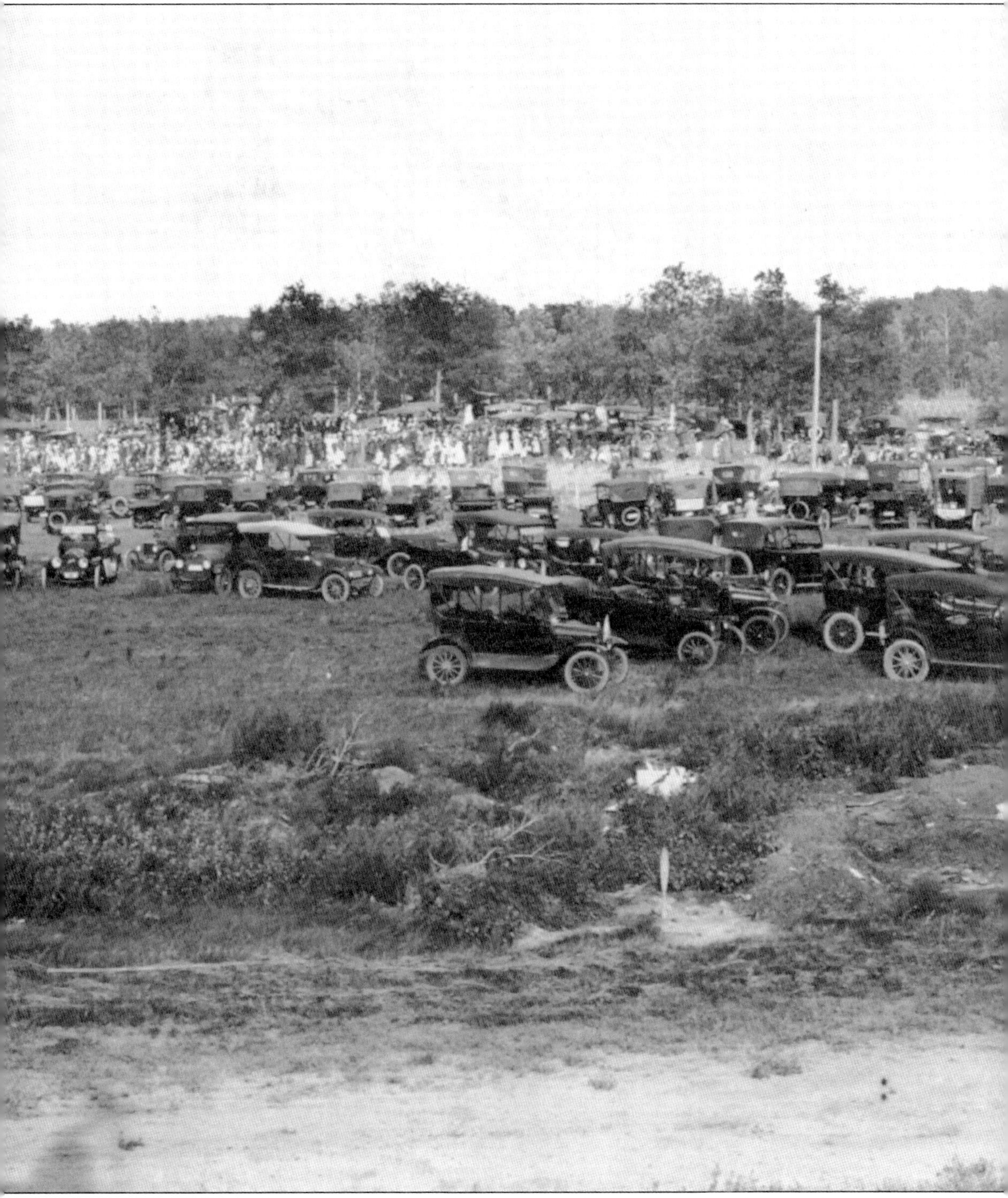

"Senior High School" sign leading into the current high school parking lot stands now. Back then, the Todd County Fair was known for holding some of the best horse-racing events around. One can see "turn 3" in the foreground of this photograph. (Author's collection.)

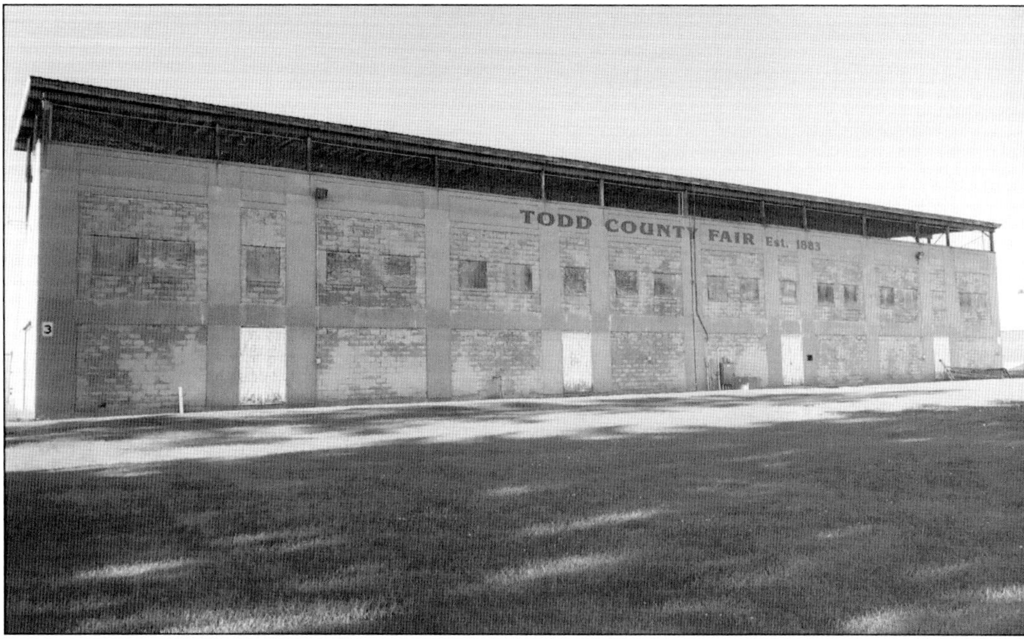

The Todd County Fairgrounds grandstand remains the focal landmark of the fairgrounds, greeting fairgoers still today as it has since its construction. Displaying historical items from the county in its caverns every August, it serves as a reminder of the great history of the Todd County Fair. (Author's collection.)

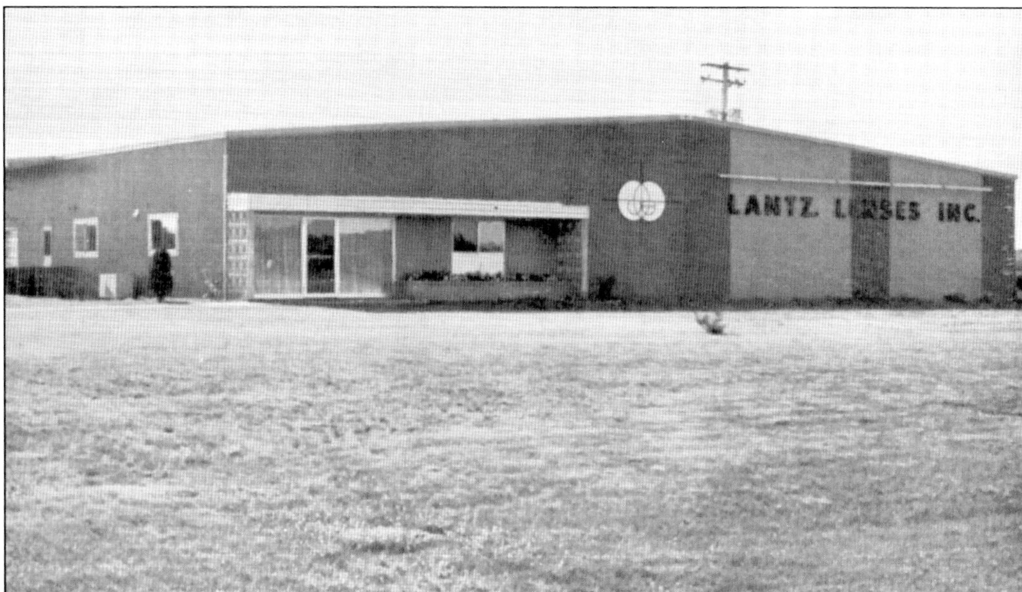

Lantz Lenses, Inc.—Long Prairie, Minn.

Lantz Lenses, a St. Cloud, Minnesota, company that operated in Long Prairie, is seen here in the 1970s. This building is located at 513 Sixth Street Northeast. When Lantz Lenses moved to its St. Cloud location, this building became Lake Country CNC for a time. This building is currently Chandler Industries, a machine shop where mechanical gears are produced and assembled. (Author's collection.)

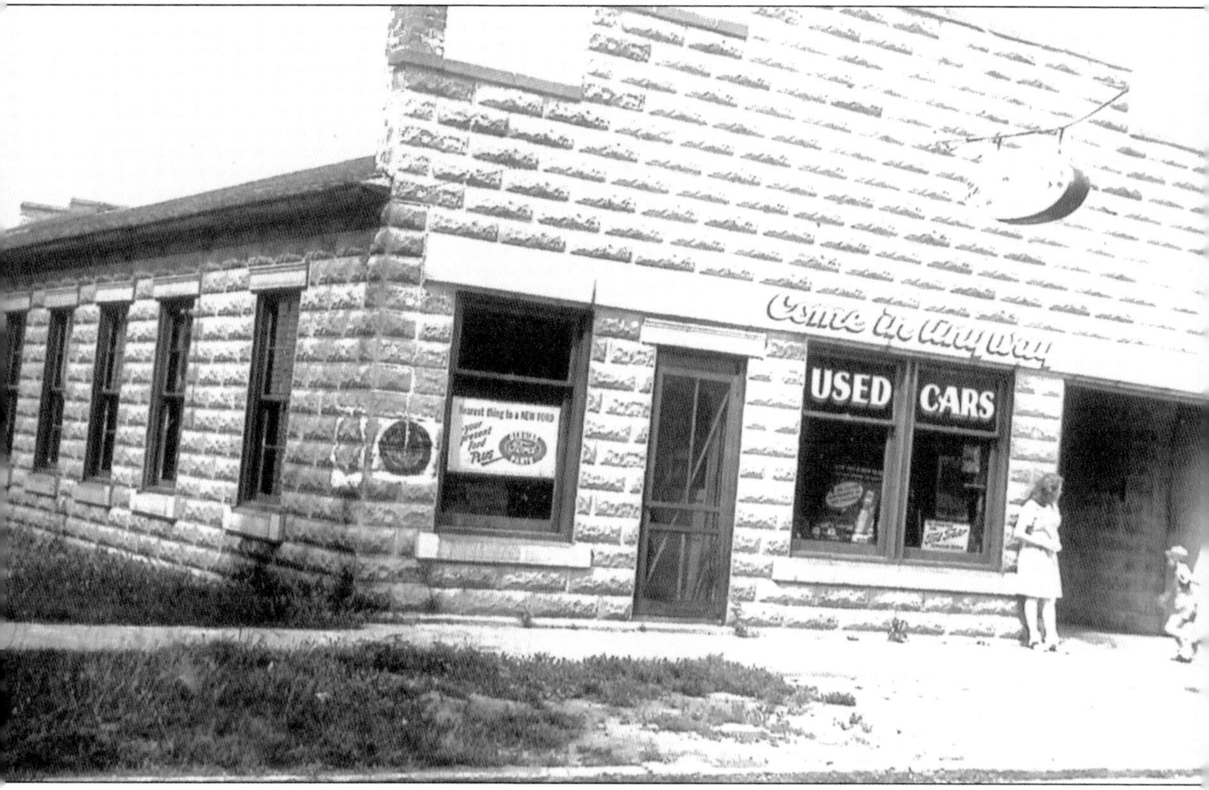

This building was erected by Phillip Petrie, a pioneer resident and blacksmith by trade. It was constructed for use as an automobile and machine shop: Hershof Auto and Acme Farm Machinery, respectively. In the late 1930s, George Tronsrue, after his stint as postmaster, tried his hand at the Nash Auto Sales and Service business in this one-story block building. The building later became the Cunningham Ford and Mercury dealership in the 1940s and 1950s, the predecessor of Blaise Ford. This 1945 photograph captures Barb and Dan Cunningham in front of the building. Arnie Westerberg and Hank Shinabarger started Long Prairie Plumbing and Heating. The author's parents, Jerry and Glenda Lucas, in partnership with Bud and Irene Pederson, purchased this building and business from Arnie and Florence Westerberg in 1975. The author's parents bought out the Pedersons in 1980. It was about 1990 when they sold the building to Jim and Barb Fahlin, who then sold it to Karen St. Germain, the current owner, who operates Pastimes Antiques at this location. (Courtesy of Karen St. Germain.)

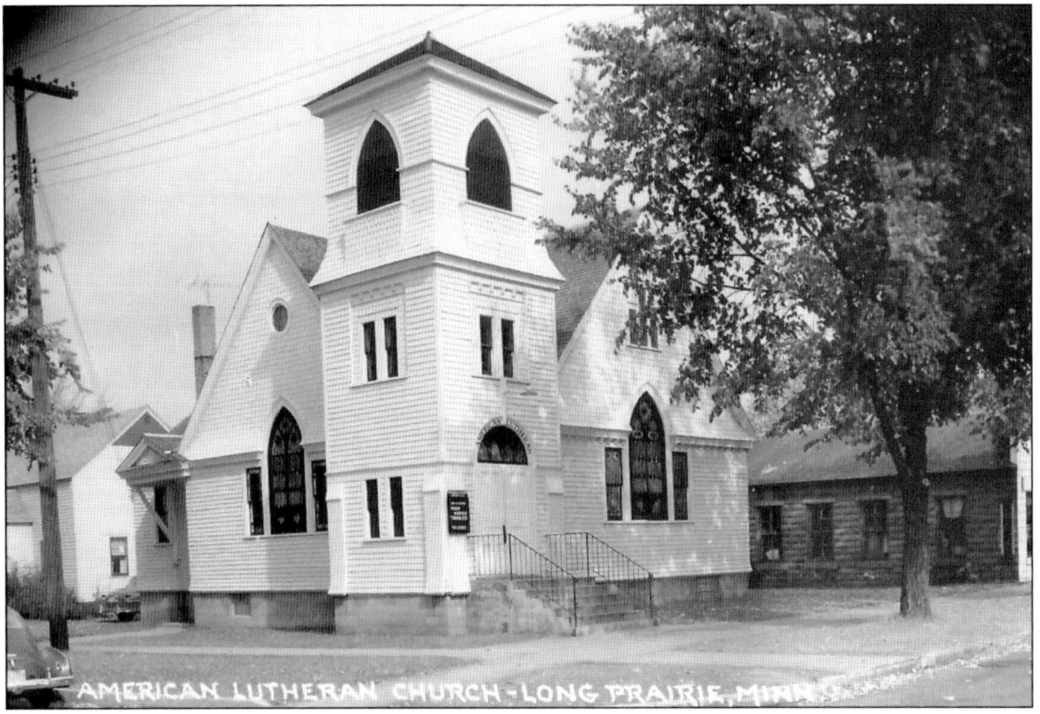

The congregation of the First Presbyterian Church held its first services in this structure in Long Prairie on October 28, 1900. The church, minus its upper steeple, became an Assembly of God and also housed the American Lutheran Church for a number of years. It was then converted into the Prairie Arts Center. Most recently, it has become the Iglesia Apostolica Long Prairie. (Courtesy of TCHS.)

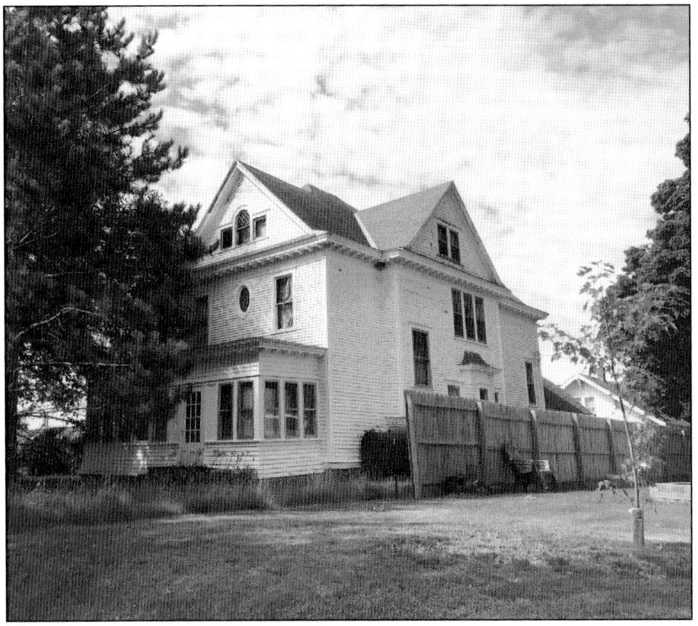

This large home at 101 First Street North was built by John Handy. He moved to Long Prairie in 1877 and opened a furniture and undertaking business where the post office now stands. Often referred to as the "twin" to the Christie home, this house was known as Riverside Hospital and used as a chiropractic center at one time. Dr. George Christie would walk from his residence to the hospital daily. Maria Handy was a vivacious musician, presenting musicals and dressing luxuriously. (Courtesy of the Christie Home Museum.)

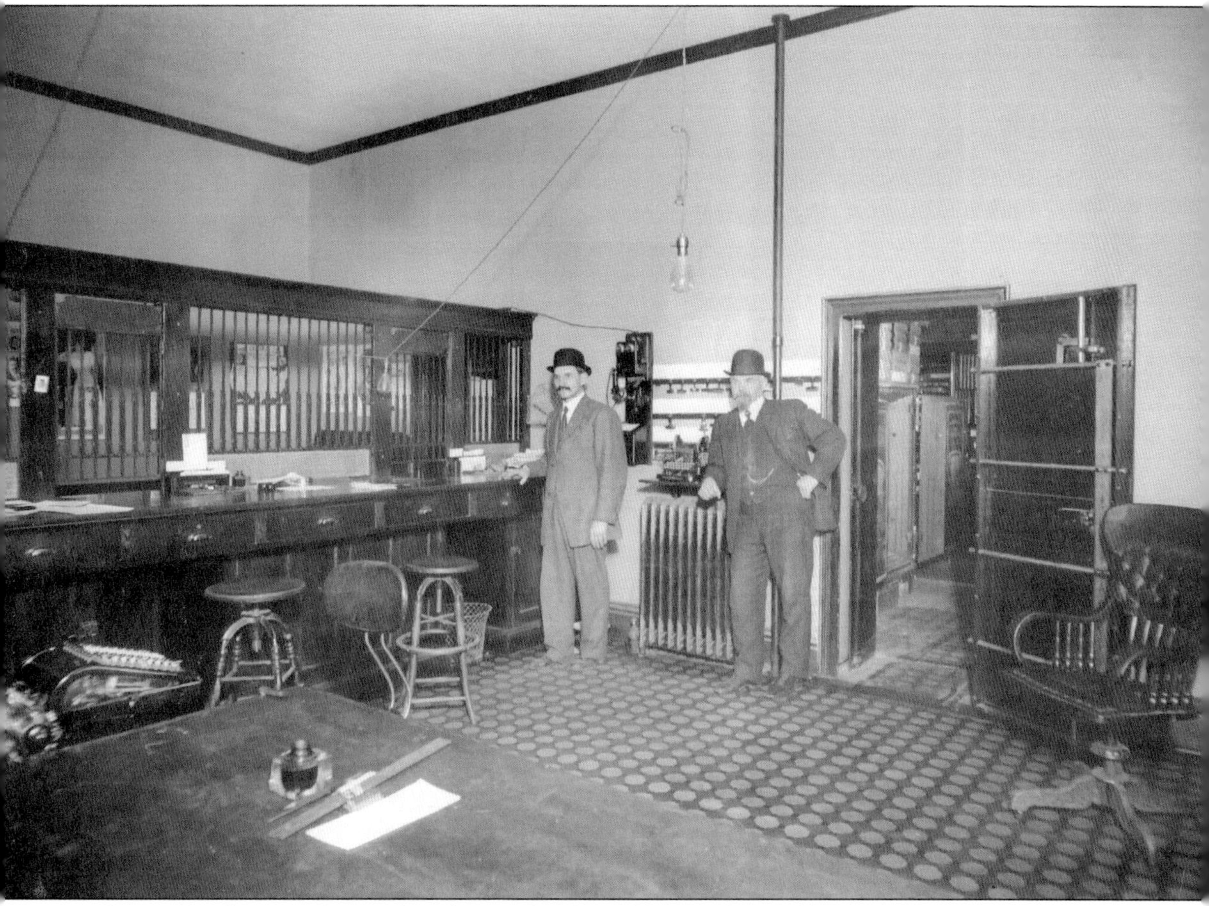

This undated image shows what the inside of an office in the Todd County Courthouse looked like prior to the remodeling project. The courthouse was extensively remodeled in 2012, with many of these old offices removed. The door to the large walk-in safe seen in this photograph was saved and incorporated into the new layout. The two gentleman in the image are unidentified but are probably staff of this office. (Author's collection.)

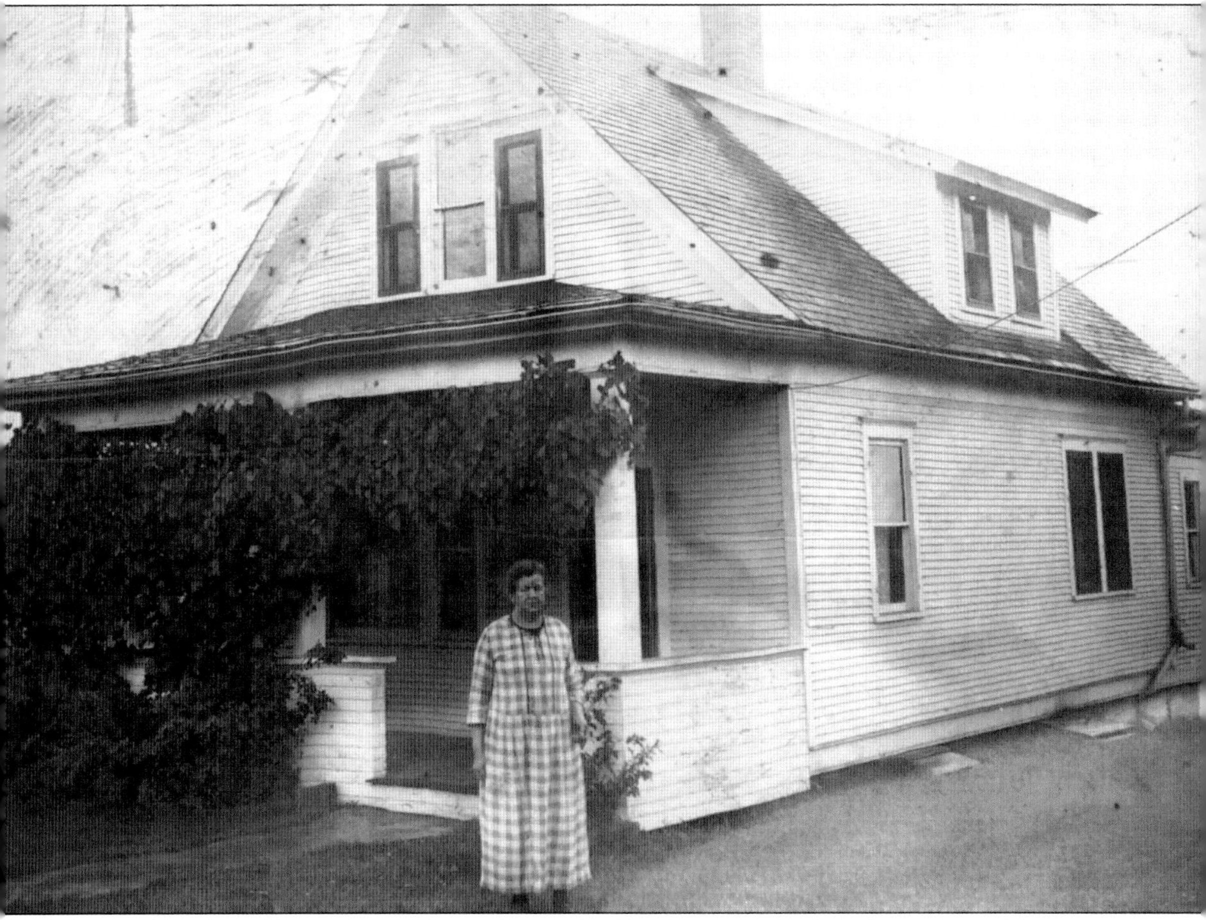

This home still stands at 145 Todd Street South in Long Prairie. Todd Street was originally known as Elm Street before the name was changed. The streets in Long Prairie were renamed in 1952. Taken in the 1930s, this photograph shows Lena Titzke in front of her home. Lena was a great-great-grandmother of the author. She was born in Germany and arrived in the United States in 1868. Lena passed away in 1937. (Courtesy of Glenda Lucas.)

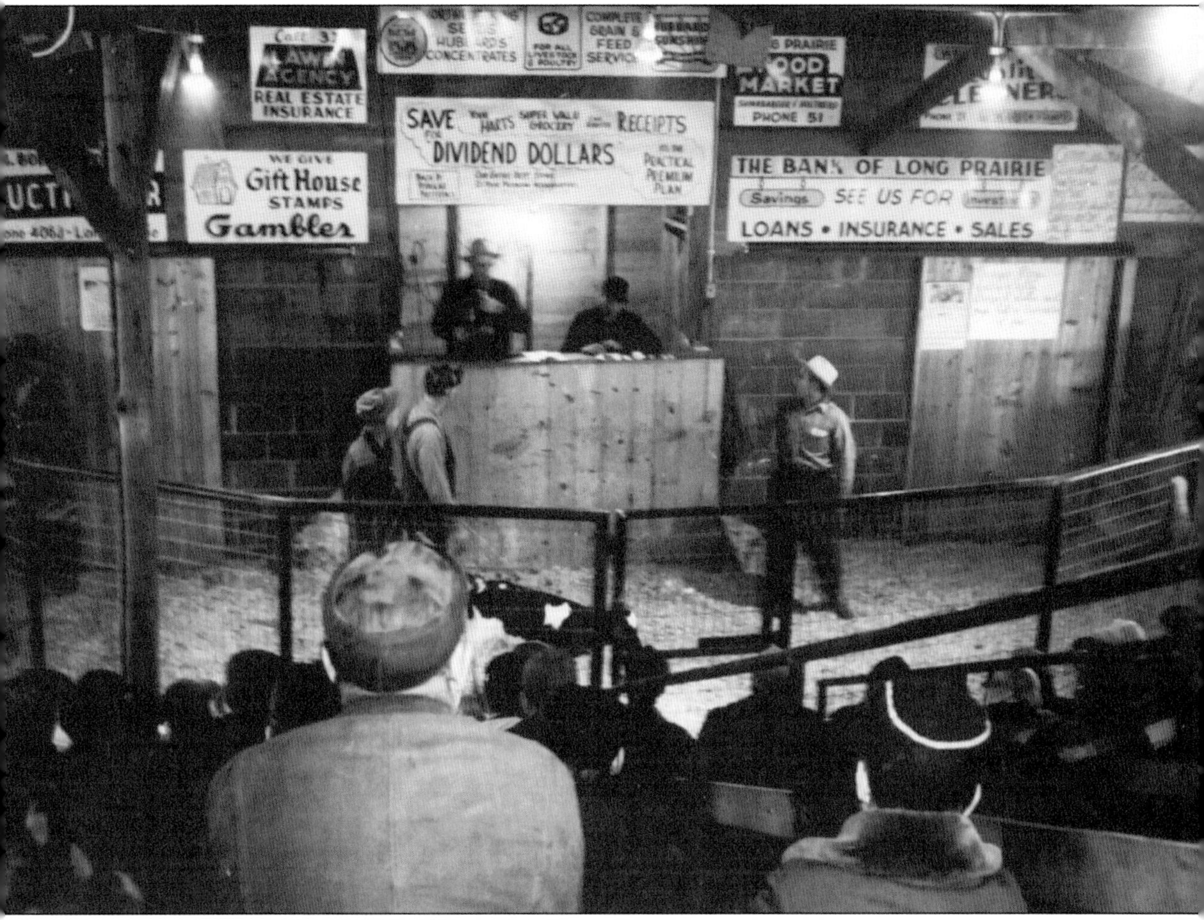

Built around 1950 by the Long Prairie Enterprises group, the Long Prairie sales barn has been active for over 70 years. Bob Eldred purchased the sales barn in 1958. During this time, the sales held every Tuesday afternoon drew crowds of people from as far away as the Dakotas, Iowa, and Wisconsin—as seen in this 1958 photograph. Along with livestock, farmers would bring such things as tools, machinery, household goods, and feed to sell at the auctions. Eldred sold the sales barn to Ray Timmer around 1962. (Courtesy of Glenda Lucas.)

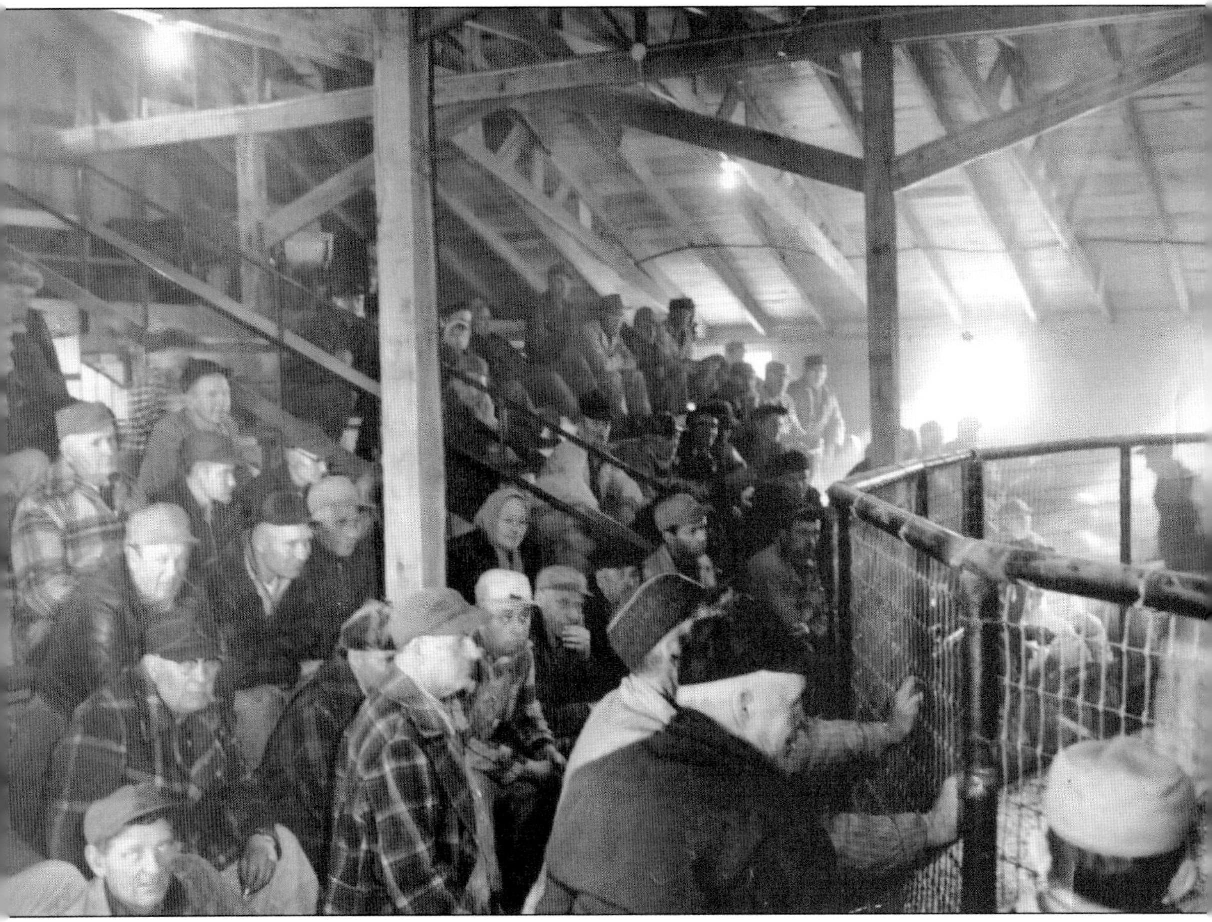

The 1958 sales barn staff, seen here from left to right, was made up of Bernice Gruening, Lucille Eldred, and Everett Whelan of the Bank of Long Prairie. All sales were clerked by the bank. The man at the window is Vic Winter of Sauk Centre. The sales barn had a lunchroom staffed by Elaine Asmus in the 1960s and Ruby Alsleben in the 1970s. (Courtesy of Glenda Lucas.)

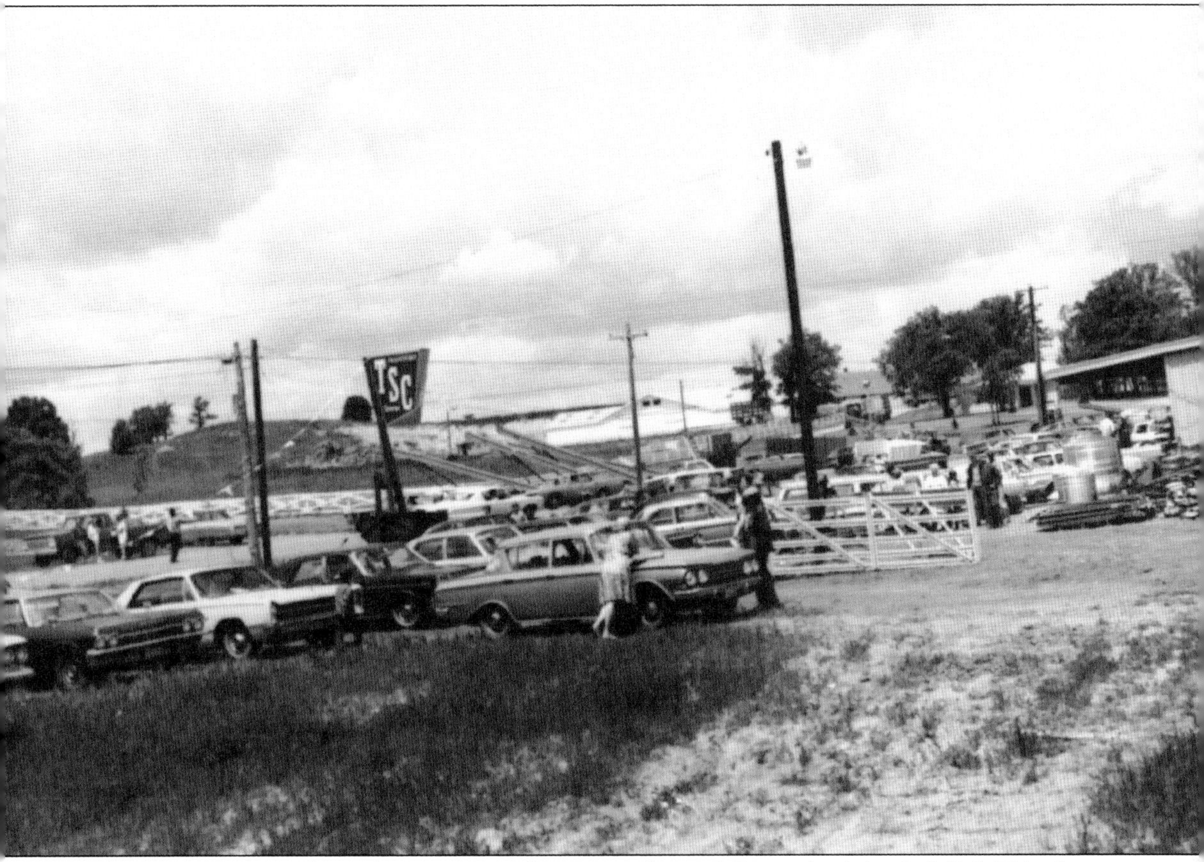

The TSC store, seen here during its grand opening about 1969, was built by Col. Bob Eldred, one of the author's grandfathers. Located at 34 Riverside Drive, this store was a type of fleet supply business offering agricultural products to the rural customers in and around Long Prairie and Todd County. Its location next to the Long Prairie packing plant drew many customers through its doors. This business held other names throughout the years, such as Big Bear supply. This building is currently owned by the Long Prairie Packing Company. (Courtesy of Glenda Lucas.)

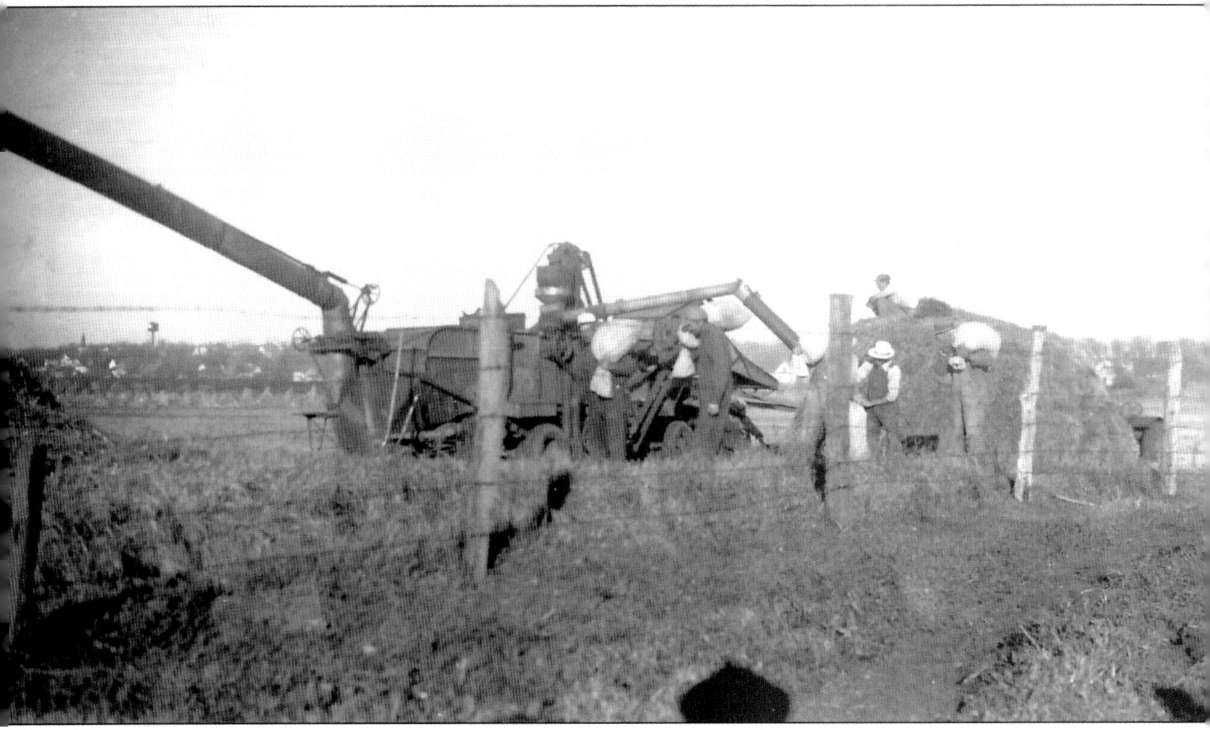

This photograph captures the Rohner pasture in the 1920s. The pasture was located where the current high school football field and track complex sit today, with this photograph being taken from about the location of the parking lot entrance, with a view looking northeast. Prior to the Long Prairie school system constructing the sports complex in the mid-1980s, it had been a wet slough area. Many longtime residents of Long Prairie will recall this area as being an excellent duck-hunting location. The housing development south of this area began in the 1970s. (Courtesy of Brian Cowdery.)

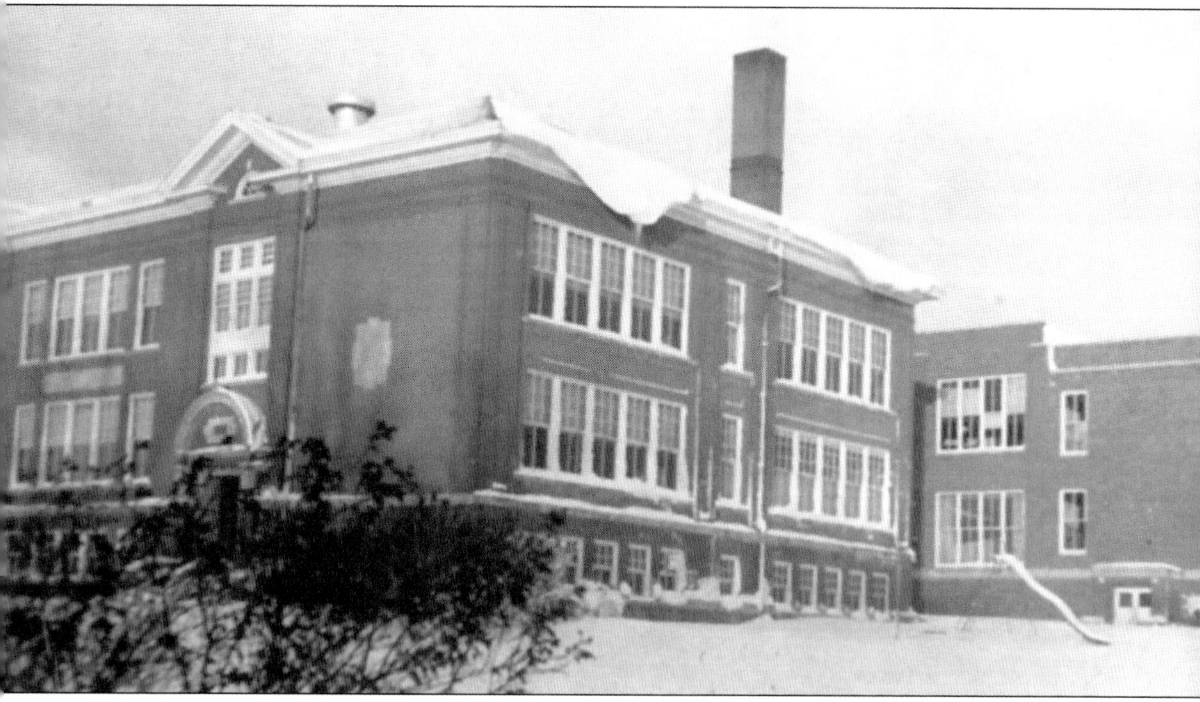

This photograph of the 1908 and 1921 Long Prairie high school buildings captures a typical winter scene of the Long Prairie area. Not deterred by the weather, the children of Long Prairie would gladly participate in recess in these conditions. For reference, this image would have been captured from near the intersection of First Street South and Third Avenue Southeast, with a view looking northeast. (Courtesy of Val Hoeschen.)

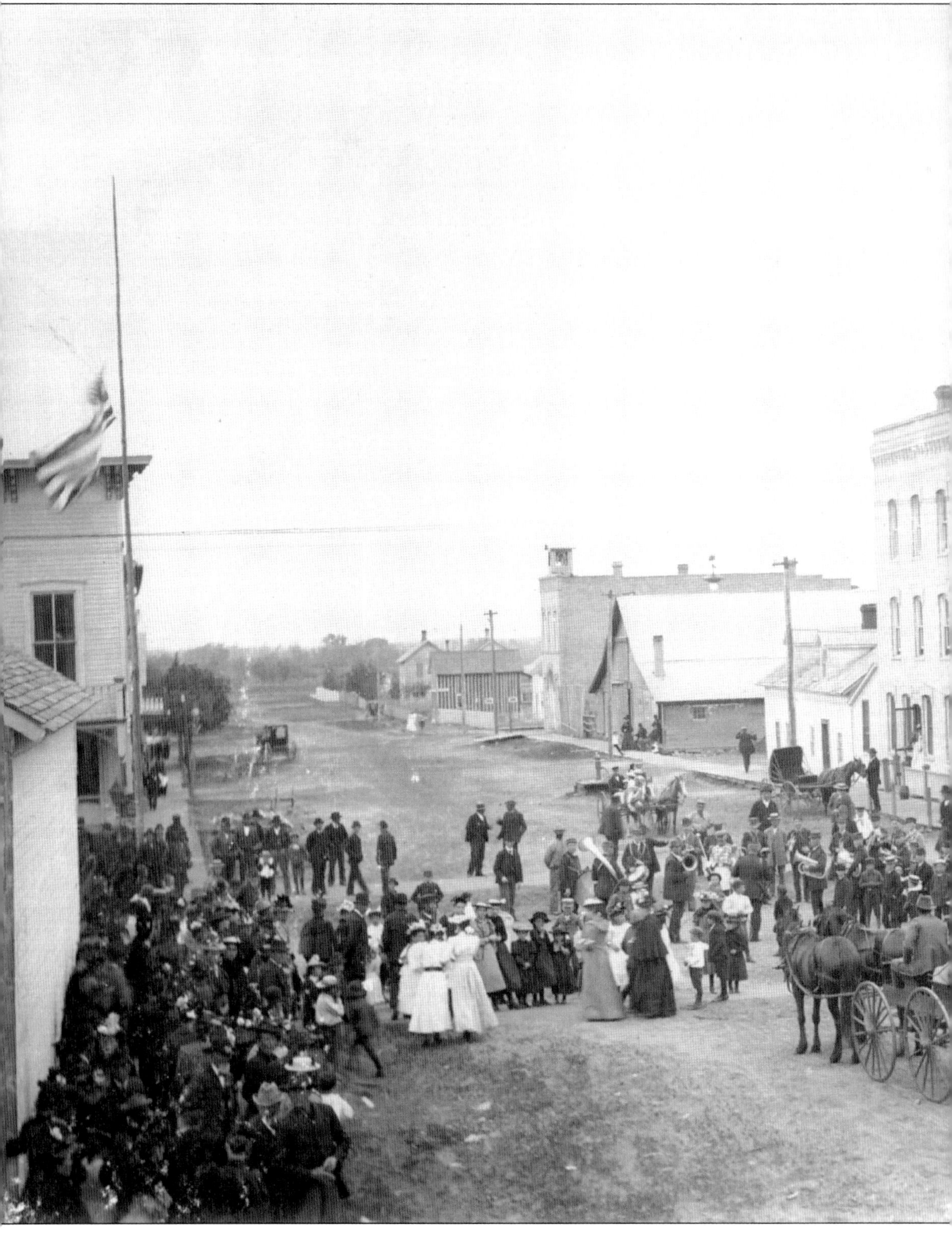

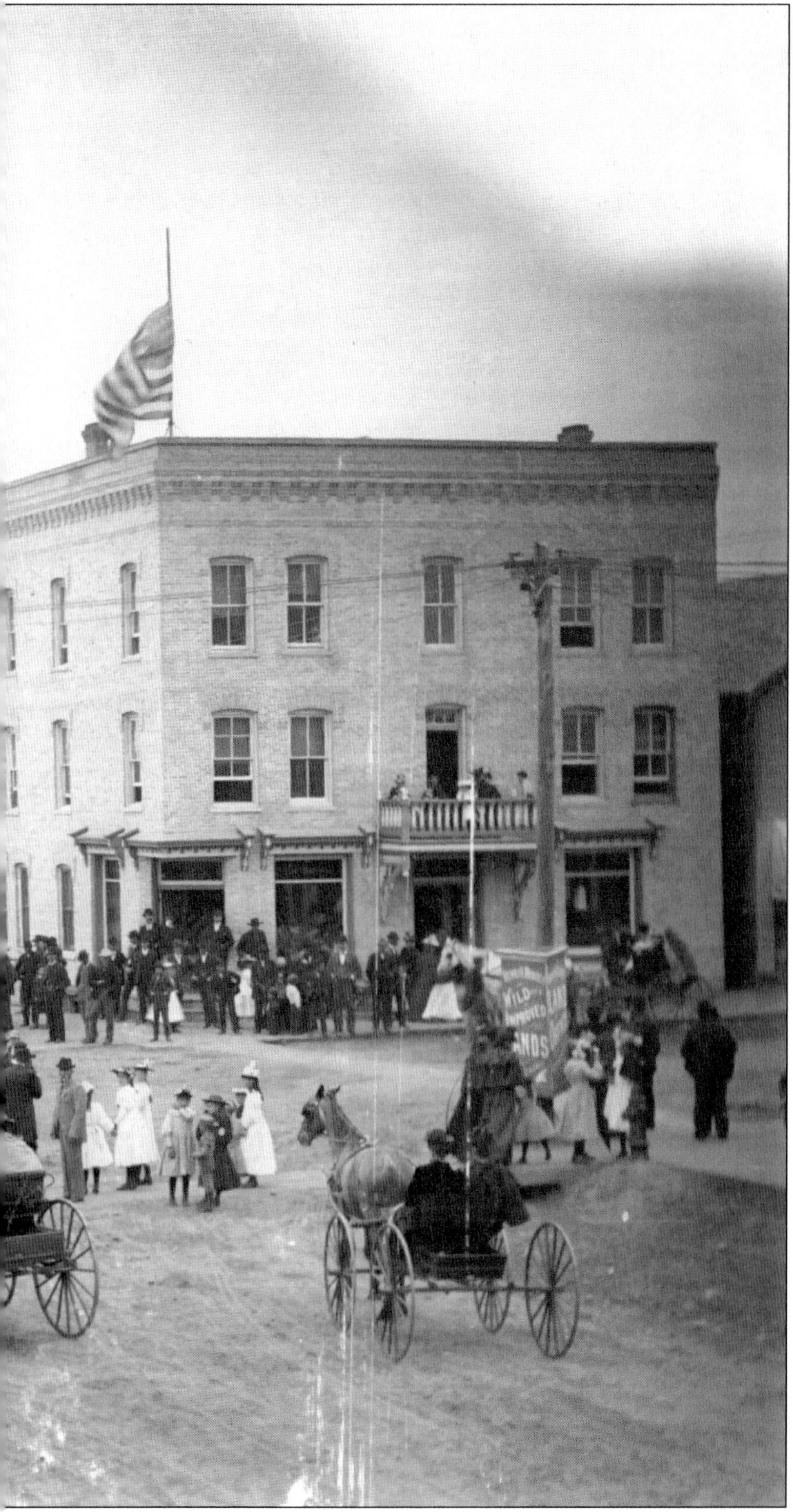

This undated pre-1899 image captures a village gathering, possibly the beginning of a parade, as there are band members standing in the intersection in front of the Long Prairie House hotel, which was destroyed by fire in 1902. With a view looking north up Third Street, across Central Avenue, this photograph was taken from a vantage point of where the Long Prairie Leader office is now. Note the wood-frame building on the far-left edge of the photograph. This is the post office building that sat on the corner location of the current Arcade Building. (Courtesy of TCHS.)

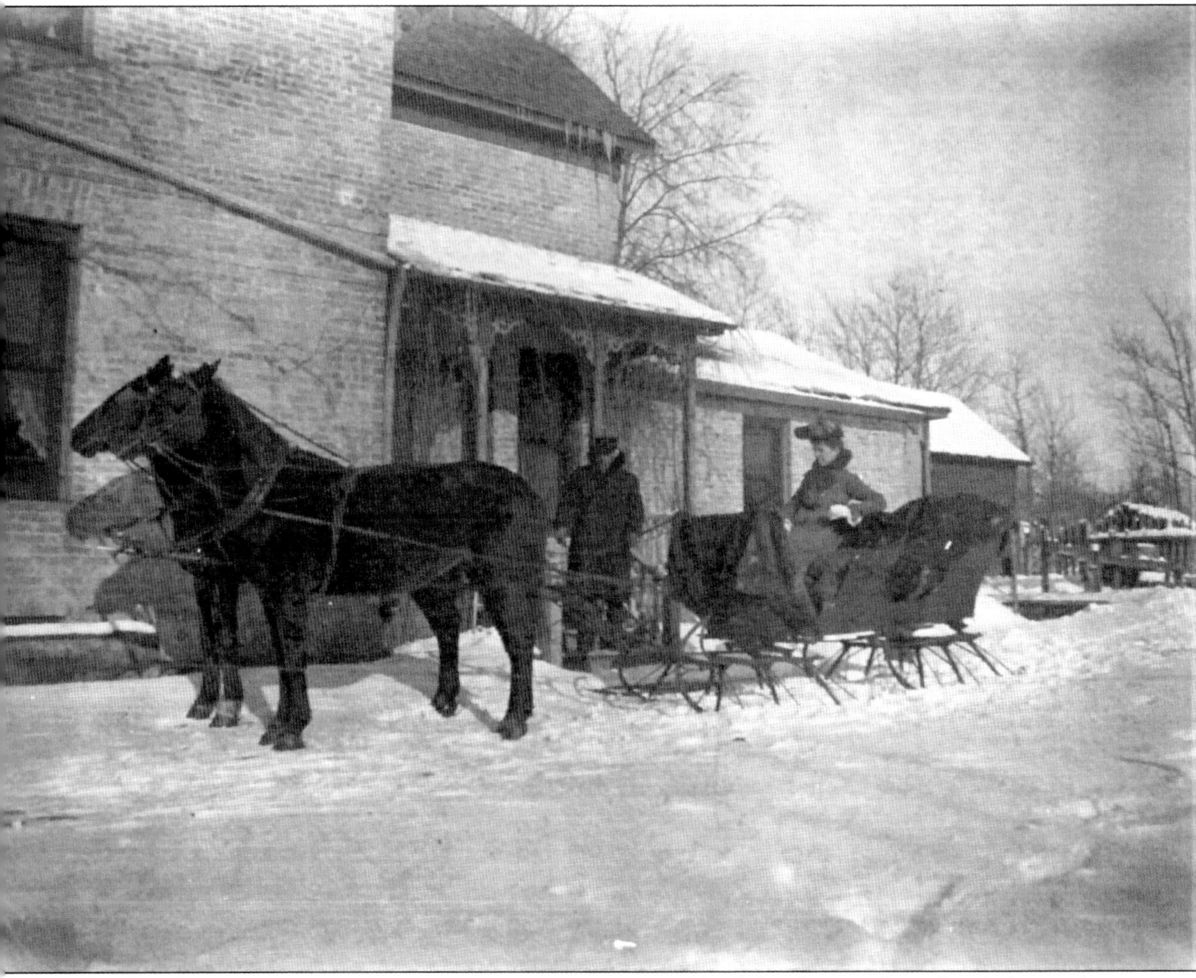

This undated photograph is a winter scene of the home built by the Reichert family located at 120 Eighth Street Southeast. This view looks south, facing the side of the house prior to the addition of the porch and extended second floor. The people in the photograph on the horse-drawn sleigh are unidentified but more than likely members of the Reichert family. (Courtesy of Ron Wienhold.)

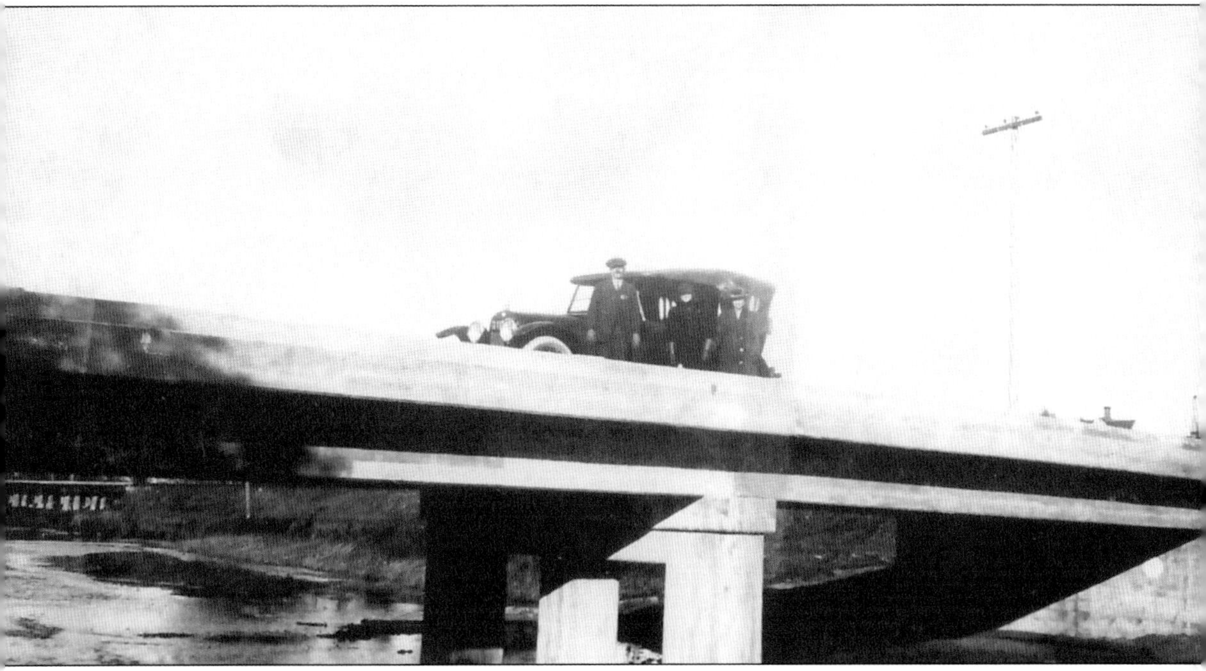

This undated photograph shows the Long Prairie River bridge just west of the intersection of US Highway 71 and State Highway 27. Originally, US Highway 71 turned west over this bridge, continued past the Long Drive-In, and then went on to Browerville, Minnesota. This bridge holds sad history in the story of Long Prairie. On July 29, 1922, the Long Prairie village marshal George Williams attempted to stop men on this bridge who had robbed the bank in Hewitt, Minnesota. During the stop attempt, the marshal was shot and killed. A memorial to Marshal Williams, dedicated in May 1998, stands just south of this location. (Author's collection.)

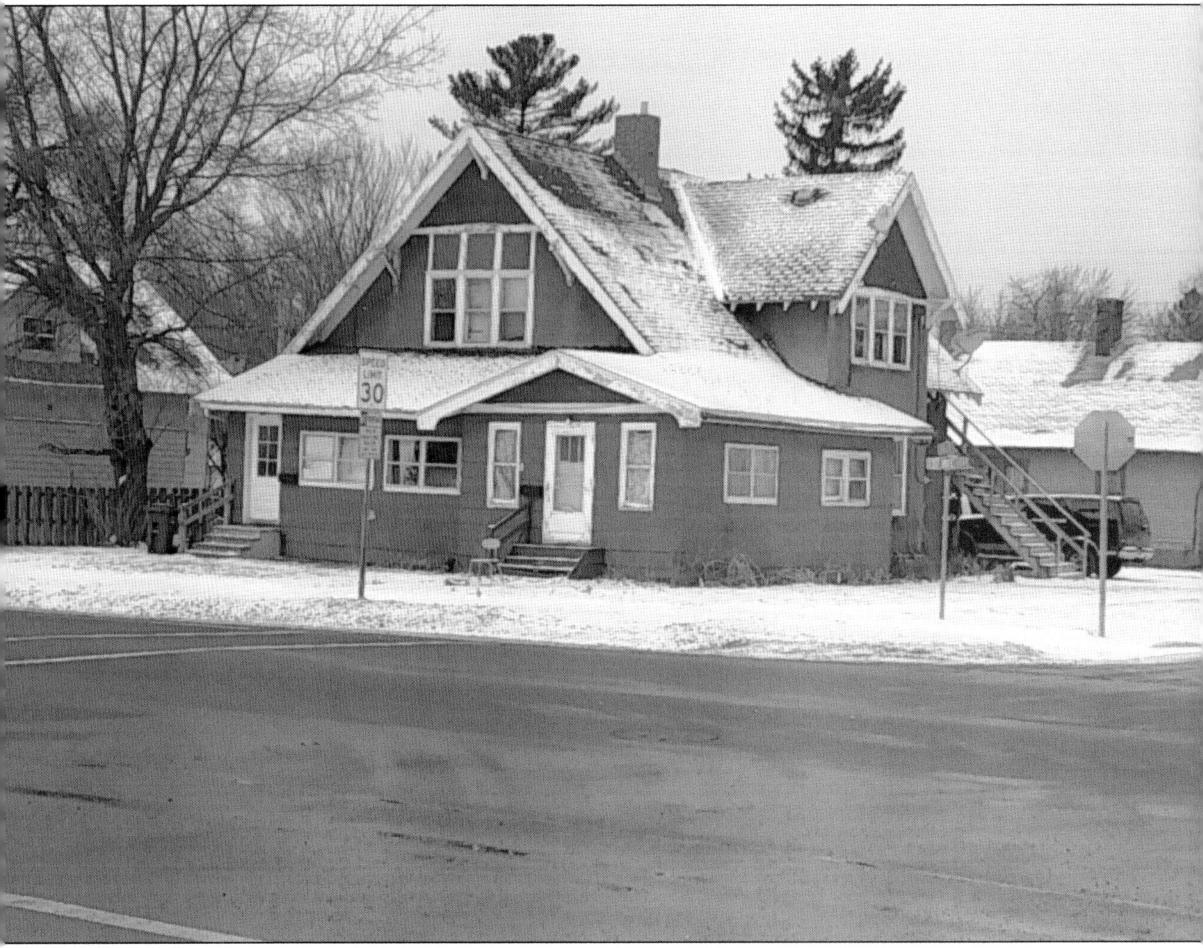

Of the different hospitals that have been around Long Prairie, such as the Riverside Hospital, the Van Hospital, and the current hospitals on the east end of town, one of the least-known that existed was the Losey Hospital. This hospital was located in the upstairs space of the home at 230 First Avenue North. This house was built by Lew Losey in 1930 with lumber purchased at the Steiner Lumber Company. Losey was a partner with Lewis Laugeson in the grocery store business. They had a store in the Hansmeyer Building before that property burned down. Ruth Losey, Lew's wife and a licensed nurse, ran the hospital in this home. (Courtesy of Lorna Hunter.)

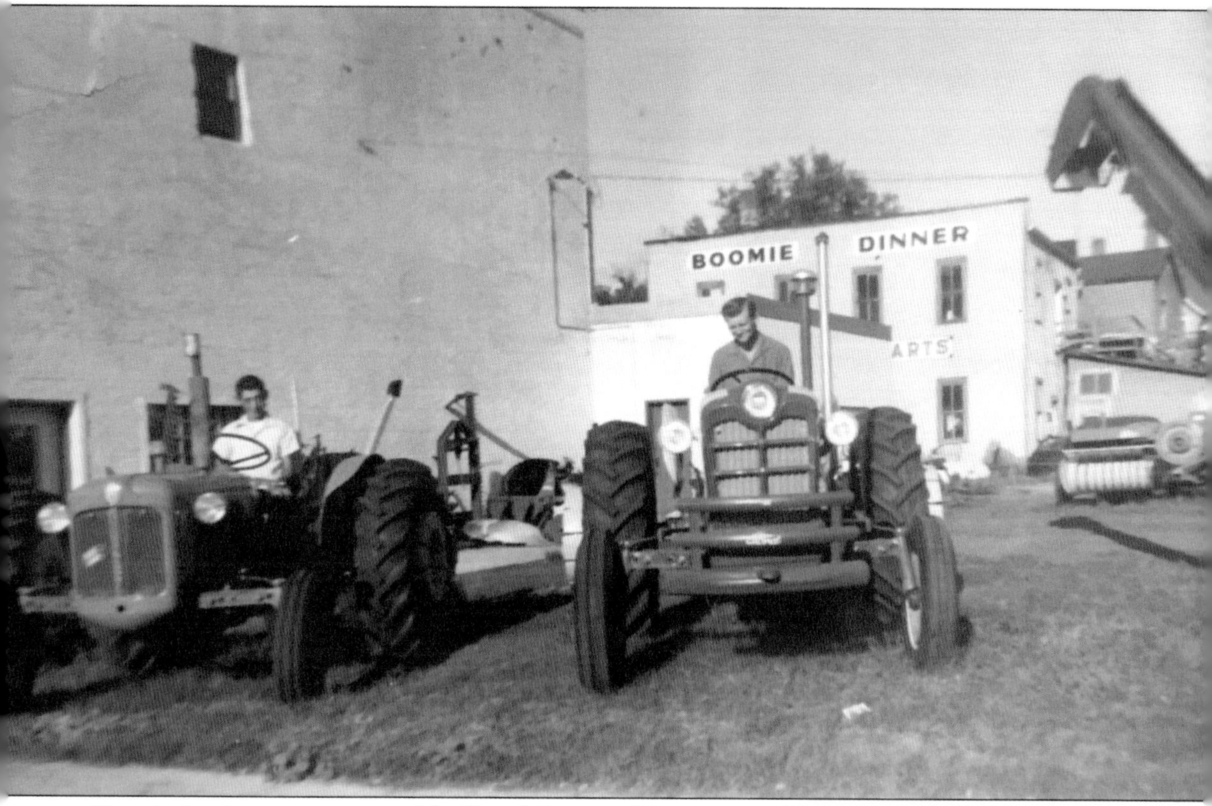

Garmin Implement was owned by Royal Garmin. The view in this photograph looks east. The two-story building on the left is currently the one-story Senior Citizens Day Center. The tractors sit on an empty lot where the building that houses the Long Prairie Library and Long Prairie Area Chamber of Commerce is now. Abraham "Boomie" Dinner is remembered by those who knew him as one of the all-time characters of Long Prairie. Boomie dealt in auto parts and scrap metal. His shop building, seen here, sat between the senior center and the funeral home. This location is a parking lot now. (Courtesy of Rose Hillig.)

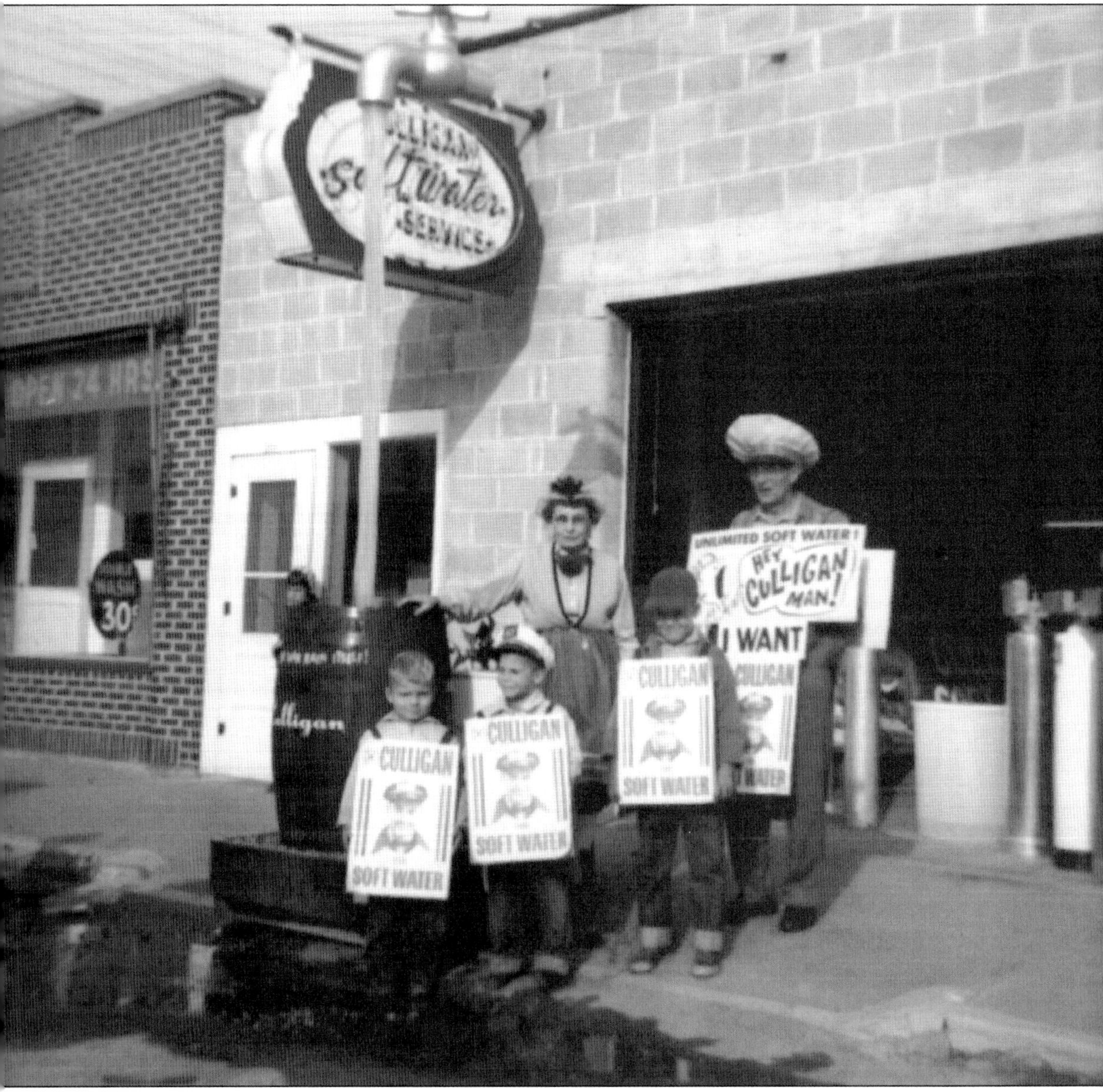

Nick Visser came to the United States in 1925 and, soon after, moved to Long Prairie, where he worked at Lano Hardware. In 1929, he rented a small building, which sat across Third Street Southeast from the *Leader* office, from C.F. Miller. Visser opened the Tin and Plumbing Shop. In 1936, he needed more space, so he purchased a building that sat east across the street from the Long Prairie Creamery at what is now the site of the parking lot for the American Heritage National Bank. Visser Plumbing closed its doors in 1959. Visser purchased Culligan Water Conditioning in 1954. His son, John Visser, bought it in 1968, selling it in 1976. In this 1961 photograph, from left to right, are Bruce Rosenow, Tom Visser, Laura Muenzhuber, and Nick Visser. (Courtesy of Doris Visser.)

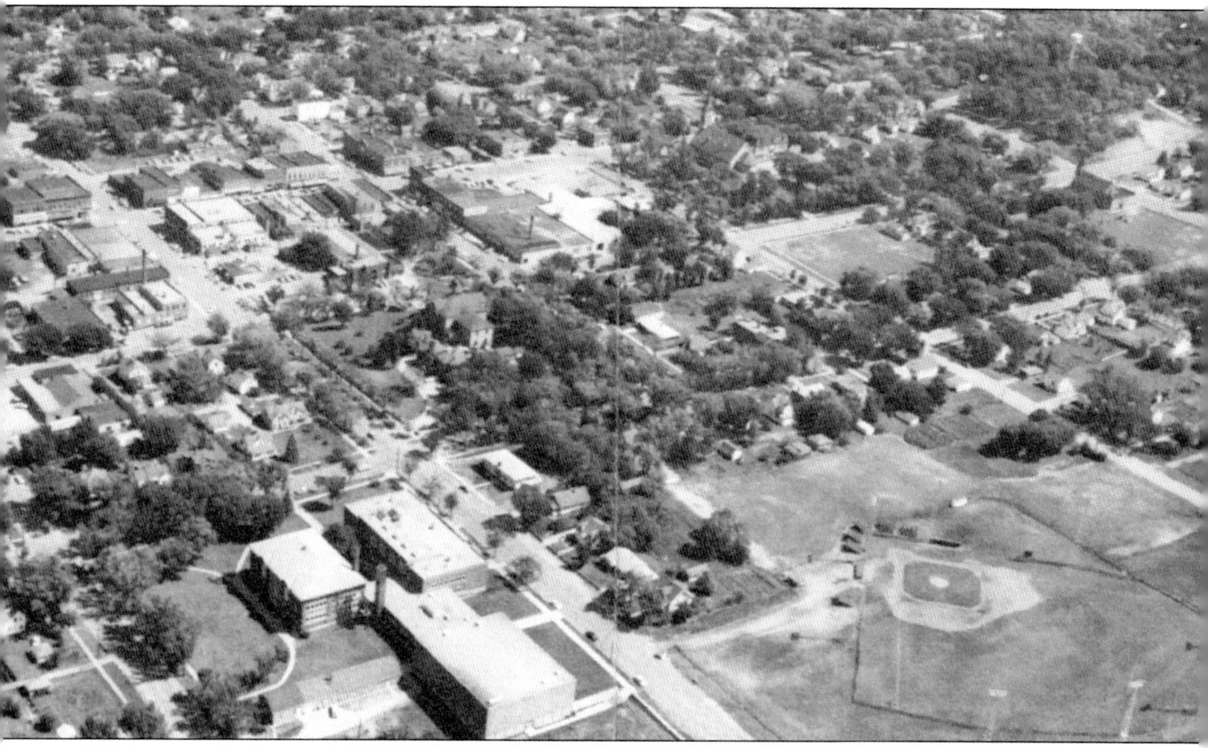

With a view looking northeast, this aerial photograph of Long Prairie shows what the city looked like in the mid-1960s. Some items of note in this image include the old Trinity Lutheran Church, on the corner just southwest of the water tower; the old Hart Press office building that currently houses the Todd County Historical Society has not been built yet. Other items of interest include the area north of the baseball field, where the future tennis courts have not been constructed yet. The buildings of Visser Plumbing that sat east of the creamery are visible north of the courthouse. (Courtesy of TCHS.)